# Journals of the Siege of Detroit Including the Pontiac Uprising

# Journals of the
# Siege of Detroit
# Including the
# Pontiac Uprising

The Commandant's Secretary's Diary
and
Journal of the Siege of Detroit
Published by Robert Rogers of the Rangers

LEONAUR

*Journals of the*
*Siege of Detroit*
*Including the*
*Pontiac Uprising*
*The Commandant's Secretary's Diary*
*and*
*Journal of the Siege of Detroit*
*Published by Robert Rogers of the Rangers*

First published under the title
*Diary of the Siege of Detroit*
*In the War With Pontiac.*
*Also a Narrative of the Principal Events of the Siege,*
*A Plan for Concluding Indian Affairs*
*And Other Authentic Documents,*

Leonaur is an imprint
of Oakpast Ltd

ISBN: 978-0-85706-128-7(hardcover)
ISBN: 978-0-85706-127-0 (softcover)

**http://www.leonaur.com**

Publisher's Notes

In the interests of authenticity, the spellings, grammar and place names
used have been retained from the original editions.

The opinions of the authors represent a view of events in which he
was a participant related from his own perspective,
as such the text is relevant as an historical document.

The views expressed in this book are not necessarily
those of the publisher.

# Contents

Introduction                                                        9

Diary of the Siege of Detroit                                      19

Journal of the Siege of Detroit Introduction                     105

Journal                                                          106

Gen. Bradstreet's Statement Upon Indian Affairs                  113

Papers Relating to the Indian Wars of 1763 and 1764,
and the Conspiracy of Pontiac                                    125

Sir

The Contemporary Records of the hostilities which followed the surrender of Canada in 1760, must ever possess an unusual degree of interest, as illustrating the Indian Character, and the success of the line of policy adopted by the French in their Northern Colonies of America, as contrasted with that of the English.

Having early acquired an intimate knowledge of the *interiour*, by a series of enterprising explorations, the French adopted a rational method of securing the benefits to be derived from a monopoly of the Indian trade, and with such success that the friendship they gained could not be annulled by Treaties, or readily assigned to a nation whom they had been taught to hate.

Deceived by the statements of zealous partisans in the French interests, the natives fondly hoped for the return of their ancient allies to power, and in the ardour of their enthusiasm they fought to merit returning favours by anticipating the arms of France in the reconquest of the country, and the expulsion of the English.

The journal and documents here printed , from their undoubted authenticity and great diversity of subject, are believed to offer a valuable addition to our previous knowledge of the events attending the Indian Wars of 1763; and the publisher, by inscribing these pages to a zealous and discriminating student of American history, has the gratification of believing that his own labours for the extension of historical literature have met with an intelligent approval.

# Introduction

Notwithstanding the English found themselves masters of Canada, by the capitulation of Montreal in September, 1760, the French retained a place in the memory of the Indian tribes which could not be alienated by treaties; and this regard, which was gained by a long series of kind offices and well-timed presents, was strengthened rather than diminished by the neglect and ill-usage which these sons of nature received at the hands of the English.

There was no longer any European rival to contend against; no competition existed for the monopoly and profits of the Indian trade, and no risk of an alliance with any civilized power, to molest the long frontier which had through many years been desolated with fire, and kept in mourning by the cruel hand of a lurking enemy. The motives for cultivating the friendship of the Indians, which had been dictated by policy, no longer existed, and those of humanity and common justice soon proved inadequate to secure those favours which the natives had long been accustomed to receive from the whites, and which the introduction of the weapons and some of the arts, if not the vices, of civilization, had to a certain degree rendered necessary to their comfort and contentment.

It was impossible for them to fall back upon the use of the bow and arrow, and the club, after having become accustomed to firearms, and the only means of their procuring these articles which had thus been made necessary to their existence, was from the English, now sole matters of the country, upon such terms and with such sacrifices as unprincipled traders or haughty military officers might exact or permit, and if any grievance arose there was no longer an appeal to a friendly ear, or hope of better times for themselves or their children.

It will be remembered that the French still retained command of the posts upon the Mississippi; that most of the inhabitants of this nation, who were scattered around the military posts in the *interiour*, garrisoned by English troops, were still living in terms of intimacy with the Indians, and although yielding a formal allegiance to their new masters, were still national in language and in heart, and finally that French missionaries and emissaries were still living in the Indian villages throughout the country. The war between France and England, although settled in North America, was still raging in Europe, and a series of successful operations in the old world, might have still enabled the French to claim the relinquishment of Canada, as one of the conditions of peace, as had occurred but a few years previous in the resurrender of Louisburgh, upon the Island of Cape Breton, after its capture by New England Troops.

If in addition to these we remember, that the indians had been taught by their French allies, that the Grand Monarch of France was scarcely less omnipotent than deity, that he loved his red children and would ultimately protect them, and that greatly perverted accounts of the true relations existing between the two countries were circulated among the indians, we shall have sufficient reasons to account for the war which devastated the frontiers in the summer of 1763, and in which Pontiac, the great Ottawa chief, acted so conspicuous a part.

Sir William Johnson, whose opportunities for knowing Indian affairs were unsurpassed, and whose judgement is entitled to the highest respect in every thing that concerns these people, thus wrote to the Lords of Trade at the period under confederation:

> Without any exaggeration, I look upon the Northern Indians to be the most formidable of any uncivilized body of people in the world. Hunting and war are their sole occupations, and the one qualifies them for the other; they have few wants, and those are easily supplied; their properties of little value, consequently expeditions against them, however successful, cannot distress them, and they have courage sufficient for their manner of fighting, the nature and situation of their countries require not more.

> As the French well knew the importance of the indians, they wisely took advantage of our neglect, and although they were not able to effect a proper reconciliation with the Six Nations, took care to cultivate a good understanding with the Western Indians, which the safety of their colony, and their ambitious views of extending their bounds, rendered indispensably necessary; to effect this, they were at an immense expense in buying

the favour of the Indians.

On the reduction of Montreal, whereby the Frontiers claimed by Canada were ceded to His Majesty, I thought it prudent to send Mr. Croghan, one of my deputies, with the troops, who were to take possession of Detroit, etc., whereby I reconciled the change to the neighbouring Indians, then in arms against us, and the next year went in person to Detroit, where I held a conference with the several neighbouring nations, the particulars of which will appear from my transactions last year transmitted to your Lordships; but apprehensive that our occupying these outposts would never be approved of, unless the indians shared our favours, as they had been accustomed to those of the French, I represented to the commander-in-chief, the necessity of weaning them therefrom gradually, as well as the repeated accounts I had constantly transmitted me of the uneasiness amongst the Indians, and my apprehensions thereon.

The Indians of the Ottawa Confederacy (and who begun the present war) and also the Six Nations, however their sentiments may have been misrepresented, all along considered the northern parts of North America as their sole property, from the beginning; and although the conveniency of trade (with fair speeches and promises) induced them to afford both us and the French, settlements in their country, yet they have never understood such settlement as a dominion, especially as neither we, nor the French ever made conquest of them; they have even repeatedly said at several conferences in my presence, that 'they were amused by both parties with stories of their upright intentions, and that they made war for the protection of the Indians' rights, but that they plainly found it was carried on, to see who would become masters of what was the property of neither the one nor the other.'

The French in order to reconcile them to these encroachments, loaded them with favours, and employed the most intelligent agents, of good influence, as well as artful Jesuits, amongst the several western and other nations, who by degrees prevailed on them to admit of forts, under the notion of trading houses, in their country; and knowing that these posts could never be maintained contrary to the inclinations of the Indians, they supplied them thereat with ammunition and other necessaries in abundance, as also called them to frequent congresses, and dismissed them with handsome presents; by which they enjoyed an extensive commerce, obtained the assistance of these Indians, and possessed their frontiers in safety; and as without these measures, the Indians would never have suffered them in their country, so they expect that whatever European power possesses the fame, they shall in some measure reap the like advantages. Now, as these advantages ceased, on the posts being possessed by the English, and especially as it was not thought prudent to indulge them with ammunition, they immediately concluded we had designs against their liberties, which opinion had been first instilled into them by the French, and since promoted by traders of that nation and others who retired amongst them on the surrender of Canada and are still there, as well as by belts of *wampum* and other exhortations, which I am confidently assured have been sent amongst them from the Illinois, Louisiana and even Canada, for that purpose.

The treatment which the Indians were accustomed to receive from the English Traders has been specified by Sir William Johnson. [1]

The frontier traders, sensible they have little to apprehend from their conduct, went still greater and more dangerous lengths than their superiors; from a variety of unheard of frauds, I shall select a very few instances which will tend to shew to what lengths some of that character will go when subject to no control, and because two of these instances were the occasion of our losing the trade and affections of some powerful tribes of the Ottawas, who were persuaded to come the length of Oswego to trade with us, and the last instances caused the defection of the most powerful tribes of the Senecas.

Several of the Ottawas having traded for a considerable time at Oswego, where they got some articles which they could not procure from the French, an Ottawa chief of great influence with his family, brought his packs to a trader there, in order to try the market; the trader, after the usual practice of deceiving him in the weight, hurried the peltry into a private room, telling the Indian that all merchandise was very dear, owing to the severity of duties (a stale, but dangerous artifice still practised) desired him to choose out what goods he wanted; the Indian having made a choice, was astonished to find that his

---

1. Col. *Hist. of N.Y.*, 7, 955.

skins produced not one third of what he had been accustomed to receive for the like quantity (for the trader had besides his extortion on the goods reckoned the peltry at only one third of its real weight) went away discontented, but returning said, he was ashamed to go back with such small returns, and begged for a small keg of rum, which the trader gave him, as he said, as a high favour, but on opening the keg soon after his departure it proved to be water.

Another trader for some valuable furs, which he received from an Ottawa chief of great influence, who came likewise to try the market, and desired to have his returns in rum for a general feast, gave the Indian thirty small kegs with directions not to open them by the way, otherwise the trader would be punished for letting them have so much; but the Indian before his return to Niagara, being desirous of some liquor, opened them and found them all water. This has been often acknowledged by these traders, and on its coming to the knowledge of the French, they made so good a use of it, that these people and all their friends were ever after our most implacable enemies.

The next instance is that of a Seneca warrior, whose influence and abilities were so well known, that I found it a very hard task to bring them over, which however I at length effected in 1756, when he came to me with a large party of warriors, who were to set out on public service in a few days, but having some furs to dispose of, I gave them at their desire a passport to Schenectady, wherein I recommended it to a merchant and trader there, to use them very kindly, and to do them the strictest justice, notwithstanding which, this enemy to the interests of his country, imposed upon them in the grossest manner; it appearing from their account, and his own confession since, that as they were strangers, he had doubled the prices of his goods and allowed them but half the weight of their peltry; this was resented accordingly, the Indians took another route back, and the chief sent me a belt of *wampum* with a message informing me of the imposition (the particulars of each article being marked on the handle of an axe) and assuring me that he would always continue to have a personal regard for me, but not the least for the English who had served him so often, but the last instance was of such a nature, that he had accepted of an invitation from the French, who knew how to treat them, and their services; he made his words good; in a few days cut off a large settlement, and continued our most violent enemy ever since, particularly at Niagara in 1759, whilst it was not in my power to have the unworthy author punished.

To this I must subjoin an instance in the case of the chief of all the Senecas, a warrior, whose influence and capacity were, and are well known here, whom I had steadily preserved in the British interest, when we were almost totally abandoned, this man at the eve of the late war, was through the means of liquor seduced by some agents at Albany to subscribe his name to an Indian deed for a tract within the bounds of Pennsylvania, but claimed by the Connecticut people, in virtue of their obsolete charter, which extended their western limits to the South Seas.

This being a most iniquitous proceeding highly resented by the Six Nations; the few who subscribed to it became obnoxious to the rest, particularly the chief before mentioned, so that he was obliged to fly to the French for protection, who so far won upon him, that he with a powerful party who followed his fortunes took up arms shortly after, attacked a body of provincials at Lake George, whom they totally defeated and killed 45. Since which he was concerned in the most important services against us, cut off some of our settlements, and occasioned the deaths of more than 400 of our people. These, it is presumed, will suffice to shew the effects of the resentment of a few Indian individuals."

Such being the causes of disaffection, and such the motives still remaining with the French to encourage Indian hostilities, there was wanting only a leader around whom to rally and upon whom to rely for direction counsel, and such a chieftain was found in the person of Pontiac, by merit as well as by birth he had gained the position of principal chief of the Ottawas, and his achievements and talents had gained him an influence scarcely less powerful over the Ojibwas, Pottawatamies, and in fact over almost all the races of the Algonquin stock. The Seneca tribe of the Six Nations were also brought into this alliance, and led by this energetic, crafty and vindictive enemy of the English to unite in a plan for the simultaneous destruction of the posts along the whole Frontier, as the prelude of a general war of extermination.

Pontiac was about fifty years of age. He was a friend to the French, whose fortunes he ardently desired to retrieve in Canada, and from whom he had without doubt been promised large reinforcements and unlimited supplies. The merchandise stored at Detroit and other posts in the interior, at the time hostilities began, were alone sufficient to provoke the cupidity of the savages, with much fewer grounds for grievance than actually existed, and at Detroit alone, the value of goods was estimated at half a million pounds sterling.[2]

In the code of Indian warfare, that measure is honourable which is successful, and treachery, craft and force may be alike employed, as circumstances favour one or another. With these people, a parole of honour or the observance of a truce, would have been faithfully kept only so far as a fear of consequences compelled them, and the incidents concerning the detention of Col. Campbell and Lieut. McDougal, as related in the following pages, furnishes but one of a multitude of instances which history affords in proof of the fact, that the natives knew no code of honour where an advantage could be gained by a breach of trust.

The hatred felt by the Indians towards the English, began to assume a centralized and efficient form in 1762, in the fall of which year Pontiac sent messengers with war belts far and wide, calling everywhere upon the warriors of his race to unite and at a concerted moment to fall upon and destroy the nearest military posts of the English, assuring them that their Father, the Grand Monarch, would sustain them in their effort, and that they would be able to drive these hated English from their land.

The incidents which marked the execution of this design are related in the following pages, and the high degree of military merit which saved Detroit from the fate of many other Frontier Posts, will long remain a subject of admiration.

The *Diary* printed in the following pages, we believe to be now for the first time published, and although its Author is unknown, we have reason to infer from several allusions to himself, and references to other records kept along with it, that he was the secretary of the commandant, and that he was fully in his confidence. The manuscript is all in one handwriting, and is written upon about half a dozen sizes of paper, which were evidently in loose sheets at the time, and have since been bound in one volume.

It was purchased from a bookseller in London, and its former owner had begun to print it; but finding, after getting through thirty-two

2. Lanman's *Hist. Michigan*, p. 107.

pages, that the sheets had not been bound up in chronological order, the enterprise was abandoned, until it came into the hands of the publisher of the present series. It bears conclusive evidence of authenticity, and is believed to offer new and valuable contributions to our knowledge of the events to which it relates.

The tribes, one by one, were gradually won back to peace with the English through the address of Sir William Johnson and others, whose sagacity led them to this pacification by detail, rather than to attempt a general treaty with all the hostile tribes, as this might lead to a union among them that would be dangerous in its tendencies and difficult to control.

The pride and hatred of Pontiac long kept him aloof from these negotiations, and many an ineffectual effort he made to interrupt them; but the final and conclusive intelligence of peace between France and England, received from the French themselves, at length convinced them that the last hope of succour had vanished, and that no effort of theirs could benefit their loved and cherished allies, or control the progress of the English.

Pontiac concluded a peace with George Croghan, Deputy of Sir William Johnson, at Detroit, in August, 1765, and promised to meet Sir William at Oswego in the spring following to ratify the peace in person, and from this visit he returned laden with gifts to the Maumee, where he spent the succeeding winter. In 1767, new sources of annoyance to the Indians were encountered by the insults and aggressions of the frontier settlers, and a brief but bloody war ensued on the borders of Virginia, in which Pontiac is not known to have been concerned. During the Summer of 1767, he went to the Illinois, and soon after repaired to St. Louis to visit his friend St. Ange, who then commanded at that post. He was treated with great kindness, and two or three days after, hearing that a large number of Indians were assembled at Cahokia, on the opposite side of the river, for some social purpose, he resolved to cross over and see what was in progress. He was advised to the contrary, but relying upon his own courage and seeing no danger, he went.

The closing scene of his life we cannot so well relate as in the language of Francis Parkman, Jr., of Boston, whose beautifully written *History of the Conspiracy of Pontiac*, evinces a great amount of research, and a high degree of literary merit.

The place was full of Illinois Indians; such a scene as in our own time may often be met with in some squalid settlement of the border, where the vagabond guests, bedizened with dirty finery, tie their small horses in rows along the fences, and stroll idly among the houses, or lounge about the dram-shops. A chief so renowned as Pontiac could not remain long among the friendly Creoles of Cahokia without being summoned to a feast; and at such primitive entertainment the whiskey bottle would not fail to play its part. This was in truth the case. Pontiac drank deeply, and, when the carousal was over, strode down the village street to the adjacent woods, where he was heard to sing the medicine songs, in whose magic power he trusted as the warrant of success in all his undertakings.

An English trader, named Williamson, was then in the village. He had looked on the movements of Pontiac with a jealousy probably not diminished by the visit of the chief to the French at St. Louis; and he now resolved not to lose so favourable an opportunity to despatch him. With this view, he gained the ear of a strolling Indian belonging to the Kaskaskia tribe of the Illinois, bribed him with a barrel of liquor, and promised him a farther reward if he would kill the chief. The bargain was quickly made. When Pontiac entered the forest, the assassin stole upon his track, and watching his moment, glided behind him, and buried a tomahawk in his brain.

The dead body was soon discovered, and startled cries and wild howlings announced the event. The word was caught up from mouth to mouth, and the place resounded with infernal yells. the warriors snatched their weapons. The Illinois took part with their guilty countryman, and the few followers of Pontiac, driven from the village, fled to spread the tidings and call the nations to revenge. Meanwhile the murdered chief lay on the spot where he had fallen, until St. Ange, mindful of former friendship, sent to claim the body, and buried it with warlike honours, near his fort of St. Louis.

Thus basely perished this champion of a ruined race. But could his shade have revisited the scene of murder, his savage spirit would have exulted in the vengeance which overwhelmed the abettors of the crime. Whole tribes were rooted out to expiate it. Chiefs and *sachems*, whose veins had thrilled with his eloquence, young warriors, whose aspiring hearts had caught the inspiration of his greatness, " mustered to revenge his fate, and from the North and the East, their united bands descended on the villages of the Illinois. Tradition has but faintly preserved the event; and its only analysts, men who held the intestine feuds of the savage tribes in no more account than the quarrels of panthers or wild-cats, have left but a meagre record. Yet enough remains to tell us that over the grave of Pontiac more blood was poured out in atonement than flowed from the hecatombs of slaughtered heroes on the corpse of Patroclus; and the remnant of the Illinois who survived the carnage remained for ever after sunk in utter insignificance.

Neither mound nor tablet marked the burial-place of Pontiac. For a mausoleum, a city has risen above the forest hero; and the race whom he hated with such burning rancour trample with unceasing footsteps over his forgotten grave.

The papers which follow the diary in this volume are now mostly printed for the first time, from original manuscripts in the state library at Albany, and will be found to have an interesting relation to the conspiracy of Pontiac and the wars of that period. The alarms which these events occasioned on the Frontier were scarcely less distressing than actual hostilities, and these were often greatly aggravated by rumours of invasions and murders which proved groundless and absurd. The resources of the country, and the spirit of the inhabitants were, however, tested by this crisis, and history is enriched with details, which might not have been otherwise preserved.

Albany, Feb. 1, 1860.                                        F. B. H.

# Diary of the Siege of Detroit

BY THE SECRETARY TO THE COMMANDANT

*Detroit, May 1,* 1763.

The 1st of May, Pontiac, the most considerable man in the Ottawa Nation, came here with about fifty of his men,[1] and told the commandant [2] that in a few days when the rest of his nation came in he intended to come and make him a formal visit, as is the custom with all the nations once a year. [3]

The 7th he came with all the Ottawa and part of several other nations, but we saw from their behaviour and from reports that they were not well intentioned, upon which the commandant took such precautions that when they entered the fort (though they were by the nearest accounts about 300 hundred and armed with knives, toma-

---

1. The Pontiac MSS. quoted by Parkman and ascribed to a French priest, says the party numbered *forty*. The commandant in writing to Sir Jeffrey Amherst, states the number as *fifty*. They came for the nominal purpose of dancing the Calumet dance and declaring their friendship for the English, but in reality to ascertain the strength of the garrison, and the nature and extent of their means of defence. While most of them were dancing, the others were strolling about the premises, narrowly examining everything.—*Parkman's Pontiac*, p. 201.

2. Major Henry Gladwyn, had but a short time previous to this date, succeeded Major Campbell in the command of this post. He had accompanied Braddock in his unfortunate expedition in 1755, was made captain in the 80th or Gage's Light Armed Foot, Dec. 25, 1757, and commissioned Major of that Regiment, June 20, 1759. In December of the year following, he became a Major in the regular Army He continued in command at Detroit through the Siege of Pontiac, and until relieved, Aug. 31, 1764, upon the arrival of the Army under Col. Bradstreet.

He was promoted to the rank of Lieutenant-Colonel, Sept. 17, 1763, and to that of Major-General, Sept. 26, 1782. He died at Stubbing, near Chesterfield, County of Derby, England, June 22, 1791

3 Referring to the Ojibwa, Pottawattamie and Wyndote tribes, who were leagued together in enterprise.

hawks, and a great many with guns cut short and hid under their blankets) they were so much surprised to see our dispositions that they would scarcely sit down to council; however in about half an hour after they saw that we were prepared for the worst, they sat down and made several speeches which were answered as calmly as if we did not suspect them at all, and after receiving some tobacco and bread and some other presents they went away to their camp. [4] This morning a party sent by him for that purpose took Capt. Robinson and Sir Robert

Davers in a barge near the mouth of Lake Huron, which Capt. Robinson went to found. They with part of the boat's crew were put to death, [5] the rest they took prisoners as we were afterwards informed. The 8th Pontiac returned with a pipe of peace in order to ask commandant leave to come next day with his whole nation to bury all bad reports, but the commandant would not give him leave but told him if he had anything to say he might come with the rest of the chiefs and he would hear them. However instead of coming the 9th in the afternoon he struck his camp and crossed the river within half a mile of the fort, [6] but being informed by the interpreter that he would not be permitted to come in, he embarked again and he commenced hostilities by killing the King's cattle that were on an island about 3 miles from the fort, [7] with the people that took care of them, and a

---

4. Other authorities state that but sixty Indians were permitted to enter the fort. All the troops and *employées* about the premises were drawn up in military array, and as Pontiac and his men passed on to the Council house, he found Major Gladwyn and his officers sitting armed with swords and pistols. It was evident that the purpose of the visit was understood, and the crafty savage was overawed. As he came to that part of his speech in which he was to have given the signal for attack, a roll of drums and clash of arms at the entrance confused him, and he sat down. The commandant had been censured for not detaining him, which he probably would have done had he suspected the extent of the plot. 5. An anonymous letter, dated at Detroit, July 9, 1763, and printed in the *Pennsylvania Gazette*, Nos. 1,807, 1,808, states that the body of Sir Robert Davers was boiled and eaten. Mr. Paully (whose escape from the enemy is elsewhere noticed) saw the skin of Capt. Robertson's arm in use as a tobacco pouch. These murders occurred May 9, 1763.—Parkman's Pontiac, p. 207 6. The Ottawa Camp had previously been about five miles above on the east side of the river. 7. Isle au Cochon or Hog Island, is now on the American side of the national boundary. It is two miles long and one wide. 8. The person killed here was named James Fisher, who had been a sergeant of the Regulars. A further account of this murder is given in Rogers's narrative in the subsequent pages of this volume. His wife and four soldiers are by some accounts reported as having been murdered at the same time.—*Thatcher, Lanman.*

poor English family that had just built a little house there, [8] as also another English family that lived just behind the fort. [9]

He also cut of the communication from the fort to the inhabitants on each side so that we could not get the least thing brought into the fort. He told the inhabitants that the first of them that should bring us any provisions or anything that could be of any service to us, they would put that family to death.

They also surrounded the fort and fired a vast number of shots at it and the vessels which were anchored so as to flank the fort both above and below. [10] The garrison lay upon the arms all night, not being above 120 men, [11] merchants, sick and officers. The 10th they surrounded it again and fired very briskly till about 11 or 12 o'clock when they made some proposals for an accommodation (which was lucky for us, as it gave us time to get provisions in to the King's store as we had not above three weeks at short allowance), and Capt. Campbell and Lieut.

---

9. This family was that of an English woman, named Turnbull, who lived outside of the fort on a distant part of the common. Major Gladwyn had given her a piece of land for her Residence. *Lanman's Michigan*, 106.

10 There were two small armed vessels lying before the fort at this time, named the *Beaver* and the *Gladwyn*. They rendered efficient service in the siege, and kept the enemy from approaching by water.

11. The garrison at the beginning of the siege consisted of one hundred and twenty-two men and eight officers, besides about forty fur-traders and *engagées*, who were more inclined to the French and were willing to be neutral. The fort was quadrilateral, with one side near the water's edge, and consisted of a single row of palisades twenty-five feet high, with block-houses over the gates and at the angles. It contained two six-pounders, one three-pounder and three mortars, badly mounted and calculated rather to inspire terror than to do execution among the skulking savages who so assiduously watched the fort, seldom venturing in numbers within range of the great guns, but ready to take off the unlucky person who might chance to show his head above the pickets, or his body before a port hole.

This enclosure contained about 100 small dwellings, closely built upon narrow streets, a council house, a small church and barracks for the troops. A wider Street, called the *Chemin du Ronde*, led around the buildings adjacent to the pickets. The buildings were of wood and very liable to be set on fire by burning arrows. The church was particularly exposed to this casualty, as it stood near to the palisades, but the Indians were threatened by the French priest with the anger of the Great Spirit, if they did not desist from their attempts to fire this building. The garrison by keeping constant watch and plenty of water in cisterns, prevented fires from taking. The river is here half a mile wide.—*Discourse of Lewis Cass, before the Hist. Soc. of Michigan, Sept. 18, 1829*, p. 29.

12. Major Donald Campbell had been succeeded by Gladwyn but a few days before. M. Gouin, a friendly Canadian, finding that these men were in great danger, hastily sent a message for them not to come out, (Continued next page.)

McDougal,[12] with the principal part of the French, who said they would be answerable for their return, went out to hold a council with him, but as soon as Pontiac got them in his possession, he changed his mind and would not come to terms as he had a few hours before promised the French, who seemed to do all in their power to make him disperse his people, but on the contrary sent word to the commandant that he must leave the fort as M. Bell Etre did, that was to say to take provision enough with him to carry him to Niagara, but to leave all the merchandise.[13] To which the commandant answered that he could not come to any terms with him until he sent back Capt. Campbell and Lieut. McDougal, for whom he would give up the two Pottawatamies that he had detained for them.

The garrison lay on their arms all night as usual. We were at the same time told by some French that they thought the best thing we could do would be to save ourselves in the vessels, as there was 1000, some said 1500 Indians ready to fall upon all sides of the fort, but they got for answer that if in case they were three times a numerous there was not an officer or [14]

*12th.* In the morning Pontiac sent another message desiring the fort to be given up, as before, to which the commandant gave an equivo-

---

but as they had already started with La Butte, one of the interpreters and some other French, they would not heed the warning and passed on. When they came to a rising ground, beyond which the Indians lay, the latter ran yelling towards them, as if they were prisoners running the gauntlet, but Pontiac allayed the tumult, and led them to a lodge, where some few words were spoken, but on their proposing to return they found themselves prisoners. They were quartered in the house of M. Meloche, near Parent Creek, and closely guarded, but otherwise well treated for the present. Two Indians had been detained in the fort a few days before, and were still in the hands of the English, which doubtless prevented the savages from acts of violence at this time.

On the 4th of July following, a nephew of an Ojibwa Chief, was killed and scalped by a party from the fort. Upon hearing this news, the enraged uncle ran to the house of Meloche, seized Major Campbell, bound him fast to a fence and killed him with arrows. He was afterwards mockingly mangled, and it was reported that his heart was eaten by the savages. Lieut. McDougall instantly fled, and succeeded in reaching the fort in safety. Some authors have stated that the murder of Major Campbell was approved by Pontiac, while others affirm that he was highly offended, and that the murderer was obliged to escape beyond his Reach. Parkman's *Pontiac*, 211, 260; MSS. Sir Wm. Johnson, vol. 7.

13. M. P. de Beletere was the last French Commandant at Detroit, before its Surrender to the English in the Autumn of 1760. He was sent with the other prisoners under the care of Lieut. Holmes and thirty Rangers to Philadelphia. Rogers's *Journal*.

14 The sentence in the manuscript thus ends abruptly.

cal answer to gain time, to get provision, having for two nights before employed some Frenchmen to put some corn and bear's grease on board the vessels unknown to the Indians. The twelfth in the morning they surrounded the fort and fired upon it and the vessels for about four hours very briskly, though at so great a distance that we had but one man slightly wounded in the fort and another on board one of the vessels. We killed three or four of them and wounded nine or ten. We set fire to some out houses from behind which they annoyed us. The garrison lay upon their arms on the rampart all night, as they had done for three nights before.

The thirteenth in the morning we heard that the Hurons had intercepted one Chapman, [15] with five *bateaus* or canoes loaded with merchandise, amongst which they got sixteen half barrels of powder and some rum, and that they were all drunk with it, upon which Hopkins,[16] with twenty-five men, among whom were Mr. Starling, Mr. Watkins and McCormick, Volunteers went on board the sloop in order to go opposite the Huron village,[17] and under the fire of her cannon to land and burn it with their booty and their corn, the wind being favourable to go up or down the river, but unluckily before he got halfway there the wind shifted and he was obliged to return, but by the fire that the Huron kept while the vessel was under sail it did not appear that they were drunk or off their guard. They constantly fired on the fort and vessels till dark, but without doing the least damage.

This afternoon burned several out-houses from behind which they

---

15 Chapman was a trader, who, without suspecting hostilities, was approaching Detroit. Heckewelder relates (*Hist. Ind. Nat.* 250), of a man of this name, and perhaps the person here referred to, that after being kept some time by a Frenchman, the Indians resolved to burn him alive. He was bound to the stake, and the flames were kindled, when in the agonies of that moment an Indian handed him a bowl of broth. Upon touching it with his lips, it was found boiling hot, and in an instant he threw the dish and its contents into the face of the savage. "He is mad! he is mad!" shouted the Crowd, and hastily quenching the fire, they relieved him from his horrid fate and set him at liberty. The superstitious awe with which the natives regarded lunatics and idiots, has been often remarked by historians, and aids in explaining some striking incidents in their annals. Chapman was brought in and surrendered July 12th, 1763.

16. Captain Hopkins had charge of a company of Rangers, and in the numerous skirmishes and sorties that occurred during the siege, he is often mentioned as having had the command. 17. The Huron village lay East of the river, a short distance below Detroit. A missionary of the Order of Carthusian Friars, by permission of the Bishop of Canada resided there.—*Carver's Travels*, p. 92.

annoyed us. The garrison lay on ramparts as usual. The twelfth in the evening Pontiac sent in another message demanding the fort, at the same time saying that the firing should cease until an answer was sent; this was to get time to bring of the dead and wounded that had fallen in the morning as appeared from about thirty or forty of them coming about the fort without arms immediately after the messenger arrived, but not so near as to be taken; after this messenger arrived we found that the corn, flour and bear's grease that we had put on board the vessels and that we found in the fort would last us for upwards of three months.

The answer to the above message is in the memorandum of the 16th.

The fourteenth[18] they began firing at about eleven o'clock and continued till dark, not daring to approach nearer than the nearest houses that could cover them, which was upwards of two hundred yards off. They fired a great deal but more upon the vessels than on the fort. We had this day a serjeant and one private man wounded.

*15th.* Last night these Indians made a kind of breastwork between the fort and Mr. St. Martin's house of some pickets that he had for a garden. [19] This morning we cut two embrasures through the stockades for two four pounders with which we intended to dislodge them in case they should return again. But instead of their coming to fire in the manner they had done yesterday, there was only a few of them came and began firing scattering shot at eleven o'clock and continued so till the evening which we did not mind. This morning a party went out

---

18. Major Gladwyn appears to have succeeded this day in getting off a letter to Gen. Amherst, as appears from an epistle of the latter to Col. Bradstreet, Q. M. G., dated June 22, 1763:

"Major Gladwyn writes me of the 14th May, that the Detroit was inverted by a large body of Indians; but that the garrison was in high spirits, and he was in hopes of being able to defend the place untill he received some Succours from Niagara; and Major Wilkins acquaints me he had, immediately on the arrival of the schooner from the Detroit, sent off a reinforcement of fifty men with a lieutenant and non-commissioned officers, which I trust will have arrived in time to save the place. I well know that you are always ready, however I think it necessary to acquaint you to be prepared for moveing at a moment's warning, as, if the savages are not quickly reduced, I believe I shall employ you on a command which I am certain will be agreeable to you."—*Bradstreet and Amherst Papers*, p. 140.

19. St. Martin, a French interpreter, lived near the fort, and his house was a convenient Point from whence the Indians might annoy the garrison. The Owner appears to have been very kindly disposed toward the English, and on the 30th of June withdrew with his family into the fort.

and burned the remainder of the houses that was near the fort from behind which they annoyed the vessels. They day before yesterday we were informed that Mr. Rutherford, [20] who was with Capt. Robinson, was not killed but remains a prisoner with the Indians.

The garrison lay on their arms tonight as usual.

*16th.* The answer the commandant sent to the verbal message that Pontiac sent the 12th in the evening was, that he was not sent here to give up the fort to Indians, and advised Pontiac to disperse his people and take care of his ammunition to hunt with.

This morning at 11 o'clock they began to fire scattering shot from Mr. St. Martin's house and Mr. Babie's, [21] and continued till evening, but without doing us any damage.

The most of the inhabitants assembled themselves today to speak to Pontiac, who told them before he would give over his design he would send two Frenchmen and two Indians to the Illinois to inform himself whether what we had told him with regard to the peace was true or not, and as to Capt. Campbell and Lieut. McDougal he would take care of them, and deliver them to the commandant that he had sent for from the Illinois.

This day a few shot were fired as usual from Mr. Babie's and Mr. St. Martin's houses at the vessels without doing any execution. The garrison lay on the ramparts.

*17th.* This day there was not above a dozen Indians appeared within sight of the fort, who did not fire above twenty shot. The garrison lay on the rampart.

*18th.* This day a few shot were fired from St. Martin's and Babie's as usual without damage. The garrison lay on the ramparts.

*19th.* This day we were very quiet, not having ten shot fired at us. We were last night informed that there was upwards of 150 Indians

---

20. Mr. Samuel Rutherford was subsequently purchased by M. Cuesiere, from the Indians, for £80 worth in goods, but Pontiac upon learning the fact went with a body of fifty men and reclaimed him, saying it was not a good precedent to sell prisoners to the French. He escaped to the fort on the first day of August.—*Lanman's Hist. Michigan*, 108.

21. M. Babie, a Frenchman in easy circumstances, evinced the greatest friendship to the English, and secretly furnished them with provisions, at a time when they were much needed. He came into the fort with his family, July 3, bringing such of his goods as he could remove, and leaving the remainder at the mercy of the Indians. His house was burned by the English as a precautionary measure on the 25th of August.

gone to the mouth of the river to intercept some parties that we expected from Niagara, upon which the commandant ordered the schooner to be got ready for sea to send her down to cover them in case they came safe to the mouth of the river.

*20th.* We also received some letters last night from Fort St. Josephs by an Indian that we had sent from here, everything there seemed quiet and the Indians declared great deal of friendship for the garrison.

This evening a man that was taken prisoner six days ago by some Ottawas and Mingoes in the Huron River arrived here by the assistance of two or three Frenchmen that were coming down that river. He informed us that he was hired with one Crawford a trader who was on his way home, that about fifteen Indians met with them and laid down their arms and called them brothers, but after having reconnoitred them and finding they had a great quantity of peltry fell upon them and took them all prisoners and obliged them to return with them to a carrying place on a small river that runs into the Miami, from whence he made his escape as the Indians took him from a Frenchman, he speaking a little French.

The garrison lay on the ramparts as usual.

*21st.* At eleven o'clock the schooner sailed for the mouth of the river with a N. E. wind.[22] No Indians appeared near the fort today till the afternoon when a few came and fired some shot at the sloop.

At six in the evening it was reported the schooner was run aground, upon which all the Indians gathered themselves together to attack her, but the foremost canoe having one man killed by a shot from her frightened the rest so much that they put ashore again.

*22nd.* This morning at 8 o'clock we were informed that after the Indians had attempted to attack the schooner she carried out an anchor and hauled off and this morning arrived at the mouth of the river.

At 9 o'clock Mr. St. Martin came with a message from the Hurons, who desired him to tell the commandant that they had been forced into the war by the Ottawas, that they had taken Chapman and his merchandise, as also a canoe with five Englishmen coming from Sandusky yesterday, among whom were Mr. Smallman and two Jews, who

22. Other accounts state that the vessel which sailed this day for Niagara, was the *Gladwin*, the smaller of the two, and rated at about eighty tons. Carver records the fact that she was afterwards loft on Lake Erie with all her crew, through the obstinacy of her commander, who could not be prevailed upon to take in sufficient ballast.—*Carver's Travels*, p. 99.

must have all fallen into worse hands if they had not taken them, as they had not killed any of them; they desired to know what opinion the commandant had of them, that if he would make peace with them they would give up their prisoners and pay Chapman for the part of his merchandise that fell to their lot in the division of them with the other Indians; to which the commandant desired the interpreter, Mr. St. Martin, to answer that upon these conditions he would take it upon himself to make peace with them for the present and recommend them to the general,[23] who he made no doubt would make it a lasting one if their future behaviour should merit it. They also offered to get themselves entrenched on a small island at the mouth of the river and protect all merchants boats from the other nations that should arrive there. But the commandant did not ask that of them for several good reasons, but would rather they should perform their promises and remain quiet, or use their endeavours to separate Pontiac and his followers, who at this time had cut off all communication between us and our outposts, as also lay in wait at different places to intercept all merchants that might be on their way hither.

He reigned at this time with most despotic sway over the French, making several of them plough land for him to put corn in the ground, and after they had done would kill their cattle. Three days ago he sent six Frenchmen with some Indians amongst some other nations to advertise them of what he was doing and to bring him word from the Illinois whether what we had told him with regard to the peace was true or not. [24]

We had not one shot fired at us today, notwithstanding which the garrison lay on the ramparts as usual.

*23rd.* This morning Pontiac being informed that the schooner was on ground, forced Capt. Campbell to cross the river with him in order to put him on board of a canoe to go and tell the commander of her to give her to the Indians, but when he arrived at the Huron village he was again informed that she was in the lake, upon which he returned. When Pontiac proposed this to Capt. Campbell, he told

23 Sir Jeffrey Amherst, then Commander-in-Chief of the British forces in North America.

24 The commandant at the Illinois was at this time M. de Neyon, who was stationed at Fort Chartres, the principal post of the French in that region. This was located near Kaskaskia, on the Mississippi, in the present County of Randolph, Ill. It was built in 1720, under the auspices of the Mississippi Company. The capitulation of Montreal did not include the remote French posts beyond the great lakes. *Brown's Hist. Ill.,* 165.

him he might put him to death for he would not go, but Pontiac told him he would not put him to death, but he would oblige him to go, and forced him. [25]

We had not one shot fired at us today.

The Hurons promised to remain neuter for five or six days to try if they could not by some means get Pontiac to separate his people, at the expiration of which time they expected some of the Delaware and Shawanee chiefs who was to join with them and oblige Pontiac to come to their terms.

The garrison lay upon the ramparts as usual.

*24th.* At about seven in the evening the Indians surrounded us and began to fire on the sloop and continued till about ten o'clock, when the people on board observed a great number firing from one place they pointed a six pounder and fired it, after which they did not fire ten shot though they had fired upwards of a thousand before; at eleven they began to fire from Mr. St. Martin's house upon the flag bastion where we are informed there was about two hundred who brought combustibles to set fire to the fort, but none of them dare approach nearer than where they could be covered, they kept a very hot fire till after one, which we did not mind, hardly ever returning a shot, till hearing one of them speaking louder than the rest and a great many answering him, the commandant pointed a four pounder at the place loaded with a ball and grape and fired it, soon after which they went off, not firing twenty shot after it, though they had fired very briskly from 11. By the death song that they sung two or three times we imagine there was some killed or wounded. The garrison lay upon the ramparts.

*25th.* This morning everything was quiet till the afternoon all which time we employed in making a kind of cavalier[26] to flank the bank between Mr. St. Martin's house from whence they much annoyed us, but at four in the afternoon they surrounded us with combustibles as yesterday, which prevented our raising the cavalier, instead of which Mr. Watkins was sent out to take with five men to take pos-

25. Other accounts state that the schooner lay becalmed, upon discovering which the Indians came out in their canoes, with Major Campbell in the prow of the foremost as a shield against the fire of the English. The brave old officer called out to the crew to do their duty regardless of the consequences to him—*Parkman's Pontiac*, 230.
26. A mound of earth, usually built in the gorge of a bastion, and several feet higher. It is used to defilade the works from the fire of an enemy on an adjacent height, or to command the trenches of the besiegers.—*Brande's Dictionary*.

session of that part of the bank that the enemy annoyed us from the yesterday, which not only prevented them from approaching but drove them away, so that from 9 at night we had not a shot fired at us. The garrison on the ramparts.

*26th.* This morning early we put up the cavalier. At 9 o'clock we were informed that last night a party of Ottawas arrived from Sandusky who brought Ensign Paulle, [27] the commandant prisoner having entered the fort with a few that he thought were his friends, who seized him and put the garrison to death. The Ottawas that went there told the Hurons that this place was taken and that their brothers and the rest of the Hurons had taken up the hatchet against us, notwithstanding which the Hurons would not consent for three days.

This afternoon we were informed that Pontiac having understood that the vessel was still at the mouth of the river, took Capt. Campbell by force as before, with an intent to oblige him to go with them in order to take her by treachery. They also took M. La Bute the interpreter and a Frenchman that could speak English. The garrison lay on the ramparts.

*27th.* This morning at daylight we fired two cannon to advertise the vessel that they might not be deceived as Pontiac intended in making them believe it was peace. Everything was quiet last night.

At 3 in the afternoon Pontiac returned with Capt. Campbell, and said that he had demanded the vessel, but the commandant would not give her up, upon which Pontiac told him they would come and attack him, and he answered they might. Then he went and encamped on a neighbouring island, but the vessel weighed anchor and went off before day. This Pontiac says.

A few shot fired as usual at the vessel today and a few at the fort. The garrison lay on the ramparts. We were informed tonight by M. St. Martin that the Hurons were still resolved to remain neuter, and that in case the Ottawas obliged them to take up arms they would

27. Ensign Christopher Paully, of Sandusky, on the 16th of May was treacherously seized while in conversation with seven Indians, disarmed and made prisoner, most of the garrison under his command killed, the fort burned, and himself thrust into a canoe and taken on to Detroit. On the way he was threatened with being burned alive, and upon arriving at Pontiac's camp he was assailed with the barbarous treatment usually bestowed upon prisoners. An old woman, whose husband had died, chose to adopt him in place of the deceased warrior, and he accepted the alternative to save his life, but watching the first opportunity escaped and reached the fort at Detroit, July 4th. He had been commissioned an Ensign in the 60th Regiment, Feb. 8, 1761.—*Parkman's Pontiac,* 238, 260.

go off into the woods. That if the rest of their nation which were at Sandusky would not desist they would disarm them.

*28th.* Nothing of consequence today. Some councils were held between the French and Indians about their cattle. Some few shots as usual were fired at the vessel and fort. The garrison lay on the ramparts.

*29th.* This morning we were informed that there was about fifty Ottawas who lay in ambush in a hollow way behind M. St. Martin's house all day yesterday, imagining that we should make a sortie as we had done two or three days before to burn some logs that they had made a breastwork of. This we suppose was in consequence of what some of the French told them.

At 10 o'clock we were informed that two *bateaus* were cut off in the River Huron with nineteen soldiers and a woman which we suppose must have been Serjeant Shaw who went from this with provisions to Michilimackinac, the 17th April.

At 3 in the afternoon Mr. Sterling[28] received a letter from Mr. Rutherford informing him that on the 8th instant they were informed that by some French people in the River Huron that the Indians were ill inclined and begged them to go no further, but Sir Robert [Davers] and Capt. Robinson did not give much credit to it and went on, that on turning a point at the entrance of the lake they were fired upon by some Indians who killed Sir Robert, Capt. Robinson and two soldiers the first shot, the rest they took prisoners. This evening a few shot were fired at the vessel and fort as usual, without doing any damage. The garrison lay on their arms.

*30th.* This morning at 8 o' clock we had the disagreeable sight of eight *bateaus* with provisions that a party of Indians had taken belonging to a party commanded by Lieut. Scuyler,[29] the [28th] instant, about fourteen miles from the mouth of the river; as the affair hap-

28 Mr. Sterling was an English Trader then at Detroit. After the receipt of the treaty by which Canada was confirmed to the English, he was appointed to take charge of the French who were in the fort.

29 This should have been written *Cuyler.* He had left Fort Niagara May 14th, with 96 men in eighteen boats, and a plentiful supply of provisions and military stores. He had met neither friend nor foe until he landed on the 28th at Point Pelée to encamp The party was surprised by a great number of Indians in ambush. The men threw down their arms and fled to their boats, five of which pushed off, but only two of which escaped. The following letter from Niagara gave the first intelligence of this event to the Superintendent of Indian Affairs in America:(Cont. next page.)

pened in the night we have no just accounts of the killed and prisoners, but Lieut. Scuyler with two *bateaus* made their escape. When they were passing the fort at about 600 yards distance we called to them, as there was but a few Indians in some of them, and told them to push off towards the vessel and she would cover them with her fire, upon which the foremost, having four soldiers and two Indians [30] in it put off, the soldiers seizing the Indians and throwing them overboard and gained the vessel notwithstanding the fire of the Indians from the shore. The *bateau* had seven barrels of pork and one of flour on board. One of the soldiers fell overboard with the Indians whom after a great struggle they tomahawked.

At three in the afternoon the remainder of the party that was at the lake returned and brought two or three traders' *bateaus*, which they lay in wait for, being informed they were coming by the prisoners they took of Mr. Cuyler's party. The garrison lay on the ramparts as usual.

*31st.* This morning two drunken Indians came up to the fort without arms, being hot brave, to set fire to it, but were fired upon one

---

Niagara, 6th June, 1763

Honoured Sir: By my letter of yesterday you'll be fully informed of everything that come to my hands since my last of the month of May.★ I shall only signify to you at present what accounts have come here since last night: first, that the Queen's Independents upon their way to the Detroit, and a serjeant and twenty men of the 60th Regiment within 25 miles of that place, at 11 o'clock at night were attacked by a party of Indians and out of 76 of the Independents only 36 returned here.

That the Old Betts daughter has been informed this day by a Seneca *sachem* to quit this place, as they have received a belt from the Indians about Pittsburg to take up the bloody hatchet, and that all the surrounding Indians in them parts are absolutely determined thereupon.

An answer the Senecas have not given to those who sent the belt till such times as all the *sachems* must be first made acquainted of their proceedings the likewise have sent with the belt one scalp that they took in or about Pittsburg. You may depend upon me to give you the most timely Notice of everything that pertains to his Majesty's Service in the most distinct manner that my capacity will permit and never shall fail meriting honoured sir to be

your faithful servant,        De Couagne.

The Honourable Sir Wm. Johnson.

—*MSS. of Sir William Johnson*, vol. 7.

★ This letter relates the insolent demands of the Indians for rum, but no hostilities had then been heard of.

30. Other accounts state the number of Indians in this boat as *three*. The *soldier* that perished was drawn overboard by the Indian he was throwing out, and some authorities relate that they perished in each other's embrace. Another writer affirms that the Indian swam ashore.—*Parkman's Pontiac*, 233.

of which fell on the spot and the other ran away but fell in our sight, and we since hear is dead. The Indians have been so drunk this two days past that they did not fire five shot at us. The garrison lay on the ramparts.

*June 1st.* This morning at about 3 o' clock two men called from the hill behind the fort who told us they were two traders that had made their escape from the Indians who we let in at a small port. A quarter of an hour after a man called to the vessel for a boat from the other side of the river, but thinking it might be a decoy, we got two Frenchmen in a canoe who went brought over a man of Capt. Hopkins company who made his escape from the Indians after Mr. Cuyler's defeat and crossed the country from lake; he brought his arms with him. This day some Indian canoes went down the river as we suppose to cut off some more traders' boats that is expected from Niagara. The garrison lay on the ramparts.

*2nd.* This morning about fifteen canoes went down the river as we imagine to intercept some more traders that are on the way between Niagara and this place. In the afternoon a Frenchman brought in a letter that was enclosed to me from Niagara which Capt. Campbell gave in, by which we were informed that the definitive treaty was signed at London the 20th February. Not a shot was fired today. The garrison lay on the ramparts.

*3rd.* This afternoon a few shots were fired at the fort and vessel as usual. The garrison lay upon the ramparts as usual.

*4th.* This morning Mr. Cuesiere purchased Mr. Rutherford from the Indians on condition that he should keep himself. A few shot were fired at the fort and vessel as usual. This evening some Indians arrived with four prisoners and some scalps and reported that Miamee was taken,[31] and that the Shawanees and Delawares had commenced hostilities at Fort Pitt.[32]

---

31. Fort Miami, on the Maumee, under the Command of Ensign Holmes, was treacherously captured on the 27th of May. Holmes was enticed away from the fort by a young Indian girl who lived with him, and represented that a squaw lay dangerously ill in a wigwam not far off. He was shot; the sergeant who came out to learn the cause of the firing, was taken prisoner, and the remainder surrendered at discretion.—*Parkman's Pontiac*, 244. A similar version of this affair is recorded in this *Diary* for June 8, and a further statement June 15th.
32. On the 27th of May a party of Indians approached Fort Pitt and encamped. The next day they came to the fort with pack horses laden with valuable furs, with which to purchase ammunition. (Continued next page.)

*5th.* This afternoon about fifty Indians fired for an hour or two at the fort and vessel without doing any execution. The garrison lay on the ramparts.

*6th.* This day we were informed that the commandant of Fort St. Joseph was prisoner with the Pottawatamies; we imagine that he was obliged to evacuate his post not having more than a hundred weight of flour the 12 May and in attempting to come here was taken. [33] It was also reported that Miamis was taken, but it was reported so many different ways that we did not believe it.

Some days ago Mr. Cuesiere purchased Mr. Rutherford from the Indians, but a Mississague Indian arriving the day before yesterday and informing Pontiac that they nor the Six Nations had not struck nor would not strike if the peace was made, alarmed him, upon which he went with fifty men and took back the prisoner, saying that it was not a good president [34] to sell their prisoners, that when things come to be accommodated they could exchange them or give them up as they saw occasion. Everything quiet today. The garrison lay on the ramparts.

*7th.* This day the Indian chiefs had a council at the Pottawatamies but for what end we know not. A few shot were fired at the vessel and fort as usual. The garrison lay on the ramparts.

Yesterday Pontiac took two prisoners from Mr. Babie that he had purchased from the Indians, telling him the same that he told Cuesiere.

*8th.* The council held yesterday as we are informed was to conclude upon a method to attack the vessel, which they intend by fitting up eight *bateaus* and lining them, with which they are to fall down the

---

Tidings of murders and burning were soon after brought in, and the country around was speedily visited by a distressing warfare in which many persons were killed, and communication with the rest of the province was entirely cut off. On the 28th of July it was vigorously besieged, but on the 1st of August the enemy withdrew to attack Gen. Bouquet, by whom they were defeated in the memorable fight at Bushy Run.—*Parkman's Pontiac*, 359.

33. The post at St. Joseph in charge of Ensign Schlosser with fourteen men, was surprised on the morning of May 25th, by a large number of Pottawatamies, who came into the fort in an insolent and disorderly manner. At a given signal, those within rushed to the gate, killed the sentinel and ten other men, and took the commandant and the three surviving men prisoners. He was exchanged at Detroit, on 15th of June.—*Parkman's Pontiac*, 240.

Schlosser's Statement is recorded in this *Diary* for June 15th.

34. Precedent.

stream and board her, while a great number keeps a hot fire upon the fort. This to be done in a very dark night. All quiet today except a few shot from St. Martins house. The garrison lay on the ramparts.

*9th.* This afternoon three *bateaus* passed up the river that were taken by the Chippewas near the place Mr. Cuyler was defeated. There was eleven persons in them, two of whom were killed, the rest they brought here prisoners.

We were also well assured that the Miami was taken, as a Frenchman spoke to the corporal of that garrison who was prisoner with the Indians, who told him that Mr. Holmes had been informed of the designs of the Indians and that he had shut the gates of the fort, which the Indians seeing found they could not take it but by treachery, accordingly they employed a squaw that Mr. Holmes kept to bring him out of the fort to bleed her sister who was sick in a *caban*, and as soon as he came there three or four Ottawas who had hid themselves on purpose fired at him and killed him, then took one Welch whom they had prisoner and went to the fort and made him tell the men if they would lay down their arms they should be all saved, upon which they opened the gates. We hear they have carried them towards the Illinois. The garrison lay on their arms.

*10th.* This day the Pottawatamies sent Mr. Gamelin with a message to the commandant desiring to change Mr. Schlosser for one of the Indians we have in custody. To which the commandant answered that they must first let him know how many prisoners they had taken and what they had done with them, and gave leave to four of the chiefs with Mr. Gamelin to come within thirty yards of the fort to speak to the two we had in custody, at their request. In a hour afterwards the whole nation came to Mr. St. Martin's house (when the garrison was ordered on the ramparts), where they halted and sent forward four chiefs, who told they were led into the war by Pontiac, &c.; to which the commandant answered he believed it, and therefore advised them to disperse and mind their hunting and planting, for if they persisted it would end in their utter ruin. To which they hung their heads and one of them said he believed it. They said they had fourteen prisoners and Mr. Schlosser, all of whom the commandant demanded, as one of the Indians we had in custody was one of the first men in the nation. To which they did not give a positive answer but went to hold a council.

Everything quiet today. The garrison lay on the ramparts.

*11th.* This day we permitted some more of the Pottawatamies to speak to the two we had in custody.

All quiet today. The garrison lay on the ramparts.

*12th.* Yesterday one Cavalier arrived from Montreal who informed us that at Grand River, within thirty miles of the end of Lake Erie, seven English *bateaus* with merchandise was attacked by some Indians, five of which were taken, the other two made their escape; that there was one Lascelle with him from Montreal at the same time who returned to Niagara.

At five o'clock about thirty Indians arrived at Pontiac's camp from Saggina, who made with what he had in camp 168 Indians besides 250 that went down the river a few days ago as it was said to cut off the communication at Niagara. Neither Cavalier nor young Lascelle, who arrived two days before him, are yet come into the fort although Lascelle arrived two days before the other, they say the Indians have threatened to kill them if they come nearer than a certain distance.

All quiet today. The day before yesterday and today made sorties and burnt some out houses and gardens. The garrison lay on the ramparts.

Yesterday and today we buried five corpses that we took up in the river, two of whom we knew but the rest was so mangled that it was impossible for anybody to have the least knowledge of them.

*13th.* Nothing extraordinary today. Three of the Pottawatamies came and spoke with the two we had in custody, who declared to us that they knew nothing of this affair till they arrived at their village below the fort, when much to their surprise they heard a great firing. That they never had any message sent to them about it, nor was they consulted in any manner whatever, but was forced into it by the Ottawas.

Upon which the commandant asked them if they were the slaves of Pontiac, at which they hung their heads; he then told them what he had told them before with regard to their dispersing, and that they would see in the end that the Ottawas would kill Pontiac for bringing them into such an undertaking, for that they, and every one that joined heartily with them, would be ruined; as they would forfeit their lands and be deprived of all the necessaries of life. Upon which they promised to go to their camps and send in their corn, &c. The garrison lay on the ramparts.

*14th.* Yesterday we heard that Outattanon was cut off and the garrison taken to the Illinois.[35]

Everything quiet today. The garrison lay on the ramparts.

*15th.* This morning between eleven and twelve o'clock one of the chiefs of the Pottawatamies (named Washee) who took St. Josephs, came with four or five others to change some of their prisoners for the two that we had in custody, and after talking near two hours, the commandant got them to consent to give Mr. Schlosser and two soldiers that they brought with them for one of them that he had, and promised them that when they brought the rest of the prisoners he would give them the other. They did not seem to be well contented as they expected the man of the most consequence in return for the officer, but the commandant was almost sure that if he gave him up they would not give above one of the eleven that remained with them for the other, and therefore detained him.

The account Mr. Schlosser gives of the way he was taken is, that about seventeen Pottawatamies came into his fort under a pretence of holding a council, after they had engaged the young men of the nation about him to join with them, to whom they promised all the plunder after they were in the fort, Washashe the Pottawatamie chief went into his room with three or four others, to whom he had presented a belt, as he could speak a little of their language himself, for they had detained his interpreter on the other side of the river till everything was ready, but before they had made him an answer a Frenchman came in and told him their design, upon which the cry was given in the fort and they seized him immediately and the young men that agreed to join him rushed into the fort, knocking down the sentinel and before the men could get to their arms put ten of them to death, which Washashe tried to prevent but in vain, the remaining three and himself they took prisoners.

After this was done all the chiefs of the St. Joseph Indians came to Mr. Schlosser and told him that they knew nothing of the affair, that their young men crossed the river in the night unknown to them, and desired him to acquaint the commandant here that they were not concerned in the war, nor would not be.

---

35. Ouatanon was a fort on the Wabash, a little below the present town of Lafayette. It was then under the command of Lt. Edward Jenkins, who was taken on the first of June, by stratagem, with several of his men, when the remainder of the garrison yielded without resistance. The Indians, however, apologized for their conduct, by saying that they acted under the influence of other tribes and against their own better judgements.—*Parkman's Pontiac*, 243.

One of the soldiers we got today was taken at June. Miamee who gives the same account of its being taken as we have already heard, with this difference, that the serjeant after he heard the shots that were fired at Mr. Holmes went out to see what it was and was taken prisoner, after which they brought one Walch whom they had prisoner to tell them what has been already mentioned, upon which they delivered up the fort, and French colours was immediately hoisted in it, but does not know whether it was the French or Indians that hoisted them. This evening we were informed from good authority that Saggina Indians had been with Mr. Labute to desire him to speak to the commandant to make peace with them, that they had not yet entered into the war, that is they had neither killed anybody nor did they take any merchants. To which Mr. Labute answered they knew well enough he dared not go to the fort, that if Pontiac knew he spoke to the English he would put him to death, and told them they must come themselves.

All quiet today. The garrison lay on the ramparts. We are assured that all the chiefs of the Hurons are peaceably inclined but there is a band of twenty-five young men that they can't bring over part of whom are gone to Niagara with the Ottawas.

*16th.* This day at twelve o'clock Washashe with two other Pottawatamie chiefs, and two Saggina Indians [37] came with a flag to speak to the commandant. After they entered the fort one of the Pottawatamies got up with a string of *wampum* and desired to be heard. That what they had already told him was true, and that what they were going to say was from their hearts, upon which he presented the *wampum*.

He then took another string and told the commandant that the two Saggina Indians were sent in the name of all their chiefs, that they were brothers, and their hearts inclined the same way. That they the Pottawatamies knew nothing of the commencement of the war, but were hurried into it by the Ottawas, but they had now buried the hatchet and it should never rise again. Upon which they presented the *wampum*. Then took another string and said they had sent messengers for the rest of their prisoners who should be all delivered up as soon as they came in.

Then one of the Saggina Indians got up with a string of *wampum* and said he was sent in the name of their chief and desired he might be heard. That their hands and ours had always been joined since we

---

37 One of the latter was Mindoghquay. He returned to the fort Dec. 12th, tendering his friendship.

took possession of this country, and they never should be parted; that they had not entered into the war at all, that their hearts were the same as the Pottawatamies, and intended to remain so; that he spoke the real sentiments of the hearts of all their chiefs, which he desired we should believe, knowing that if he told lies the great God would be offended at him, upon which he presented the *wampum*. Then the commandant took a small belt and desired to know before he gave them an answer, whether the Pottawatamie chiefs that were there spoke only for their bands in particular or for the whole nation, to which they answered for the whole nation.

He then told them that he was glad they had opened their eyes and did not intend to persist in a thing that must end in their ruin, that the only thing they could do to convince him of their good intentions would be to give up the rest of their prisoners and go to their villages and tend their corn and hunt. That he would then recommend them to the general, and that they would find everything he told them was true. That the peace was actually made between the French and us, and if they persisted in a thing of this kind we should not only fight against them, but the Canadians (the people they thought they were fighting for) would also take arms against them as we were all one. That he knew they were made to believe there was no peace and that there was an army coming from the Illinois, but those that told them so, told lies, and were their enemies, which they would soon see. That if they took his advice and did as he desired them they might live for the future in tranquillity as they had done before, and see the Ottawas starving in the woods for want of the necessaries of life that they could no ways get but from us. Then presented the belt.

The Saggina Indians further said that the Michilimackinac Indians would not strike and if Pontiac attempted to go towards that post they would prevent him.

The commandant then took another string and told the Saggina that he was glad to hear they were so well inclined and that they had more sense than to be lead into a thing by the Ottawas (that would be their ruin). That he never intended anything but peace with them, that the Ottawas began the war without any reason, that he was well pleased with their behaviour and would also recommend them to the general if they continued at their villages in the same tranquillity that they said they were then in. That they might be sure everything he said was true which they would find in the end, and desired them not to give ear to any lies that might be spread amongst them. Then

38

gave the *wampum*. Upon which the Saggina Indian said he was glad to receive it, that the chiefs would believe when they saw his mouth (as he called the *wampum*) they were pitied. All quiet today. The garrison lay on the ramparts.

*17th.* All quiet today. This evening we was told that a cannon was heard at the mouth of the river about 11 o'clock this morning, which must have been the vessel; a little after sunset we fired another to answer her. Upon the report of the cannon in the morning several Indians were sent off to see if she was there or not. The garrison lay on the ramparts.

Since the first information that we had of the Indian intention of attacking the vessel with *bateaus*, Capt. Hopkins lay on board of her every night.

*18th.* This day the Jesuist arrived from Michilimackinac, with the disagreeable news of its being cut off by treachery. The particulars not yet come to hand. All quiet today. The garrison lay on the ramparts.

*19th.* This day the Jesuist came into the fort, and brought a letter[38] from Capt. Etherington by which we were informed, That the 2nd June the Chippewas were playing at Cross[39] at Michilimackinac (three days after they had a council with him and professed a great deal of friendship. That upon the arrival of a canoe from Saggina, one Mr. Tracy a merchant went to the waterside to speak to them which the Indians seeing said to themselves now is the time, for if these people enter the fort they will tell our design, upon which they tomahawked Mr. Tracy and gave the cry, and in an instant seized Capt. Etherington and Lieut. Lessley who were at the gate of the fort looking at them playing, forced by the centry and entered the fort where they found their squaws (who had been previously placed with their tomahawks)

---

38 This letter, dated June 12th, is published in *Parkman's Pontiac*, p. 596, from the original, as preserved in the State Paper Office of London. It is substantially the same as that of Capt. Claus, given on the following pages. The Jesuit referred to was Father Jonois, then stationed at L'Arbre Croche.

39 The game of La Crosse, or Baggattway, is played with a bat and ball; two posts are planted in the ground, about a mile apart, and each party having its post, the object is to propel the ball, which is placed in the centre, toward the post of the adversary. In the ardour of contest, if the ball cannot be driven to the desired goal, it is struck in any direction by which it can be diverted from that designed by the opposite party.

A game much similar is still played by the Iroquois of New York and Canada.— *Carver's Travels*, 201; *Smith's Hist. Wisconsin*, 1, 137; *N.Y. Senate Doc.*, 1850, No. 75, p. 81.

with which they forced the guard before they could get under arms, killed thirteen men on the spot with Lieut. Jamet who fought with his sword against five for a long time, but after receiving thirty-six wounds fell in their hands after which they cut off his head and killed six of their prisoners; they pillaged all the merchants and got fifty barrels of powder with lead in proportion.

The Ottawas took the officers and eleven of their prisoners from them whom they keep at the priest's house. Capt. Etherington then gave a written authority to Mr. Langlad [40] to command in the fort till further orders, and recommended him Mr. Langlad and one Mr. Farli to the commandant here as good men and who did all in their power for the good of the service, as also the Jesuist who has a great deal to say among the Indians. [41]

40 Sieur Augustine du Langlade, about 1750, became the owner of most of the lands around Green Bay, and his descendants still reside there. He was a man of character and education, and retained the polished manners of the French Metropolis. His son, Charles Langlade, was a native of this country and in 1760 was commissioned by Louis XV, and appointed Second in Command at Michilimackinack, where he was residing at the time of the massacre. The narrative of Alexander Henry, the trader, gives an unfavourable impression with regard to the humanity of M. Langlade. At the time of the attack, as the Indians were pursuing the English from one retreat to another, Henry rushed into his house and besought him to afford an asylum. The Frenchman, who stood at his window watching the slaughter, looked at him a moment and then turned again to the window, shrugging his shoulders and remarking, "*Que voudriez-vous que j'en ferais?*" "What would you have me do?" He afterwards willingly submitted the keys of his house to allow the savages to search his premises for English.—*Smith's Hist. Wisconsin*, 1, 346; *Henry's Travels*.

41. The circumstances attending the attack upon Michilimackinack and its capture by the Indians, on the 4th of June are also set forth in the following extract from a letter written at Montreal by Capt. Daniel Claus to Sir William Johnson:
"......6th Aug. Whilst I am writing this, my landlord tells me that Capt. [George] Etherington and Lieut. [James] Lessley passed the door coming from Michillimacki-nack who I heare with all the traders except one Trasey [Tracy] who was killed by the enemy Indians were escorted here by the Ottawas as living near that place. I followed them immediately to the Governor's, and there learned the news of them parts, which is that a parcel of Chippeways to the number of 100 assembled near the fort as customary in the beginning of summer, and diverted themselves playing foot-ball, and Capt. Ethrington and Mr. Lessley (not suspecting the least treachery, having then not heard a word of Detroit being besieged by the enemy Indians) stood out of the fort to see the Indians play: that on a signal given by a yell, they both were seized and bound, and that the same instant the sentries were tomahawked, likewise Mr. James, who was officer of the day in the fort, together with 18 soldiers killed and taken. Then the traders were plundered and taken prisoners; that afterwards themselves were dragged to the Chippeways' encampment where the spoil was divided, and a council held, (Continued next page.)

All quiet today. The garrison lay on the ramparts.

*20th.* This morning the commanding officer gave the Jesuist some memorandum of what he should say to the Indians and French at Michilimackinac, as also to Capt. Etherington, as he did not choose to carry a letter saying that if he was asked by the Indians if he had any he would be obliged to say yes, as he never told a lie in his life. He gave him a belt to give to the Ottawas there, desiring him to tell them that he was very well pleased with their not meddling in an affair that must end in their ruin.

That if they send their prisoners to Montreal, it will convince the general of their good intentions for which they will be probably well rewarded.

in what manner the officers were to be put to death. In the meantime the news reached the Ottawa town thirty miles from Michillimackinack, who without any delay set off armed to Michillimackinack, and inquired into the reason of the Chippeways' behaviour, The latter had nothing to say but that a few days before the blow, they received belts of *wampum* from Pontiac, the Ottawas' Chief at Detroit, in conjunction with ye chiefs of their nation living there, informing them of the rupture with the English, and desiring them to cut off Michillimackinack. The Ottawas were surprised and chagrined and insisted upon the Chippeways delivering up the prisoners, &c.

"The latter to reconcile themselves with the Ottawas, made up a heap of goods and put Mr. Lassley and two soldiers by them as their share of the prey, but they would not accept of it, and demanded all the prisoners. The Chippeways at last gave way and delivered over Mr. Lassley and the soldiers and demanded a ransom for the traders, which they agreed to, and being every one exchanged they took them into their care and afterwards escorted them safe to this place. The officers and traders cannot say enough of the good behaviour of these Ottawas and General Gage is resolved to use and reward them well for their behaviour. As Capt. Etherington is going to Gen. Amherst, you will doubtless hear the particulars of the whole affair. By what I can find none but the Chippeways at Michillimackinack and those of the same nation and Ottawas at Detroit, are concerned in the present breach.

"All the rest of the western nations, and even some Chippeways living at the Falls of St. Mary would not engage or receive the belts sent by Pontiac, and on the contrary are very well inclined to our interest, in particular the nations living at La Bay, and the Sioux, who are always at war with the Chippeways; and if the Indians now here (among whom there are some other nations as they come here in behalf of eight nations to the westward who assure us of their friendship) leave this satisfied; it may be of infinite service which I intend to represent to General Gage, and I believe you will approve of making them handsome presents as an encouragement for their good behaviour, and the only means of chastising those villainous nations who are the occasion of this unhappy event. . . . "—*MSS. of Sir William Johnson*, vol. 7.

The circumstances of the capture of Michillimackinack, have been related with great minuteness by Alexander Henry, an eyewitness, who narrowly escaped the massacre.—*Henry's Travels.*

To give his compliments to Mr. Langlad and Mr. Farli and thank them for their good offices which he exhorts them to continue. To desire them to try and prevent as much as possible all commerce with our enemies, above all ammunition and arms. That he authorizes Mr. Langlad to command in the fort according to the orders given him by Capt. Etherington till further orders.

To desire Capt. Etherington to try to advertise the Governor of Montreal of what has happened as soon as possible, and to send back all merchants that may be on the way, English or French, if they find from circumstances of affairs it is necessary. To tell him all the news that he has heard from us that might be depended upon regarding the posts that has been surprised and murdered, and that the definitive treaty was signed at London the 20th of February according to the *Articles of the Cessation of Arms*.

This day we heard that some Shawanese were arrived at the Hurons who say that all this nation (except a few who watch the motions of the army near Fort Pitt) are several leagues below on the Ohio, who remain there to intercept the army that is coming from Fort Pitt.

That upon their receiving the belt, they were ordered to strike against the English, upon which they commenced by killing fifteen merchants that was amongst them in different towns.

Yesterday a Saggina that was in the fort with the Pottawatamies was here and received a belt from the commanding officer which he was to present to the nation to tell them that it was his advice that they should remain quiet as they said they had done, as those that entered in the war would surely be ruined in the end. Some few shots fired today at the vessel at a great distance. A sortie was made today to cut down and burn some pickets between Mr. Babies and the fort. The garrison lay upon their arms.

*22nd.* This morning fired two guns down the river, being informed that the vessel was there. Made a sortie and pulled down a good many pickets and cut an orchard that was near the fort.

At eleven o'clock about fifty Indians came to Mr. Babie's and fired briskly at the vessel and fort, they killed one man on board the vessel and wounded another.

Two hours after which they went over the river and the Hurons joined them and the Pottawatamies to attack the vessel, but we do not know yet whether the vessel is there, or whether that was their real design. The garrison lay on the ramparts.

*23rd.* This day a few shot were fired at the fort and vessel as usual.

This evening we were informed that the vessel was not at the mouth of the river, but that the Indians thought she was and went and made a kind of an entrenchment at the Isle au Deinde[42] where the channel is narrow in order to fire upon her as she passed. The garrison lay on the ramparts.

*24th.* Some few shots were fired at the fort this morning. Capt. Hopkins with twenty men made a sortie this afternoon, imagining there was some few Indians in the neighbouring houses but did not find any. The garrison lay on the ramparts.

*25th.* A few shot fired as usual at the vessel and fort today. The garrison lay on the ramparts.

*26th.* [Sunday.] This day Pontiac went to mass on the other side of the river and after it was over he took three chairs that belonged to the people for himself and his guard to ride in to look for provision making the French his chairmen. He gave billets to the people for their cattle signed with his mark, with the imitation of a coon drawn on the top of each billet.[43]

Nothing Extraordinary. The garrison lay on the ramparts.

*27th.* Pontiac sent another message to the commandant telling him there was nine hundred Indians assembled at Michilimackinac, and that as he had compassion on him desired him to surrender himself, that the garrison would be well used, but if he waited till those Indians arrived he would not be answerable for the consequences. That the roads were all shut up round us and we could receive no succour.

To which the commandant answered as he had done before, that he would not give him an answer to anything he asked till he sent back Capt. Campbell and Lieut. McDougal, whom he kept contrary to all the laws of even savages. That he might save himself the trouble of sending any more for he would not answer to anything till these two gentlemen were returned. Soon after Pontiac sent word by one that was passing, that he had too great a regard for Capt. Campbell and McDougal than to send them to the fort, for if he did that, as the ket-

---

42. Turkey Island, on the east side of the main channel, and now included in Canada.
43. These bills of credit were drawn on birch bark, and were promptly redeemed by Pontiac. Rogers states that they bore the figure of an otter. The great Indian chieftain was evidently assisted to the idea by some of the Canadians. The contributions were all collected at the house of Meloche near Parent's Creek, and a vain and conceited old Frenchman, named Quilleriez, acted as commissary.—*Parkman's Pontiac*, 225.

tle was on the fire he should be obliged to boil them with the rest.

A few shot fired at the fort and vessel as usual. The garrison lay on the ramparts.

*28th.* This afternoon at five o'clock we were informed that the schooner [44] entered the river at 10 this morning; at 6 she came in sight after passing the Isle au Deinde where there was at least 160 Indians hid in holes who fired upon her all the while at a little distance, as the channel is not above a hundred yards wide. The wind failing her she dropped anchor about four miles from the fort.

A few shot were fired today at the vessel and fort as usual. The garrison lay on the ramparts.

As it was imagined the Indians would attack the schooner, the commanding officer made a feint as if he would land some troops in *bateaus* which the Indians hearing so alarmed them that they guarded the edge of the river and dropped their intention of attacking the Schooner.

*29th.* The wind contrary all day till about 6 o'clock, when it came a little favourable for about half an hour, of which the schooner profited, weighing anchor and coming in sight of the fort beyond the Huron village.

This day we heard that the Indians that went from this about twenty days ago had taken Presque Isle, that they lost three men there, that the way they took it was by setting fire to a small house that was close to the fort and which communicated the fire to it, that they killed but three, and the officer with several prisoners was given to the nations near that place. [45]

---

44. This was the schooner *Gladwyn* that had failed for Niagara on the 21st of May, and was now returning with Lieut. Cuyler and the remainder of his company, together with such troops as could be spared from Niagara, in all numbering about fifty men. To encourage an open attack from the Indians who swarmed upon the shores of the river and the islands which divided its channel, the greater portion of her men were kept out of sight, ready to appear at a moment's notice.—*Parkman's Pontiac*, 253.

45. The fort at Presque Isle, was a large block-house of solid timber, the upper story projecting on all sides and roofed with shingles. It stood on the shore of Lake Erie, a little below the present business part of Erie, Pa. It was assailed on the morning of June 15th, by 200 Indians, chiefly from around Detroit, and after a resistance of three days, which presents few parallels in desperate labour and unavailing courage, the little garrison under Ensign Christie surrendered on condition that they should be allowed to withdraw to the nearest post. With characteristic disregard of this treaty, the unfortunate men were seized and sent prisoners to Detroit. Christie was brought in by the Hurons and surrendered with several other prisoners, July 9th.

This day a few shot fired from over the river, &c., as usual. The Indians guarded the riverside tonight fearing a sortie. The twenty-fifth at night it was so cold here that there was a very white frost. The garrison lay on the ramparts.

*30th.* At 12 o'clock the wind sprung up favourable for the schooner when she weighed anchor and reached this about 3, with a detachment of twenty-two men from the 30th Regiment and Lieut. Cuyler and twenty-eight men of Capt. Hopkins's Company of Rangers, with 150 barrels of provision and some ammunition. Lieut. Cuyler informs us that Presque Isle was burned the 22nd instant after being attacked three days.

We were informed this evening that Pontiac had been demanding of the inhabitants to assemble to dig trenches, that if they refused it he would put them to the sword. The Hurons fired upon the schooner all the while she was passing and a great number from Pontiac's camp assembled at Mr. Babie's and fired at the boats that went and came from her after she came to an anchor.

One serjeant and four men were wounded in the schooner a coming up the river. The garrison lay on the ramparts, except those that came in the schooner, who lay in their quarters.

*July 1st.* The garrison was employed this morning in unloading and putting ballast on board the schooner. Mr. St. Martin and his family came into the fort today, he being informed that the Hurons intended to take him to their town to interpret for them. This afternoon the Pottawatamies came with a flag to speak about giving up their prisoners, five of whom they said they had at their village and whom they promised to bring in the next day. The commandant recommended to them to bring them in as soon as possible and retire to their villages, as he should now make sorties with great bodies of men, and if he should meet with them should treat them as enemies as it was not possible for him to distinguish the nations one from another.

A few shot were fired today at the fort and vessels.

The garrison lay on the ramparts.

*2nd.* At three o'clock this morning Lieut. McDougal with an Albany trader arrived at the fort, having made their escape from the Indians; about half an hour afterwards, another prisoner arrived at the schooner that made his escape from the Hurons, who had been taken with one Crawford a trader some time ago. [46] Lieut. McDougal

46. Crawford's Capture is related in this Diary for May 20.

informed us that the council the Indians held yesterday to demand the French to join them and make trenches, which was promised by one in the name of all the young people. A party was sent out to Mr. St. Martin's house to cover a working party near the fort, which the Indians came to fire upon, and upon our fending out a reinforcement all the Hurons crossed the river and came running up as far as Mr. Gamelin's and after firing a few shot at the fort went back.

This morning took post in the two block houses on the height that commands the fort, and from which a chief of the Saggina's was wounded in passing by the edge of the woods an hour after.

This evening we were informed that Pontiac had taken away Mr. Navarre, Mr. Hecotte and all the heads of families on that side of the fort, but nobody knew for what.

This evening threw a shell to try a mortar that we had enlarged about half an inch. All the garrison except the old Guard lay on the ramparts.

*3rd.* This day Mr. Navarre wrote a line to the commandant informing him that the inhabitants were obliged to write to him in Pontiac's name for the last time to surrender the fort, and to let him know that if he would not give it up they would oblige all the inhabitants to take up arms. Accordingly Mr. Louis Campo came in with the message in the evening, and at the same time asked permission to come into the fort, which the commandant agreed not only to him but every one that could bring provision with them. Mr. Babie and Mr. Recme who lived opposite the fort came in with their families between eleven and twelve at night, abandoning all they had except a few moveables that they brought with them.

All the garrison lay on the ramparts except twenty men that were finishing a small ditch round the fort.

This day the commandant collected the inhabitants of the fort and read the *Articles of Peace* to them and sent a copy of it over to the priest on the other side of the river.

*4th.* This morning early made a sortie with thirty men to cover a party to bring in some powder and lead that was in Mr. Babie's house, after which we destroyed an Entrenchment that the Indians had made, from which they annoyed us. The Indians being advertised that we was out came down and Capt. Hopkins was sent out with a party of twenty men more, who with nine or ten Frenchmen and the party that was first out, pursued them as far as it was safe; we took one scalp and wounded two or three more, [47] we had one man wounded. While we were at dinner Dr. Paully entered the fort having made his escape in open daylight, by whom we were informed that the Indian we killed this morning was the son of the most considerable chiefs of the Chippewas, and that we only wounded another. That upon their arrival at the camp he was informed that they were gone to look for Capt. Campbell to kill him, upon which he formed a resolution to attempt to save himself. He was dressed so like an Indian, his hair being cut and painted in their fashion that nobody knew him when he was brought in. This evening we were informed that there was 140 Frenchmen gathered at the Hurons' who had made an agreement to defend one another against all enemies. Mr. Navarre published the *Articles of Peace* both to the French and Indians.

The French were assembled today by order of the commandant, who all rejoiced to take up arms to the amount of about forty, and chose Mr. Sterling to command them.

The garrison lay on the ramparts. Yesterday we wounded an Indian with a grape shot from the vessel behind the breastwork at Mr. Babie's house.

*5th.* This morning Mr. Labute came into the fort, and informed us that as soon as the Chippewas were informed that we had killed the son of their great chief they went to Pontiac and told him that he was the cause of all their ill luck, that he caused them to enter into the war and did nothing himself, that he was very brave in taking a loaf of bread or a beef from a Frenchman who made no resistance, but it was them that had all the men killed and wounded every day, and for that reason they would take that from him which he intended to save himself by in the end, then went and took Capt. Campbell, stripped him, and carried him to their camp, where they killed him, took out his heart and eat it reeking from his body, cut off his head, and the rest of his body they divided into small pieces.

He likewise informed us that in a quarter of an hour after Mr. Paully made his escape upwards of a hundred Ottawas left their camp in search of him.

This evening we were informed that the Ottawas found one of

---

47 The sortie of this day was led by Lieut. Hay. One of his men had long been a prisoner with the Indians and had acquired in some degree their ferocious habits. Coming up to a wounded savage, he tore off his scalp and shook it with an exulting cry towards the enemy. This act cost the unfortunate Major Campbell his life.— *Parkman's Pontiac*, p. 260.

their men dead in the edge of the woods opposite the fort, who we supposed must have been killed from one of the cavaliers. The garrison lay on the ramparts.

*6th.* This morning we were informed that we killed three Indians and wounded one in the affair of yesterday.

At 12 o'clock the commandant sent the sloop up to Pontiac's camp under the command of Capt. Hopkins and Ensign Paully, but the wind being very weak they had time to remove almost all their things out of their *cabans* and send their women and children away before she arrived, however they fired near fifty cannon at those that were there, and threw several shells amongst them, we have not heard what number was killed or wounded.

The Pottawatamies came with a flag while the sloop was battering their camp, and after telling the commandant that they had heard the peace between the French and us proclaimed, and that they believed it, and the several chiefs with their bands were gone and going to leave Pontiac, they asked him to give them the Indian we had for two of our prisoners that they would bring in.

Upon which the commandant told them that he would still stand to what he had told them before with regard to changing prisoners, that notwithstanding all they had promised the last time they were with him, they went down the river and fired against the schooner when me was coming up, and a few days before stole two horses from him, notwithstanding all which, to show that he pitied them if they would bring in all their prisoners and the horses, and promise not to do any more mischief either to the French or English, as we were now one, he would give up the Indian he had, and would recommend them to the general, but if they made the least difficulty in it he would not hear them anymore and they must take the consequences of his displeasure, upon which they hung their heads and said they found everything that he had told them to be true, and could not deny what they were accused with, and not only promised to do all he asked of them, but that none of their nation was to come nearer the fort than Mr. Campo's Mill, about a mile from it.

Pontiac who always told the French that we were all dead men that were in the fort, could not help acknowledging today that we were come to life and that he was ruined. The garrison lay on their arms.

*7th.* This day the Pottawatamies came with a flag for a belt of *wampum* that the commandant promised them to carry to the rest of their nation at St. Josephs and to the Miamis to tell them what they had done and how much they were pitied by the commandant whose advice they must always follow; which belt they got with a letter to the interpreter there desiring to tell the Indians what he had promised the Pottawatamies here as they were the first that offered to make peace, *viz*. if they continued quiet for the future and minded their hunting he would recommend them to the general, who he made no doubt would forgive them, as he believed they had no hand in the war, further than that some of their young men were led into it before they knew what they were doing.

The Hurons came at the same time and told the commandant that neither they nor the Pottawatamies knew anything of this affair at the commencement, for Pontiac never consulted them about it until he had got such a number of men together that overpower them both, and then he told them his design and threatened them that if they would not join with him he would cut them to pieces. That notwithstanding which they never did anything but fire one day against the fort except a band or two of their young men whom they could not then command.

The commandant told them he believed it, and asked them if they did not now see that everything he told them was true, which they could not deny. He then promised them the same he had done to the Pottawatamies, if they would give up all their prisoners and behave well for the future. He told them he could not make peace with them, but as he told the Pottawatamies would recommend them to the general.

They promised to do all he desired of them, but told him it would take them two or three days, as all the prisoners that were adopted in the room of the people they had lost must be given up by the consent of those that had them, as they were given to them by the nation.

We imagine that the reason of the Hurons coming today was in consequence of the commandants sending the sloop yesterday to batter the camp of the Ottawas and Chippewas, by which they saw how much they were in our power. The garrison lay on the ramparts.

*8th*. All quiet today except a few shot being fired as usual at the fort and vessel at a great distance. Several of the principal inhabitants brought in their goods yesterday and today, and one Maisonville brought five *pittiaugers* [48] loaded with 10,000 weight of lead and peltry

---

48. *Perigua*, a narrow ferryboat, carrying two masts and a leeboard.—*Webster's Dict.*

into the fort though the Indians knew he was coming with it; if it had fallen into their hands it would have been a fine prize, but he being resolute and acquainted with their manners and customs took such opportunities that he arrived safe. He was at Outattanon when it was taken. The garrison lay on the ramparts.

*9th.* This morning six of the Huron chiefs came in and brought Ensign Christie, a soldier of the R.A. Rangers, a woman and child and five other prisoners, and after telling the commandant that they were drawn into the war before they knew where they were and many things to the same purpose of what they had told him the 7th instant, they asked him if it was not advisable for them to retire until such time as we received succours enough to assist them in case they should be attacked, which he told them to do, and when the army arrived desired them to come back that they might show their sincerity.

They intended to go and join the Pottawatamies and build a kind of stockade upon the River Huron to defend themselves against the Ottawas in case they should declare war against them. All quiet today. The garrison lay on the ramparts.

*10th.* Last night at twelve o'clock the enemy made a large float with four *bateaus*, which they filled with faggots, birch bark and tar, and other combustibles which they brought into the middle of the stream about a half a mile above the vessels and set on fire, but the vessels being properly moored let go one of their cables and sheered off from it, letting it pass at about a hundred and fifty yards distance.

This we suppose was not entirely the invention and work of Indians.

At 4 o'clock some of the Miami Indians came within three hundred yards of the fort with a flag, with an intention to speak to the commandant about one Levy they had prisoner, but not daring to come any nearer they sent in a list of things by a Frenchman that he had promised them if they would give him up. But the commandant sent them word he would not give them anything.

The garrison lay on the ramparts. Not a shot fired today.

*11th.* This day the Hurons brought in the goods (that had fallen to the share of three or four bands) that belonged to Chapman and Levy and others, as also a Panee that had been adopted in the family of one Babi, which was a very extraordinary thing, as they seldom give up a prisoner that is adopted.

Yesterday Pontiac was at the Huron village with fifteen of his best

50

warriors completely armed to frighten them, but it had no effect with Babi and Theata and two or three other chiefs as appeared from their testimony today. They told the commandant that they had not yet brought the rest of the nation to reason, but hoped in a little time to do it, when they would give up their prisoners and their merchandise; they also told the commandant the name of a Frenchman who had bought a gold watch of them for 2000 *wampum*.

The commandant told them that if they could not bring the rest of the nation to do as they did they must abandon them, as by and by when the army came it would be too late for them to make any offers.

We heard today that the Miami Indians were gone off with Mr. Levy.

This night and between 12 and one o'clock the Indians sent down another large fire float which passed without doing any damage. They had made two, but Capt. Hopkins, who was on board the sloop, fired a cannon at them as soon as he perceived the first and frightened them so that they jumped out of their canoes and let the other go without being lighted, which we towed on more. The garrison lay on the ramparts.

*12th.* This morning the Pottawatamies came again with Mr. Chapman, one Crawford and another prisoner of Capt. Hopkin's company, and promised to bring the rest as soon as they arrived. Accordingly at 4 in the afternoon they came with four Royal Americans two of the Rangers and one of Mr. Crawford's men, and demanded their brother, but the commandant told them what he told them before, that when they brought in all the prisoners he would let him out, knowing by our prisoners that they had some more, they promised to bring them the next day or as soon as they could be got together, and would bury everything that had passed in their next speech.

They brought an Ottawa with them which the commandant was informed of, and upon enquiry found that he came to see where the fort was most acceptable, that they might set fire to it, upon which he told the Pottawatamies that they had an Ottawa with them. They then seeing he was discovered said he was left with them by a band that was gone home, to bring them the news of the finishing their peace with us, but the commandant told them if he let him out again the Ottawas would laugh at him and desired them to ask him in case he should send one of his to their camp if they thought their chiefs would not do the same.

He then desired the interpreter to tell them that he would not use him as they had done Capt. Campbell and the rest of our prisoners, but would guard him for the security of the rest until they brought them all in.

At 4 o'clock this afternoon the schooner set fail for Niagara, but the wind failing she dropped anchor about 4 miles off.

Since the proclamation of the peace, the French that were in the fort were put under the command of Mr. Sterling. The garrison lay on the ramparts.

*13th.* This morning at about half past two, our outlying centries fired upon two or three Indians that were crawling to the fort, but one of them being a Frenchman and afraid got up and run away, calling out "*Je suis François*," at which time the Indians fired at them and shot him through the body, but he is not yet dead.

At one o'clock the Pottawatamies came in with a white belt and made many professions of friendship, but their chief errant was to try to get the Ottawa that the commandant detained yesterday. But the commandant told them they would do better if they would not even speak to that nation, as they only fought their ruin.

They promised to bring in all the prisoners they had to the number of six belonging to their village if the commandant would give them their man, which he told them he would do, as he thought they were sincere.

They gave him a white belt as a token of their fidelity and friendship and he promised them another when they came back, as he had not any then made that was proper. The garrison lay upon the ramparts.

*14th.* This day an Ottawa from Michilimackinac came into the fort and after a long story was going to say something about the Indian that the commandant detained the 12 instant, but he finding what he was going to say told him something that stopped him from making any demands. All quiet. The garrison lay on the ramparts.

*15th.* This day one Clermont who was formerly major in the Militia came into the fort and informed the commandant that most of the young men in his department were going to Illinois, and asked if he thought proper to send an order to them not to leave the settlement without his permission (though he had already given a general one) which the commandant did with power to him or any of the officers of Militia to bring them back with a party of men in case they should go off. This day we were informed that the Ottawas and Chippewas had quarrelled and were going to separate.

*16th.* All quiet. The garrison lay on their arms.

The 13 instant the wind blew fresh at N. W. and continued till the 14th when it was easterly till the evening me came about westerly and blew fresh all the next day and today S. W. so that we imagined the schooner must have been at Niagara sometime last night, or at furthest today.

*17th.* All quiet today. We heard this morning that the Ottawas were encamped on a plain about a league off. The garrison lay on the ramparts.

This afternoon we were informed that the Indians had broke down two barns to make six large rafts, which they were to tie together to burn the vessel but they did not send them. At 11 o'clock two Frenchmen came to the fort for arms and flints, informing us that the Jesuist had sent word from the other side of the river that the Hurons and Pottawatamies intend to fall upon the French on the south-west side of the fort. But they did not. The garrison lay on the ramparts.

*18th.* Yesterday the wind S. W. today N. E. This day we were informed that the float they were making was 300 foot long. We were also informed that all the young men towards the Gross Point intended to go off to the Illinois as they were afraid of being hanged.

At about 11 o'clock some Ottawas came down opposite the sloop and called out to them several times to go over to them with some rum, &c. which they answered. When the garrison called all was well, they were very angry and fired over the river, which the people on board observing fired three or four muskets in return, and by accident wounded one of them. The garrison lay on the ramparts.

*19th.* This day about sixty Indians as near as we could guess, came within about 350 yards of the fort in some orchards and fired upon the fort. We threw a shell amongst them but unluckily it did not break, which gave them great joy by their crying; however we prepared another, and while they were taking the first one up we fired it and it fell directly amongst them and burst about three foot from the ground, and as they run away fired another after them, but have not yet heard whether any of them was killed or wounded, though everybody imagined there was, as they went off without making one cry.

This evening we were informed that the enemy were making twenty-four rafts of about 30 foot long each, four of which were finished. The garrison lay on the ramparts.

*20th.* This day we fitted up a large *bateau* with a *pattararoe* that carried a three pound ball.

We were informed that there was one Indian wounded with the shell yesterday. The garrison lay on the ramparts. The wind westerly and fresh.

*21st.* This day fitted up a second *bateau* as the one mentioned yesterday. The wind S. W. all day and pretty fresh. The garrison lay on the ramparts.

*22nd.* This morning Mr. L. Campo informed us that about the middle of June the Ottawas of Michilimackinac brought off the garrison at La Bay, [49] without doing any further harm than killing one man, who was killed by the Chippewas; the Renards [50] and Foles a Voines [51] Nations came with them to Michilimackinac, but finding them well disposed turned back.

The Ottawas of Michilimackinac say that they brought off Mr. Gorrel and his garrison fearing the Chippewas would kill them. The wind S. W. all day and pretty fresh. The garrison lay on the ramparts.

*23rd.* The wind S. W. and fresh the most part of the day. The commandant and several officers went out of the fort, some on horseback and some on foot, at whom the Indians fired a good many shot but without doing execution. The garrison lay on the ramparts.

*24th.* The wind S. and S. W. the most part of the day. This day the two *bateaux* were sent up the river to look at the situation of the enemy's camp and try to bring off any canoes or fire floats that might be convenient, but there was none to be come at without running a

---

49. The post at Green Bay, was then garrisoned by Lieut. Gorell, who, upon receiving a letter from Captain Etherington of Michilimackinac, informing him of the events at that place, and advising him to withdraw and join him, summoned the neighbouring Indians, stated to them that the public service required him to leave them for a while, and committing the fort to their care during his absence, departed. The Dacotahs were hereditary enemies to the Ojibwas, and in case of hostility would have been active auxiliaries of the English.—*Parkman's Pontiac,* 321.

50. Renards, the Foxes. This tribe belonged to the Ottawa Confederacy and numbered about 320 warriors.—*Sir William Johnson's Report,* 1763.

51. The Voiles Avoines (Wild Oat) Tribe, according to Sir Wm. Johnson's Report to the Board of Trade, dated Nov. 18th of this year, numbered 110 warriors, and he formed a part of the Ottawa Confederacy. In 1736, they numbered 160 warriors, resided North of Lake Michigan and bore as their armorial device the large tailed bear, the stag and a kilion (a species of eagle), perched on a cross.—*N.Y. Col. Hist.,* 7, 582, 9, 1055.

risk of losing more men than they were worth; however they obliged them to throw away their ammunition, as they lined the sides of the river and fired very briskly from each side without even wounding a man. The *bateaux* now falling down with the stream and then rowing up again, on purpose to draw their fire, as we were well informed they had not much ammunition.

This day we were informed that there was about 70 Chippewas arrived from Michilimackinac, among whom were five of the Foles a Voines but not one Ottawas. The garrison lay on the ramparts.

*25th.* The wind S. and S. westerly all day, but not strong. Nothing extraordinary today. The garrison lay on the ramparts.

*26th.* This morning Mr. Nauvarre sent in some letters that were brought from the Illinois in consequence of some that were wrote by the inhabitants of this place sometime in May. The messengers also brought some for Pontiac.

This morning were informed that yesterday there was a council at the Huron village with the Shawanese that are come; that one Andrew, a Huron who undertook to go to Fort Pitt some time ago, came with them and says he was hindered by them to go on, that he was at Venango when it was taken and that all the garrison was put to death without exception; it was taken in the same manner with the rest, fifteen went in to speak to the commandant and forty remained without, and while they were in Council the forty rushed in and put the garrison to death. [52] The wind westerly. The people in general seemed to be a little cast down on the return of their messengers from the Illinois, from which we imagined they had not received such answers as they expected. The letters they wrote were sent from this about the middle of May, unknown to the commandant. The garrison lay on the ramparts.

*27th.* This morning Andre the Huron came into the fort, who told us that he was not at the taking of Venango and that the reason he said to the Ottawas that he was there, was because they would suspect him, but that all the Indians that he saw near the Ohio told him so. That he was stopped upwards of twenty days by different parties of Indians

---

52. Venango was garrisoned by a small party under Lieut. Gordon, and as every man within it perished, we have no history of the details except the narrative of Indians, and the traces of its ruins. The men were all slaughtered on the first attack, except Lieut. Gordon, who was reserved for the most refined tortures by fire that savage ingenuity could invent. This done, they burnt the place and departed.—*Parkman's Pontiac*, 337.

and that in trying to cross a river to get from one of them, he lost his letters, that he did not dare to go into the fort as he would have nothing to show, and knowing that the Indians had commenced hostilities there, although he was on the opposite side of the river. He likewise informed us that the Delawares had killed all their prisoners in consequence of the prophecies of one of their nation who pretended that he had been to Heaven and was told by God that they must put all the English to death, but not to burn any as was sometimes their custom, otherwise we should overcome them. He also informed us that all the Hurons except the bands of Babi, Theata and another chief, with part of the Pottawatamies had sung the war song again, but that the Hurons, or Wyndotes told the Ottawas that notwithstanding that, they would not fight.

He also told the commandant that as he was suspected, being so long away and not being at Fort Pitt, if he would give him letters again he would go and return in twenty days. Upon which the commandant told him he did not suspect him, and as proof would send him again and desired him to come the next day in the evening and he would have everything ready for him, though at the same time he could not be otherwise than suspected, but as he was a very knowing fellow and had a good deal to say among the Indians it was thought best by the Interpreter and everybody that was present to try him again, as he might change seeing the confidence we put in him, though he had been acting the knave before. The wind southerly.

*28th.* This day we were informed by Mr. Sterling that Mademoiselle Cuersiere told him that Godfoy told Pontiac when he returned from the Illinois that he could not send him any succours yet as they had heard by a Spanish vessel that the peace was made, but that as soon as his couriers arrived that he had sent to New Orleans if he found the News to be false he would see what he could do, and desired that the inhabitants should not appear in it at all, but keep themselves quiet.

This morning six Frenchmen set off in a birch canoe for Niagara with letters from the commandant. This evening Andre came in and took the commandant's letters for Fort Pitt. The wind southerly.

*29th.* This morning at half past four o'clock, it being very foggy, we heard the report of several musquets and now and then as we thought swivels at the Huron village, which we [thought] to be some Indians firing at the schooner, as she might have come that far up the river without our seeing her in the night, but in about half an hour to our great surprise, we saw about twenty *bateaus*, which upon their coming near we found to be English boats, with a detachment of about 260 men under the command of Capt. Dalyel.[53] They came the south side of the lake and burned a small Indian village near Sandusky that the Indians had abandoned. They had fourteen men wounded in passing the Huron village.

In the evening we saw some fires at the Huron town which was said to be some canoes that they set on fire as they were gone away. It was given out by the French to Pontiac (as we were informed) that it was not a new detachment, but that the commandant had sent out his young men as they could under the cover of the fog, and rowed up the river again to make them believe it was succours that arrived. The wind S. westerly all day.

*30th.* The wind S. westerly. This morning Andre set off for Fort Pitt. Nothing extraordinary today. Two prisoners saved themselves to-night from the Indians.

*31st.* This morning at three quarters after two a detachment of 247 men under the command of Capt. Dalyel marched out with an intention to surprise the Indian camp about three miles and a half from the fort.[54]

But whether the enemy were informed of it or discovered them in marching out is not known, but when they were within a half of mile of their camp they were fired upon by a great number of Indians from behind orchards, fences and entrenchments that they had posted

---

53. James Dalyell (sometimes written Dalzell) had been appointed a lieutenant in the 60th Regiment or Royal Americans, early in 1756, and in 1760 obtained a company in the 2nd Battalion of the Royals, or the 1st Regiment of Foot. He perished in a brave but indiscreet attack upon the enemy soon after his arrival at Detroit, as stated in the following pages.

54. The following paragraph had been written in the MSS. next following this, and erased:

"It was given out yesterday morning by the French that we intended to attack them, but they did not know when. Their reason for thinking so was, because we were mending some old canoes, but we gave out we should not want them in less than four or five days, imagining that news would be carried to their camp with everything else, as we never could do anything in the fort without their knowing; for even if the gates were shut and nobody permitted to go out, yet they knew everything we did, as one may see from the other side of the river every movement made inside of the fort. The detachment was three quarters of an hour from the fort before we heard any firing, when it commenced and continued four to five minutes very heavy, at which time our people were approaching the bridge on the side of the river."

themselves in for that purpose, which put them a little in confusion at first, but they soon recovered their disorder and forced the enemy from their lodgements. They then finding that their scheme could not be put in execution, they thought of making the best retreat they could, the enemy being twice as numerous as they were, and knowing they could not expect any more succours from the garrison, for which purpose they took post in several houses that was most advantageous for to prevent the enemy as much as possible from getting between them and the fort.

Capt. Dalyel, who behaved with all the bravery in the world, was unluckily killed; after receiving the fire from the enemy, though Capt. Grant begged of him either to push on immediately, make a retreat without loss of time, he remained almost in the same place for at least three quarters of an hour, soon after which he was killed, and Capt. Grant then with the assistance of the two row galleys made as good a retreat as was possible for anybody to do, after fending off all the wounded and all the dead except seven.

We lost in this affair, Capt. Dalyel killed, Capt. Gray, Lieut. Luke and Lieut. Brown of the 35th wounded, one serjeant and 13 rank and file killed and one drummer and 25 wounded. 60th Regiment one private killed and seven wounded. 80th Regiment two killed and three wounded. 2nd R. A. Rangers two killed and one wounded, and a trader's servant wounded. Total, officers included, killed and wounded, 61. The Indians say they had five killed and eleven wounded. [55]

*August 1.* Last night about ten o'clock a prisoner was brought in that was wounded at Mr. Cuyler's affair.

The wind S. and S. westerly all day, and at night changed all round the compass.

This day we were informed that part of the Hurons were encamped on the upper end of the Gross Isle, [56] where they had some corn, that they had sent their chief who was wounded in yesterday's affair to the Grand River with a belt to desire the Pottawatamies to

---

55. Parents Creek, ever since this memorable affair called Bloody Run, enters the Detroit River about a mile and a half above the site of the fort, and near its mouth was crossed by a narrow wooden bridge. The surface beyond was broken by ridges parallel with the stream, and Pontiac, forewarned by Canadians in his interest, had ample time to remove his camp, and conceal his warriors along every hollow and behind every building and tree along the route of the devoted band.

56. An island about twelve miles below Detroit and still known by this name. It is seven miles long and about two wide at the widest part.

join them.

This morning about two o'clock Mr. Rutherford arrived at the sloop, having made his escape from the Indians about nine mile from the fort, seven of which he came by land, when finding a canoe he embarked in it and came to the vessel.

Young Mr. Campo brought in the body of poor Capt. Dalyel about three o'clock today, which was mangled in such a horrid manner that it was mocking to human nature; the Indians wiped his heart about the faces of our prisoners.

Since the detachment arrived the garrison has been less fatigued than before, as instead of everybody lying [upon] the works, a Capt. Picket of 80 men and three subalterns took their place every night.

*2nd.* The wind wavering today, but mostly S. and south-westerly.

Since the last sortie the people have brought in several cattle for the King, and offered anything they had, which we imagine was partly owing to some disorders that the soldiers committed the 31st in the morning by plundering several houses, and partly as they see we are so strong that we can defend ourselves both against the Indians and them, that is to say to maintain the post without their assistance.

The commandant has not yet been able to get a copy of the letter that the inhabitants wrote to the Illinois, nor a copy of the answer that Mr. Noiyon sent back to them, by which it appears they had a great share in the affair, though they try to hide it.

*3rd.* The [wind] N. Easterly and pretty fresh. This day we began to fit up another *bateau* for a four pounder.

*4th.* Since the sortie there has been every night as we are informed at least two hundred and fifty Indians dispersed in party round the fort to watch our motions. About two o'clock about fifteen were seen at a house about a quarter of a mile from the fort, upon which a party was sent out, but whether they were seen in going out or no we can't tell, but the Indians went off immediately.

*5th.* This morning at half an hour past three o'clock, Capt. Grant with sixty men of the picket was sent out to take post in some houses near the fort that the Indians made a practice of coming to in the daytime, where he rested till one o'clock, but none came near enough for him to hurt them.

The wind S. Easterly and pretty fresh. At four this afternoon the schooner appeared in sight.

*6th.* This morning at 8 o'clock the schooner anchored before the fort; she brought but eighty barrels of provision, a good deal of naval stores, and some merchandise.

At 3 in the afternoon a Frenchman came in from Michilimackinac which he left fifteen days ago and informs us that Capt. Etherington and his garrison, with that of Fort Wm. Augustus[57] and all the English merchants were gone down to Montreal guarded by the Ottawas, a detachment of one subaltern, four serjeants, four corporals, one drummer and —— as also Commodore Lorain with sixteen sailors.

This day unloaded the schooner and made the sloop ready to sail.

*7th.* This day the commandant received a letter from Capt. Etherington dated at Michilimackinac the 18 July, who with his garrison and that of Fort Wm. Augustus was then going into the boats to go to Montreal, as also all the English merchants, for whom he had obtained permission of the Indians to carry all their merchandise.

*8th.* This morning at two o'clock Capt. Hopkins and two subalterns with 60 volunteers went down in boats with an intent to surprise an Indian *caban* at the Pottawatamie village. We went down undiscovered to the place we intended to land, and in turning in the boats to the shore the row galley which was commanded by Lieut. Abbot being heavy did not follow so near as could be wished, by which means, it being foggy and dark under the land, she lost sight of us and dropped down with the current so far that before Capt. Hopkins got her up again it was broad daylight and we was discovered and obliged to return back without attempting anything. The fog continued so thick that my boat and the row galley was lost again; the row galley at last threw out her anchor and lay there till it began to get clear, but the other boats could neither do that nor go to the shore, as the enemy followed us on each side of the river.

*9th.* The wind has been up the river ever since the vessel arrived that she could not go from this.

57. This fort was near the Grand Portage on Lake Superior and subsequently became an important station of the Northwest Fur Company under the name of Fort William. Another fortress of this name stood on an island in the St. Lawrence, at the foot of sloop Navigation, three miles below the present village of Ogdensburgh. This island was named by the French Isle Royal, and by the Indians Oraconenton. From the ruins of its barracks and other buildings, it is now known as Chimney Island. This island was fortified in 1759 under the direction of Chevalier Levi, and from him was named Fort Levi. In the Summer of 1760, while under the command of M. Pouchot, it was attacked and reduced by Lord Amherst and its name changed to Fort William Augustus. This was the last resistance made by the French against the English in Canada.

*10th.* Both vessels were made ready to sail today, fifteen of the wounded were put on board the sloop to be sent to Niagara as they could be of no use here this year, and it saved provision, as also fourteen or fifteen merchants that had been prisoners with the Indians.

*11th.* The wind straight up the river all day. This day we were informed that the Pottawatamies and Hurons were all coming back.

This night one Jacob Taylor a trader came in, having made his escape from the Indians.

*12th.* The wind almost West, the vessels could not stir.

*13th.* The wind a little to North of W., the vessels weighed anchor at 10 o'clock and in two trips got below the Huron Point, from where they had a large wind to Sandusky. [58] The Indians did not fire one gun at them.

*14th.* This morning the wind W. and fresh.

*15th.* The wind West and fresh all day with a good deal of rain. This day threw a Coehorn shell to the other side of the river.

*16th.* The wind westerly all day with rain. This day we were in-

---

58 The Arrival of these vessels was announced to Sir William Johnson in the following letter:

Niagara, 24th August, 1763.

Sir: Being allways glad to selebrat all oppertunityes of giving you the earlyest inteligence of anything perticular intreduces me to trouble you with this. The Commodore arrived here on the 22nd inst. and allso the schooner and the sloop from Detroit. By them we have the following account of the grate luck and safe arrival of Capt. Duel [Dalyell] and his armiment at Detroit being somewhat remarkable, as the Indians was lying in ambush for him which he knew of, but the night and morning that he arrived being fogee weather he got in to the garrison without the knowledge of the Indians, who were soon made acquainted with it, not only his arrival but his intentions, which was the next morning he marched about two miles distance from the garrison being informed of some intrenchments they had there, where he was fired on very warmly by a party of Indians, as he was crossing a wooden bridge which was behind some pickquets, notwithstanding which the brave and undaunted Capt. Duel [Dalyell] marched the men on to the brest work or trench which the English soon got possession of, and the Indians retreated to another trench they had some distance in the rear of the intrenchment where Capt. Duel behaved with the greatest courage and resolution imaginable, but soon told Capt. Grant he was wounded, notwithstanding which his bravery in the command was the same as before, but sometime after Lieut. McDougle informed Capt. Gray, belonging 55th [35th], that Capt. Duel [Dalyell] was wounded again and dead. Then Capt. Gray took the command and being informed that the Indians were surrounding them fast by the directions of their Sachem Pondeack and takeing possession of the French houses.

formed that Pontiac had given out that the commandant only sent the vessels out into the lake to make the Indians believe that they went to Niagara, but he knew better for they neither brought provisions nor men. That when they arrived opposite the fort we always sent two or three *bateaux* along fide of them full of men who were all hid except those that rowed, and as soon as they got on board huzzad, by which means we made them believe that we received succours.

*17th.* The wind still westerly and N.W. with rain. Last night there was 150 of the enemy within about three quarters of a mile of the fort, fifty of whom were constantly centry; the night was extremely bad. They themselves say that two or three of them swum down close to the fort, but observing some soldiers that was in a *bateau* anchored above the fort with a *patteraroe* [59] in it, to put up their heads, they went back as fast as they could.

*18th.* The wind N.W. Last night and this morning before day the Ottawas changed their camp from behind the Grand Marais to the River Rouge, [60] where they will be very convenient to harass any party that may be coming up; or the vessels, as they will have early intelligence of it, and time to post themselves in the most convenient places for that purpose.

Last night Mr. Watkins with about eighteen volunteers lay in Mr.

---

Upon this news the English thought proper to retrate. Some partys were detached to drive them out and take possession from the Indians, which they soon did, at which time Capt. Gray was wounded taking possession of a mill, but hope he will recover. Also Lieut. Brown of the 55th was wounded at the same time. Then Capt. Grant had the command, who marched the men very regular on the retrate into the fort. About fifteen men with Major Rogers got in a house who was to bring up the reare and cover the retrate, which was soon surrounded by the Indians and had no other way to get clear of them but by showing them a clean pair of heels, which he did, and a corporal of the 55th had a fair tryal for, and got safe in the fort.

There is killed and wounded in this engagement about thirty English, the number of Indians is not known.

They have murdered Capt. Duel [Dalyell] in a barbarous manner by schelping him, cutting of one of his arms and one leg and takeing out his bowels, his body was brought in and buried in the fort. Last night arrived here seventy of the 46th Regiment. I am Sir, Your most Humble Servant.

T. De Couagne.

P. S. By the prisoners we have account of the Seneckees, it is suspected that they have joyned the Dellawares.

59. *Paterero*, or *pederero*, a small cannon mounted as a swivel.

60. The River Rouge empties into the Detroit River from the West, four miles below the site of the fort.

Babie's house as the Indians had past it two nights before in order to try how near they could come to the fort. But he did not get an opportunity of firing upon any of them as there was cry given as soon as he got there, which we imagine to have been one of their centries.

This evening the commandant received a letter from one Wassong, the chief of the Chippewas, to this effect: That if he had a mind to leave the fort he might do it peaceably at present, but if not that the river would soon be stopped up. That he had never yet fought against him, for that if he had the fort would have been burned long ago, with a great many threats and very insolent expressions. The commandant sent word to the Indians that if they had anything to say to come to the fort; that he knew they could not write and therefore might be imposed on by those that wrote for them, and desired the messenger to tell the French that the first that wrote another letter of that kind might expect to be hanged; which we suppose was in consequence of some *bateaux* that were sent up the river in the morning to see what the enemy were doing, as it was reported they were making a large raft.

*19th.* The wind easterly, but not much of it. This day finished another *bateau* for a four pounder.

The wind N. easterly in the morning and westerly in the afternoon, but not much of it.

*20th.* This morning at half an hour past three Capt. Hopkins, Ensign Perry and Ensign Kiggel and forty men of the picket, with Capt. Roger and four or five of his men, and Mr. Watkins and Mr. Cornwell and some other volunteers went to waylay the road that the Indians generally take to pass from the Pottawatamie village to the camp up the river, to favour which the commandant sent up four *bateaux*, two with a four pounder in each, and two with *patteraroes*, they went as far as the upper end of the Isle au Cochon, [61] and drew a good many of the Indians that way, but Capt. Hopkins being discovered returned without being able to do anything.

*21st.* The wind S. and S. easterly, but very little of it. This day part of the picket was out about four hundred yards from the fort lodged in houses to try to catch or kill some Indians that daily came near the fort, but their intelligence was so good that they always knew of it and never came near enough. A woman was wounded through the arm by accident at the door of a house behind which were two Indians.

---

61. Nearly five miles from the fort.

*22nd.* The wind southerly in the morning, from 12 till night S. E. pretty fresh, then more southerly. This day part of the picket was out as yesterday and fired a great many shot at the enemy, but was so far off that they could not do any execution. On their going out they saw two Indians whom they followed in pursuit of whom we had one man mot through the thigh, for the Indians ran away (as is their custom) as soon as they saw our men, and when they returned the Indians returned also and generally got a shot at our men without exposing themselves, however we heard that one of the two that ran away this morning was shot through the body.

At half past nine this evening a Negro made his escape from one Marsacks who had bought him from the Indians.

*23rd.* The wind S. and S. westerly all day. This morning we were informed that one of the Indians died last night that was wounded yesterday and that two others are wounded.

This day the picket was at Mr. Barrois and a little beyond it skirmishing with the Indians the most part of the day, we fired a good many shells in the garden where some of them was and fired several shot through the houses they were in, so that we imagine they received a. good deal of damage. About half an hour before sunset the party was ordered in, and as soon as the rear of the party was well in the fort they were impudent enough to come to Mr. St. Martin's house and fired several shot in at the gate and set fire to two or three little out houses that we had possession of all day, which the commandant thought so insolent that he sent out Major Rogers with the picket to take possession again, and upon his appearing the Indians run away and he remained there all night. We had three men wounded today.

*24th.* The [wind] S. and S. westerly but not much of it; in the afternoon Rain, the wind changing all round the compass.

This night the commandant sent out an officer and thirty men of the picket to keep possession of Mr. Barrois's house and barn to protect it and Mr. St. Martin's, which the Indians said they would burn, which he intended to do till they had thrashed their corn, &c. This day we had two men wounded, but one of them very slightly.

This day a Bennickee[62] Indian came into the fort for a pass to go to Montreal, being the third time within this five days; he said he had been at war against the Cherokees, and that his brother who came with him last winter with Mr. Ferguson went a hunting when

---

62. Abenaque.

he went away and he had not heard of him since. But one —— an Albany trader who was taken with one Meldrum between Miami and Ouiattanon, came in this evening and informed us that he had been four days in the woods without anything to eat, having made his escape from one of the Puttawattamee villages about forty miles off, where he heard the Indians say that in Capt. Dalyel's affair there was six Ottawas, two Chippewas and one Bennickee Indian killed, which Bennickee we suppose to be the brother of this one that is in the fort.

At ten this night the Indians set fire to a small house that we had possession of all day from which we galled them. It was too far from the other houses that we had possession of to keep men in, as they were always liable to be cut off

*25th.* This day in the afternoon the Indians came to their post and fired a good deal at our men that kept possession of Mr. Barrois' house &c., but without doing any harm.

*26th.* This morning Mr. Cecote and Mr. Forville came to the commanding officer in the name of four of the most principal chiefs of the Ottawas to ask Mr. Labute to come to speak to them, but Mr. Labute did not choose to go, and the commandant would not order him. In the afternoon they fired a great deal and exposed themselves more than usual. At four o'clock they set fire to Mr. Babie's house which burned to the ground in a few minutes. This day we had one man wounded. The wind S. and S. westerly.

*27th.* The wind S. This morning we were informed that there was one Indian killed yesterday and three wounded. This day did not fire so much as yesterday, wounded one Indian.

*28th.* The [wind] S. W. Very little firing today at the advanced post.

*29th.* The wind weavering from S. S. E. to W. N. W. This day by accident found two keys that had been lately made, one of which opened one of our small gates and the other a large one. Yesterday about fifty Indians arrived here, thirty of whom had been opposite to the landing place nine mile up the river, and say they saw a great many English carrying provision on their backs and otherwise, are likewise informed that the Indians that [went] to Montreal with Mr. Lerond by Pontiac's leave are come back, who met Cap. Etherington and garrison about twenty-five leagues from thence.

*30th.* The wind changed all day from S. E. to S. and S. S. W. This evening we were informed that four Hurons arrived from Sandusky to inform the Indians here that there was an army of two thousand men between that and Fort Pitt on their way hither, that the Indians had been near enough to fire upon them, and the English returning the fire killed seven of the Miami Nation.

The Indians fired a good deal from their breastwork at the outlying picket today.

*31st.* The wind changed all round the compass. This morning we were informed that a chief of the Missisagues was badly wounded yesterday.

*Sept. 1.* The wind almost due East all day. This day we were informed that the chief of Missisagues who was wounded the 30 August died yesterday. This day the nephew of a great chief of the Ottawas was killed at their retrenchment that they were trying to open again, as Mr. Brehm destroyed it yesterday morning.

*2nd.* The wind East and a little to the southward of East all day. The Indians fired a good deal today at the advanced picket.

*3rd.* The wind a little to the southward of East. This morning we were informed that the schooner was in the river near the lowermost inhabitants and that there was some Mohawks in her, as four of them had landed and sent for Babi [63] and Theata of the Hurons to come and speak with them and then went on board again.

At one o'clock the Indians came and set fire to a windmill about three hundred yards from the fort. At half an hour apast 2 one Mr. Petet and another Frenchman arrived from the Illinois by way of Fort St. Joseph, who informed us that 28 days ago Mr. Neyon the commandant there had not received the account of the peace from authority but expected it every day. He had heard it from New Orleans by an English merchant that was arrived there from Martinico.

That the Outattanon Indians had been with Mr. Neyon for ammunition and he had given them about three barrels of powder and lead in proportion, enough to keep them from starving a little while.

*4th.* The wind East the most of the day. Last night at about 9 o'clock 340 Indians embarked in canoes and went to board the schooner. The merchants were on shore. The channel where the vessel lay not being very wide and rushes growing on each side of it, they came within a little more than a hundred yards of her before they were discovered

---

63. Babie, the Huron chief, signed the treaty at Fort Niagara, July 18, 1764. His Indian name was Odinghquanooron, and he appears to have possessed considerable influence among his tribe.

and then rushed in at once upon her surrounding her with canoes and *bateaux* and under a very brisk fire attempted to cut holes in her stern and the cable. The cable they cut, but notwithstanding there was but twelve on board, two of whom Mr. Horsey and another was killed and four wounded at the beginning, they never was able to board her, but obliged to fly with the loss (as the French tell us) of eight killed and twenty wounded. When the commanding officer was informed that there was Indians on board and but twelve men, he sent off an express with a letter to Mr. Horsey, but they did not get down till the attack began, and consequently could not get on board, and this morning, the fifth, when we were informed that she had been attacked, the commandant sent down four row galleys.

*5th.* The wind S. E. At 9 o'clock the row galleys returned, Capt. Hopkins and about twenty men including some volunteers remained on board.

At 11 the wind spring up a little and the schooner came in sight and at half apast three cast anchor opposite the fort. She brought 47 barrels of flour and 160 of pork.

*6th.* The wind S. W. This day we heard that the Indians were watching near the mouth of the river to pick up those that were killed. The Mohawks say that the Hurons kept them prisoners after they went on shore, but from all appearance they are great rascals and came with an intent to betray the people in the vessels.

*7th.* The wind S. W. This day we were informed that seven Indians died of their wounds. The commandant being informed by the people in the schooner that there was two more Indians coming in the sloop, who with those that came in the schooner might have laid a scheme to come on board with other Indians as friends and endeavour to take her by treachery, thought proper to send a man with a letter to the River Cannard (as if he was going a hunting) with orders to remain there till the sloop came into the river, and then to go on board of her and give the letter to the commander, to whom he gave orders for preventing any treachery that they might think to practice against him.

*8th.* This morning the commandant was informed that it was really the intention of the Mohawks to betray the sloop if they could and for that purpose they were gone to the mouth of the river, upon which the wind coming about he ordered the schooner to make ready to sail, and wrote a short letter to the general telling him the reason of his being obliged to send her away before he had time to write all that he intended, and wrote a letter to the commander of the sloop with orders and directions how to behave in coming up the river. The wind N. W. when the schooner failed at half past one and continued so till about half after four, when it came about to East and continued all night.

*9th.* The wind E. Last night at about 11 o'clock the Indians burned the barn of Mr. Reaume[64] on the other side of the river with about 1000 bushels of wheat in it, some peas and some hay.

This morning we were informed that seventy Pottawatamies arrived from St. Josephs.

*10th.* The wind S. W. Nothing extraordinary today.

*11th.* The wind westerly all day, and at night blew pretty fresh.

*12th.* The wind westerly.

*13th.* The wind S. and S. West. This day we were informed that there was a vessel seen at the mouth of the river yesterday morning.

One of the sailors that was wounded in the schooner told us yesterday that the sloop was going to land 200 men and provision at Presque Isle and was then to return to Niagara for provision for this place, which if true is very surprising, as they knew we had but six weeks provision in store when she went away, and the schooner was sent loaded with pork, all to about forty barrels of flour.

*14th.* The wind S. W. This day we were informed that forty Pottawatamies were gone to their village at St. Josephs.

*15th.* The wind W. and S. W. For two or three days past we have had accounts of the vessels being at the mouth of the river and of boats being at Sandusky.

*16th.* The wind westerly. Today we heard that the Indians were making ready their canoes to go off.

*17th.* The wind S. and S. W. Last night a soldier that was taken the 29th May coming from Michilimackinac and a merchant made their escape and came into the fort. The soldier says that he was told by a Frenchman that the reason that the people ask *billets* or certificates from Pontiac for their cattle was because the people in Canada were

---

64. In 1777, one Pierre Reaume was a prominent settler at Detroit, and the next year Charles Reaume was a captain in the British Indian Department at that place. The latter settled at Green Bay in 1790, and after holding a civil office many years died between 1818 and 1824.—*First An. Rep. State Hist. Soc. Wisconsin*, 61.

to pay half their losses. That he spoke with Aaron the Mohawk, who told him he was sent here by Sir William Johnson to find who were the cause of the war.

*18th.* The wind S. and S. W. This day we were informed that the Ottawas, Pottawatamies and Wyndotes were to go off tomorrow. That a canoe with some Hurons was arrived from the East end of Lake Erie who said that they saw a number of troops embarked on board the sloop and a great number of *bateaux* on their way hither. The wind W. and N. W. Very fresh all day and last night from 8 o'clock it blew very hard squalls from the same quarter with a great deal of rain.

*19th.* This day we were informed that the Pottawatamies were all gone, and that the Ottawas were angry at Pontiac for proposing to go, and they chose one Manitoo for their chief in his place.

*20th.* The wind W. and N. W., very fresh all day and very cold for the season. Last night twelve Frenchmen got a pass for Montreal and took some letters with them.

*21st.* The wind W and N. W. and very cold. We were informed a few days ago by Monsieur Fortville that Baptiste Deriverre with his party who came from the Illinois with Monsieur Sabole fought in conjunction with the Indians against the vessel when Mr. Horsey was killed.

*22nd.* The wind West till 12 o'clock when it changed to the Eastward of South, and continued all day a light breeze, the air not being so cold as it had been for two or three days before. Yesterday the Indians sent word to all the inhabitants not to offer to go into the fort for three days, and if any came out of the fort they were to tell them to go back and inform those within not come out during that time, under pain of having their houses and barns burnt.

*23rd.* The wind S. and a little to the Eastward of S.

*24th.* The wind S. E. and E. S. E. all day. Last night at about a quarter after eight o'clock Serjeant Fisher in passing from the fort to Mr. St. Martin's house was fired upon by two Indians as we suppose and was killed, which gave reason for us to think that it was scheme laid by the French and Indians to get an officer prisoner, as they knew the commandant and many of the officers walked there (since we took post at Mr. Barrois's) after night, and for that reason the French was neither to come in nor go out of the fort; as otherwise they might fire upon some of them instead of us.

This day at about one o'clock Babi the Huron came into the fort but brought nothing extraordinary. He said that the most of his errant was to see the major and pay him his respects, it being the first opportunity he had since he was in before, as the Ottawas and Pottawatamies were always being along the road to watch our motions.

*25th.* The wind S. and S. E. till twelve of clock then changed to the West with rain.

This evening we were informed that the enemy intended to attempt to surprise the advanced post. The night was very bad, it raining very hard and the wind shifting with hard squalls from South to West.

*26th.* The wind pretty fresh from the West with rain. This day we were informed that some Indians came in last night that had been to see whether there was an army on the lake or no, who reported that there was a vast number of boats between this and Sandusky which they imagined would be here this night or tomorrow.

*27th.* The wind westerly all day with rain. This day Aaron the Mohawk sent word to the commandant that he would come into the fort tonight or tomorrow night.

*28th.* The wind N. W. and N. all day.

*29th.* The wind W. all day, hazy weather. Last night at seven o'clock Aaron the Huron [Mohawk] came into the fort with his pass from Sir William [Johnson] and five other Mohawks who were to join Capt. Dalyell, who said that he was sent to find out the reason of the War, and that he was convinced the French were great rascals, yet the first belts came from the Five Nations, and that the Mr. Horsey sent him ashore before the schooner was attacked, contrary to his own judgement, to buy vegetables; that the vessel was attacked in consequence of the intelligence that was given the Indians by the two Frenchmen that went on board of her, and not from any that he or his people gave, and that the people on that side of the river furnished them with canoes and everything they wanted. That many of the inhabitants were going off to the Mississippi with quantities of merchandise that they had bought of the Indians, that they had taken from our merchants . He promised to return in three or four days.

*30th.* The wind S. to N. E. 3

*Oct. 1st.* The wind N. and N. E. and some part of the day N. W.

This morning a Frenchman crossed the river a little above the fort with his goods on his way to a house down the river that he had hired, but being called to, to come in shore, and not obeying was fired upon, which he did not mind but went on. The commandant then ordered a boat to bring them back, which they seeing coming after them obliged them to put in shore opposite the fort. But as no enemy was to be seen, the boat went in under the bank to bring her off, but before they got thirty yards from the shore two Indians came running down and fired upon them and killed one man.

*2nd.* The wind N.E. This morning, at 10 o'clock, Lieut. Brehm, Lieut. Abbot, Ensign Riggell and myself were sent up the river with four armed *bateaux* to reconnoitre an island in the mouth of Lake St. Clair to see if it was possible to bring wood from it for the garrison and to try to bring off a ship's boat that the Indians took from Capt. Robinson, when we were about four miles from the fort the Indians began to fire upon us from holes they had made on the side of the river, and two or three times attempted to put off in a *bateau* and two or three canoes as we imagined to cross the river to fire upon us from each shore, but we drove them ashore as soon as they were well on board, but at last seeing we only lost time with them, pushed on to perform what we were sent about, when we had gained the upper end of the Hogg Island we saw them push off with nineteen canoes and *bateaus* and seemed to follow us, and when we were in the narrow part of the river surrounded us under a brisk fire from each shore; upon which we turned to attack them, they still pushing on with great bravery all open to our fire, making a great hallowing; at length Lieut. Brehm got a good shot at some of them with a four pounder charged with grape at about forty or fifty yards distance, which he so disabled that out of about fifteen or sixteen that were in it we could not see but two that paddled.

They then put on shore some on one side of the river and some on the other, and cried two death hollas; we then rowed up and down in the same part of the river and called to them to put off again, that we were waiting for them. But they were then very quiet and did not holla as in the beginning, and chose rather to fire few straggling shot from shore than attempt coming off again. Then finding it too late to proceed we returned to the fort. We had one man killed and three wounded, two of which were very slight. We have not yet heard what number of them were killed or wounded. Upon our return we were informed that one of the vessels were in the mouth of the river.

*3rd.* At 12 o'clock, the wind being almost South, heard firing of cannon and small arms down the river, and at one or half past, the schooner came in sight; about half past three she arrived at the fort, in which came Capt. Montresor, who informed us that the sloop was lost the 28th of August between Presque Isle and Niagara, [65] the provision and guns were all lost except 185 barrels, which they brought in the schooner; the rigging was all carried to Niagara.

*4th.* The wind S.W., pretty fresh with showers of rain. Last night the enemy set fire to a barn about sixty yards from the post occupied by our outlying picket, and crawled about the whole night to try to get a prisoner and kill a centry, but they did not succeed if that was their design, but on the contrary had one man killed as our people fired at everything they saw move. Another had a spear run through his body by one of their own people, and we hear is like to die.

*5th.* The wind west and very fresh. This day the schooner was made ready to sail. This day we were informed that there was two hundred Indians and twenty five canoes when they attacked the boats.

*6th.* The wind west. Aaron the Mohawk came in today to see his

---

65. Letters to Sir William Johnson:

Niagara, 8th September, 1763.

Sir: In my last I wrote you that ye sloop was lost upon Lake Erie, since ye have been on shore they have been attacked by a few straggling Indians, we have lost three men in ye breastwork and one out that was scalped. Daniel and ye rest of the Indians behaved very well

De Couagne.

Cat Fish Creek, 9th September, 1763.

14 Mills on Lak Eria.

Dr: According to Daniel Oughnour's desire I now take the freedom to write to you. The 8th *ult.* we have been cast away at this place which detained him from proseiding to Detroit, but he says he'll go forward and deliver your belts and bring you an answer from the different nations according to your directions. The 3rd inst. we had 3 men kill by a small partey of Indians. Daniel spoke to them at little distance from the breastwork but they would not tell what nation they were, he says he believes they arc Cinices [Senecas]. We expect the scooner from Detroit dayly. Aaron and 5 Indians went in her to Detroit. Daniel gives his compliments to you and familey and desire the favour of you in case you see his wife to tell her that he is well. Sir excuse my freedom in writing in such a maner for I have had the fever and eague those several days.

I am Sir your most obedient humble servant,

Collin Andrews.

P.S Capt. Coghran gives his complements to you, he has used Daniel extremely well.—*MSS. of Sir William Johnson*, vol. 7.

comrades that came in the schooner, who told us that there was three Chippewas killed and seven wounded the second instant. That the Hurons were sickly with a bad fever. That seven or eight had died within five or six days past.

*7th.* The wind E. and N. E. The schooner sailed at twelve o'clock, in which went Capt. Grey, Lieut. Brown and Lieut. McDonald.

This day Mr. Campo came to the commandant in the name of Wabagommigot a Toronto chief to know his sentiments about a peace, to which the major gave no direct answer, but told Mr. Campo that he might bring him to the fort and he would speak to him. He arrived here last Sunday with twenty four men as he says not to make war, but to try to accommodate affairs.

*8th.* The wind E. and N. East. This day 60 Miamis arrived; we hear that the Chippewas are preparing all the boats and canoes they can to attack the armed boats when they go up the river again.

*9th.* The wind West and N. W. Last night a soldier, a trader and a Cherokee that was prisoner with the Indians made their escape and came into the fort.

This day we were informed that the Indians had taken all the canoes they could get from the inhabitants but know not for what end.

*10th.* The wind E. to N. E. in the morning, in the afternoon westerly.

*12th.* The wind westerly. Yesterday was held a council with the Missisagues, and this day another with the same.

*13th.* The wind from W. to N. W., pretty fresh all day.

*14th.* The wind West and a little to the North of West all day and pretty fresh.

*15th.* The wind W. and N. W. with snow in the morning.

*16th.* The wind changed from one point to another all day with now and then snow.

*17th.* The wind S. and S. E.

*18th.* The wind Easterly.

*19th.* The wind Easterly. The councils that has been held these few days past has been attended with this good effect, that we have been able to get in some wheat and some little flour, without which we should not have an ounce of flour in the garrison ten days past, as the men for upwards of seven weeks past have had only five pounds of flour per week, and for the other two pounds half a gallon of wheat each.

*25th.* This day a soldier saved himself by running off from a Chippewa who brought him to Cuesieres to sell.

*29th.* This morning Capt. Grant with a party of 150 men was sent to the Isle au Couchon to cut wood for the garrison, the commandant not choosing to let more time pass in waiting for the Troops that he expected some time ago.

*30th.* Last night Mons. Duquendse a *cadette* arrived from the Illinois and was in council with Pontiac and the chiefs of all the nations here, and this morning brought a letter to the commandant from Mons. Daneyon Commandant of the Illinois Country, with a speech which he sent addressed to all Indians with three belts of *wampum* and four pipes of peace, which he distributed to the nations as he came along. In the speech he let them know that peace was made between England and France and exhorted them to live in peace with us, telling them that fighting against us at *present* was fighting against them, and desiring them to esteem their brothers the French that remained amongst us, as they would never be abandoned by them.

That they changed their situation as the King ordered, and that they had given up those parts of the country that belonged to the King and not theirs, and desired an answer to his speech telling them they should always receive succours from them at such and such places. That their villages would be full of ammunition and merchandise. Upon which Pontiac sent in word to the commandant that their hatchet was buried and desired to have his answer in writing. To which the commandant answered that if he had begun the war it would be in his power to end it; but as it was him, he must wait the pleasure of the general, to whom he would write and inform him of his pacific inclination in case he committed no more hostilities. Pontiac then said he would not commit any more and would come when he was sent for.

The news of the definitive treaty arrived at the Illinois the 27 of September. In another letter to the inhabitants of the peace being concluded, he marked five places on the south side of the Mississippi that any of the inhabitants might retire to that had an inclination where they would receive all the succour that was in his power to give them. From which one may imagine that if one word could prevent all the nations from committing further hostilities it was in their power with a very few to do all they have done and that they will always remain in their interest as long as they have any footing on the continent from whence they can succour them.

*31st* [66] This day Mr. Jadeau was in the fort and in talking with Major Gladwyn about provision, he told that ever since the beginning of this affair, the inhabitants in his district had received orders to give Pontiac a bushel of peas or wheat pr. family, under pain of disobeying the greatest of orders, and that when the Indians were asked who gave them the orders they said sometimes Mons. Cecotte and sometimes Baptist Campo. Once in particular one of the inhabitants upon being told that it was Cecotte that gave the order tore it and told him he did not mind the order nor Cecotte and then went away. The next day the Indians came and it was much as all the rest of the inhabitants could do to prevent them from taking everything he had in the world and pulling down his house.

The following names are those people who went from the settlement and from his district within these three weeks without leave:

Grenon, an inhabitant.
Millehomme Do.
Brisar and his family.
De Roen.
Jean Faies.
Des Cheine, labourer, and one Lizott Do.

*Nov. 10.* Three days ago Aaron went from the River Huron on his way to Fort Pitt with letters.

This day by the returns from the commissary it appeared that we had upwards of 9000 weight of flour and wheat equal to about 23000 more, which would have been enough for to keep 250 men here all the winter, as the commandant had given over any thoughts of boats coming and imagined the vessel was lost, as she had been gone from this upwards of thirty days.

---

66. The following extract from a letter of Wm. Edgar at Detroit, dated November 1st, 1763, states the progress of pacific Overtures as then understood:
"I have lately received a letter from Hornlach, which came by an officer from Illinois, who brought a belt and letter to the savages, with the account of the peace between England and France which neither the savages nor the French, here believed till now. In consequence of which, our most implacable enemies, the Ottawas who were the only nation here disposed for continuing the war (all the rest having begged forgiveness for what they have done of our worthy commandant) are now with the others, suing for peace, in the most abject manner, Mr. Prentice is very well at Sandusky, as is Mr. Winston at St. Joseph's, and from the present disposition of the savages I apprehend they will soon bring them in."

This evening Mr. Jadeau came in with a letter from the schooner dated at Isle au Boisblond, informing us that the troops had left Niagara the 20th October.

Mr. Jadeau in conversation happened to tell before Mr. Duquindse that Pontiac had said he was going with nine of his men to the Illinois with him, and that he, Pontiac, had been informed that Mr. Duquendse was to take a good many French with him, which a little shocked Mr. Duquendse as he had given out that he was to pass by St. Josephs.

*11th.* At three o'clock the schooner arrived, in which came Mr. Willero of the 80th, who brought us the disagreeable account of a party of about 70 men being cut off at the carrying place at Niagara by a large body of Indians, as also the loss of most of the carriages and bullocks, which undoubtedly prevented the army from coming so soon as they otherwise would have done. [67]

---

67. The affair here alluded to, is the surprise and massacre at the Devil's Hole, three miles below Niagara Falls and on the road then recently constructed from Fort Niagara to Fort Schlosser.

In September, twenty-five wagons loaded with provisions and supplies for Detroit, and escorted by fifty soldiers and their officers, were ambuscaded at this point by Seneca Indians, and with two exceptions the whole were killed, or driven off a frightful precipice of a hundred and eighty feet. The wagons and their contents, with the ox teams attached, were also hurled down the chasm. William Stedman, the contractor, narrowly escaped on horseback, and a drummer boy, named Matthews, was caught by his belt in the limbs of a tree, which broke the force of his fall, and he fell in the river near the shore. He lived many years afterwards near Queenston. The following letters, addressed to Sir William Johnson, relate to these events on the Niagara Frontier:

Niagara, October 17th, 1763.

Sir: I have acquainted you of the sad usage of the savages to the detachment of our forces that turned out at lower landing sometime past, where the officers and men were almost totally destroyed by them together with the King's working cattle. Our endeavour since in transporting provisions to little Niagara, intended for Detroit, has been safely hurried on without their offering to disturb the troops, but a few days ago they killed a man on the race that dropped behind and scalped him. There are four men more of the flankers missed, all this without the noise of a gun. The man that was scalped was between Starling's house and the fort. They gave one fire at the troops, fort, or in the air, uncertain, none being hurt or any damage done. I have no more to acquaint you of but conclude Sir,

Your most obedient servant,

D. Couagne.

I forgot there were some cattle sent here from Ontario since which we had up at work and now they are all taken, stole by the savages or straying in the woods.

*18th.* This morning two Indians arrived from Point au Pain, with a letter one half wrote in Erse and the other in English, from Major Montcrief, giving an account of the *bateau* being cast away the seventh instant at the Highlands beyond the said point, where they lost 20 boats and 50 barrels of provisions, with two officers and a surgeon drowned, as also 70 men, and that all their ammunition, even the men's cartridges, were wet, and that they had wisely (not knowing our circumstances) taken a resolution to turn back to Niagara. But from the steps Major Gladwyn had taken some time before he was in a situation to keep a tolerable garrison here with provision till the month of May, and was in a good way of getting in enough till the month of July, though at the expense of listening to the demands of peace the Indians had some time before made, which notwithstanding he did not grant them. But put them off by telling them they must wait the general's pleasure, &c., as will appear from the councils he held commencing about the middle of October.

*Dec. 5.* This day two Mohawks went from this by land to Niagara with letters; they came from Sandusky to this place, having come with a pass from Sir William Johnson when the schooner was attacked.

This day Andrew the Huron got 6000 of *wampum* and a good deal of vermillion for the voyage he made last to Fort Pitt. The reason he took so much of these commodities was (as he said ) to send the young men of Sandusky to war against the Cherokees.

Mr. Jadeau told Major Gladwyn that Lafontaine, an inhabitant near his house, told the people that the peace was not yet made, and that the army was only come to save the 200 men who departed from hence under the command of Major Rogers to reinforce the garrison

Niagara, November 11th, 1763.

Honourable Sirs:

My last to you was to acquaint you of Daniel, &c., which I hope came safe to your hands, since which a small party went out from the lower landing to cut wood, when a body of Indians surrounded them and killed and scalped nine, one of which had his head cut off within sight of that post, it is supposed that the Indian who did this murder was wounded from the fort, as he was seen go off lame with the head in his hand, all which happened on the fifth instant.

I am in hopes of a line from you the first oppertunity wherein should be glad to know how affairs go down the country, I mean in regard to the Indians, &c.

I am Sir, your obedient humble servant,

De Couagne.

P. S. Sir here is two sisters of Silver Heells at this place who would be glad to know where he is. One of them is the lame one, the other is the young one. Neither of them dare go to the castle.

at Quebec, he likewise took the opportunity of robbing the merchants' *bateaux* that were brought in by the Indians when they were drunk. He declared before Mon. Legrand that he had no more than 17 yards of Chapman's Linen, but Mr. Jadeau has found that he had 69 yards. He broke open some cases and stole a box with silver trinkets which the Indians afterwards got from him.

Prud'homme senior is a dangerous man and animates the savages. He understands their language and told them not to go off, for if they did the English would hang the French, and as for provision they (the savages) should never want.

Michael Campeau told the Indians of two barrels of powder that were hid in Mr. Jadeau's house, he likewise animated the Indians very much. Buxton, an Ottawa chief lodged in his house.

St. Louis, an officer of the Militia on the South side of the river, said, when Mr. Jadeau was in council with the Hurons, engaging them not to strike against the English, and gave them three days to consider of it. "What!" said St. Louis, "four days? it must be resolved immediately; shall we let our throats be cut for the sake of the English?" which signified, says Mr. Jadeau, that they should rather strike against the English than have the ill will of the savages. He also said it would be a luckier thing for them to be with the Indians than the English. Another time he told the informer that he did not know what dominion he was under.

*12th.* This day Mindoghquay (a chief of the Sagginaws who was in the fort the 16 June and asked the commandant's friendship, &c. as he had not entered into the war) arrived here with three prisoners of the 60th Regiment and one sailor who was brought from the Chibbawas by one Beaulieu, and demanded the continuation of the commandants friendship as he had promised in the summer and gave him a pipe of peace and several large belts. He was very well received by the commandant, as he had obeyed all his orders from the first time he came into the fort, retiring with his people and not committing hostilities as others did.

*22nd.* Last night one Mackoy arrived here, having made his escape from the Pottawatamies about fifteen leagues from this.

*23rd.* This day Mr. Cecote came to the fort and told the commandant that the Pottawatamies intended to have brought the man in that made his escape two or three days ago, and that they intended to come in hoping he would pity them.

*25th.* This day Mr. Marsack informed us that he was assured that there was four or five of the Pottawatamies of Naintaw's family that intended to come and take a scalp if possible, and desired the commandant would not let anybody go out of the fort, as some of the merchants had straggled out in the country some days before.

*27th.* This day a Mohawk with one David Vanderhiden arrived express from Niagara, which they left two days after the arrival of Major Rogers, who was only six days in going from the Detroit River to the Niagara.

*31st.* This day six Indians (originally of the Saqui[68] Nation) but at present of the Pottawatamie came in with a prisoner, and told the commandant that they came in hopes of receiving mercy. That if they pretended entirely to excuse themselves from being concerned in the late war they would lie, but that did not signify, though they were living amongst the Pottawatamies they were not of that nation, nor like them. That what offence they committed was through fear, as they had been obliged to ask liberty to live amongst them, having been obliged anciently to fly from other nations, who had this summer made war against their brothers.

That they knew their brothers the Putts had lied, and even come and spoke to their brother and the same day fired against his fort, but begged he would not think that they had an inclination to do the same, but that they spoke from their hearts, and came to offer one of his flesh which had fallen to them by lot, and to demand mercy. That their families were starving. That they could not come into the fort in the summer as the fort was every day on fire. That in fine they begged that they might live in the same friendship with their brother that they had done when he took possession of the country. That they hoped, nor they would not return home shamefully, suppose their brothers did not listen to them, as what they did was their duty and which they would have done before but had not an opportunity. That notwithstanding they were orphans and had no chiefs, and knew that the other Indians would laugh at them, and asked them how their brother received them at his fort, they would not be ashamed as it was their duty they were doing, but nevertheless expected their brother would take them in compassion.

The prisoner being asked if he knew of their going from home during the summer said they always stayed upon their land the whole

---

68. Sacs.

79

time, except the two that was at Presque Isle where he was taken, and they never went abroad to war after he came amongst them, but once in the summer came as far as Mr. Gamelin's with him to give him up, and the other nations told them not to go to the fort as they would be killed.

*10th.* This day Babi and Theata with four or five more of their relations came in to wish the commandant a Happy New Year, as is their custom, whom he received very well.

*11th.* This day some of the Pottawatamies came to the settlement and sent in word by Mr. Cecote that they wanted to come and see their brother the commandant but Mr. Cecote was told that the commandant had nothing to say to them and they would do much better to stay at their hunting ground.

*12th.* This day Vanderhiden and Jacob the Mohawk left this for Niagara with letters.

*13th.* This day one of the Chippewas came to the settlement and sent for Mr. Labute to desire him to ask the commandant leave to come in and see him, which Mr. Labute informed him of, but the commandant told Mr. Labute not to make him any answer, but let him, the Indian, return as he said he intended to do the next morning.

*14th.* This day the Huron chiefs (Babi, Theata and the Doctor's son) went to see the commandant before they went away, and after talking of the beginning of this Indian war, &c., Mr. St. Martin said it was sure that it took its rise from the belts that passed amongst the Indians two years ago, and that it was commenced in consequence of the succours that the Indians were made to believe they might expect from the Illinois. That one Sibbold that came here last winter with his wife from the Illinois, had told at Mr. Cuellierrey's that they might expect a French army in this spring, and that, that report took rise from him. That the day Capt. Campbell and Lt. McDougal was detained by the Indians, Mr. Cuellierry accepted of their offer of being made commandant, if this place was taken, to which he spoke to Mr. Cuellierry about and asked him if he knew what he was doing, to which Mr. Cuellierry told him I am almost distracted, they are like so many dogs about me, to which Mr. St. Martin made him no answer.

*20th.* This day two Michilimackinac chiefs came in to see the commandant, with one or two Washtinon chiefs from the Grand River who were here in the beginning of the summer about fifteen days, but went away. They brought in a prisoner that was given to them by the Ottawas.

*Feb. 1st.* This day Wabagommigot, a chief of the Toronto Indians who came in last fall, returned and asked a certificate which the commandant at that time promised him of his behaviour, which he gave him.

*14th.* This day some of the Saqui's came in with the other prisoner they promised to bring in the last time they were in the fort.

This evening Aaron the Mohawk arrived from Fort Pitt with letters from the general.

*20th.* This day some of the Ottawas of the Grand River arrived with a prisoner whom they bought from some other Indians.

*March 12th.* This morning the gunner going his rounds found a Brand's end that had been set up against the magazine door the night before, which appeared to have been on fire but was gone out.

*14th.* This day a cow belonging to one Moran came in from the woods with ten arrows sticking in her, which were supposed to be shot by some party of Indians that was lying about the fort.

*18th.* This day two or three Frenchmen saw a small party of Indians back of the fort going loaded with meat, which must be the cattle that was killed and missing for two or three days past.

There has been a party of Pottawatamies in the settlement every night since the 15th instant.

*21st.* This day the commanding officer was informed that one Mintiwaby, an Ottawa chief of the Grand River, was to come in under a pretence of trade and endeavour to surprise him and put all the officers to death. M. informer.

*23rd.* This day two Saquis came in and informed the commandant that the Chippewas of the isles about Michilimackinac had sent belts this winter to their nation, to the Folavin and Puante, to strike against us this spring, but they would not receive them. That Wassong and Marchioquisse had tried to prevent that party from coming from towards St. Joseph that was here some time ago, but they would not be advised, they said they had lost a man last year and they would have revenge. That if they had known it sooner they would have advised us of it before they arrived, but they [knew] nothing of it till they were gone.

That the Delawares and Shawanese had sent belts during the winter towards St. Joseph and La Bay to invite the nations thereabout to take up arms against us in the spring.

*27th.* This day France Ruiard set off with two other Frenchmen express to Niagara.

*29th.* This day the commandant being informed that there was thirteen Indians in the woods behind the settlement, who were come to make war, sent out a party commanded by Lt. M'Dougal of twenty men to try to fall upon them by surprise; they set off a little after dark and went through the fields guided by a Frenchman to the place where their fire had been seen, but not finding them there, they returned towards a house that they had been at the night before, and fell in with them on their way, but the Indians finding they were discovered run off, after receiving the fire of the most of the party, but it was so dark that they could not see to adjust their firelocks and don't know whether they killed any or no.

*30th.* This day an Indian was seen at the edge of the woods behind the fort.

*April 12th.* This morning at ten o'clock the schooner sailed for Niagara, in which were sent the two French prisoners, as the commandant was informed that the Indians had said they should not long be prisoners, and as it was imagined if anything was intended by them, it was through the influence of the friends of these two.

*15th.* Last night at about 8 o'clock [a] prisoner came in from Saggina who reported that the day before he came away the Indians killed and eat a young girl they had prisoner and that he was to been killed that day himself, but they sent him out to bring in some wood and he run off; he was eight days a coming, but when he was asked if he was hungry he said no, that for the first two or three days he was fainty, but since he found no great alteration though he had not eat a mouthful of anything the whole eight days.

*27th.* This day Andrew a Huron and two others from Sandusky brought in one Mr. Prentice whom they had prisoner since last May. They told the commandant they were not sent by any chief, but as he (the one that spoke) looked upon Mr. Prentice as his real brother, he told him in the winter he would bring him in, for he chose to see him content at this place than discontent with him, which was the reason he brought him in. But he imagined that Mr. Prentice could have other no reason for leaving them, than because he could not get bread amongst them.

Mr. Prentice said that he never wanted for anything they had during the whole winter, and notwithstanding this man never got any of the plunder that the Indians took from him when they made him prisoner, he gave him two packs of beaver and twenty dollars when he gave him up.

*28th.* This day at four in the afternoon the commandant thought he heard a cannon down the river and fired another.

*29th.* This morning at half past four Mr. Jadeau arrived from the vessel with letters and informed us that they fired a gun from the vessel about the time the commandant thought he heard one.

This afternoon eight Huron chiefs and two or three young men came to speak to the commandant. Theata speaks:

My Brother, we beg you may take pity upon us and hear us, that the words we now say may be as a carpet for your successor to walk upon.

Brother, we beg you to have pity upon us and be assured of our good intentions, as we have most faithfully repented of all the ill we may have done, and do sincerely promise never to be guilty of any bad thing for the future, having thrown ourselves into the hands of God, if any evil happens to us it must be from him, as you may be persuaded let the earth turn how it will, we shall never be advised to a bad thing again.

This, brother, we beg you will inform the general of the first opportunity.

Gave a large white belt.

Another chief got up with a string of *wampum* and said:

Brother, ever since the English have had possession of this place we have been used very tenderly, agreeable to the promise you made us when you first came here, for which reason we hope our brother will grant us the small favour we are going to ask.

Brother, as wood and bark is very unhandy to us at our old village we hope you will give us leave to make a new one up a small creek near the bottom of the settlement, where everything will be more convenient.

Granted.

Brother, when you first came here you told us you had conquered our Father and sent him over the Great Lake, and that all that then belonged to him was yours, but that we should remain in our former possessions and be allowed the Jesuist, and now as we are going to alter our village we hope you will not prevent him going with us.

Gave a string of *wampum*.

Granted by the commandant.

*6th.* This evening four indians sent by Sir William Johnson arrived here with a speech to the nations hereabout.

*8th.* This day we were informed by Mr. Jadeau that one Rainbeau and his family with one L'esperence went off to the Illinois.

*15th.* This morning at half past six the schooner sailed for Niagara, in which went Peter and the three other Indians that came here with a speech from Sir William Johnson.

This afternoon some of the Saquis came in and informed us that one Lagasse and four other Pottawatamies were somewhere in the woods near the fort, and intended to try to take a scalp.

*June 2nd.* This morning the schooner anchored off the fort after having been kept at the mouth of the river three days with contrary winds.

This morning a band of Chippewas who were at the Gross Point dividing themselves amongst the inhabitants, asked at several Places for provision, &c., one of them being refused a cock by a farmer had a dispute with him, and because he would not let him have it fired at him and mot him through the body.

*3rd.* This day the band of Chippewas who fired at the Frenchman headed by a chief they called the Great Spoon, came with a belt and pipe to Mr. Marsack, telling him they were very sorry for what they had done, which belt and pipe he brought to the commandant next day with a prisoner they had sold him who was taken at Presque Isle. The man they fired at died of his wounds last night.

They then sent in a Frenchman to tell the commandant they had always been fools, but that their senses were now come to them and begged he might receive them, to which he sent them word that when they returned the goods that Mr. Marsack gave them for the prisoner and brought in the rest as they had promised the fall before, he would see them, but not till then.

*4th.* Being His Majesty's birthday, the garrison was under arms at 1 o'clock and fired three volleys with three discharges of the cannon in the fort and one of those in the schooner; after which His Majesty's health was drunk upon the parade by all the officers and several Frenchmen who were asked there by the commandant who afterwards dined and supped with all the officers of the garrison together. At nine at night almost the whole town was illuminated.

*6th.* Mr. Marsack after going to the priest's came in haste to the commandant to tell him that the Indians had returned him his merchandise that he had given for the prisoner two or three days before, and wanted to come in. To which the commandant sent the same answer as he had done two or three days before, that when they brought in all the rest of the prisoners and their chiefs came in a proper manner, he would receive them.

*7th.* This morning Mr. Marsack came in and informed the commandant that there was a small band of Chippewas from beyond Saggina to come in, who came with a belt and pipe of peace, and after they had smoked and told the commandant they were come to open a new road between him and their nation, as the old one had been shut up for some time; he enquired what they were and who sent them, and found that they were from the same place and village with those that sold the prisoner to Marsack a few days before, and had no authority for coming nor had no chief with them, but they were part of a party that came to the settlement about seven or eight days before, consisting of forty men, who told the inhabitants they did not come to make peace but to make war. All which they could not deny.

The commandant then took a string and *wampum* and told them to take that to their chiefs and tell them when they brought in the other prisoner they had in possession and came and asked peace in a proper manner he would hear them, and until then one of them must stay with him, as perhaps they might to fell the rest, and at the same time told them to tell their chiefs if anything happened to his people amongst them, he knew what to do with those he had. When they saw this a second offered to stay to keep the first one company; he is a son of...

The Col. then asked them if he had three or four of his nation prisoners, and would send two or three of his people to their village whether they would not keep them, to which they said they would. Then said he you would undoubtedly think me a fool to let you all go when you have prisoners of mine. They then said perhaps it would be hard for them to get those prisoners, as they did not belong to their relations. "Yes, but" said the commandant, "if they have an inclination for peace as you told me a few minutes ago, they will bring them in without any difficulty." They then said they were a little band of six or seven, everyone for himself; then said the interpreter "how came you here to make a new road for the whole nation and fight in alliance with them all last summer?"; to which they hung their heads and could not say anything.

*10th.* This day the schooner sailed with a head wind for Niagara and got below the Hurons Point.

*11th.* This day the schooner returned the wind being fresh ahead, and as Teata the Indian chief arrived at their village with Aaron and two other Mohawks who came into the fort and gave the following intelligence annexed in two sheets of paper:

Detroit, June 9th 1764.

This day a small party of Pottawatamies arrived here who informed, that an Indian was come from the Illinois to St. Josephs who informed them that he was in council with Pontiac there.

That Mr. Deneyon told him he was glad to see him and hoped that his senses were come to him.

Pontiac then took a large belt and laid it before him saying, "my father the reason of my journey is to get you and all your allies to join with me to go against the English," upon which Deneyon took the belt and told him, "your speech much surprises me, as I doubt not but you have received my message wherein I informed you that the French and English were but one," then returned the belt. Pontiac took the belt again and importuned Mr. Deneyon on the same subject. At last Mr. Deneyon grew angry and kicked it from him, asking him if he had not already heard what he said to him. He then addressed himself to the Illinois Indians and told them they saw him that day in the fort, but perhaps they would see their brothers the English the next, and exhorted them to live in amity with them, which he made no doubt of as their sentiments were very good.

Pontiac then asked for rum and Deneyon gave him a small barrel, which he took to one of the Illinois villages and with a red belt exhorted them to sing the war song with him, which some of them did, but were sorry for it when they were sober. The Indian that brought this account says that before he left the Illinois he saw three English officers who were sent on before,

before, the army being but a little way behind with a large body of Indians.

Detroit, June 10th 1764.

This day Teata a Wyndote chief arrived here from Sandusky, where he had been to carry Sir William Johnson's speech, who says that after he delivered it and left it to their deliberation, the great Chief Bigg Jaco got up and thanked him for the trouble he had been at to bring it, and immediately the whole went out. After he had delivered the speech he says he advised them to come to their senses, but in case they did not it was their affair. Aaron says they made great game of Teata on saying so to them.

Four days after, they came back and asked Teata to come and hear what they had to say in answer. The first belt they gave him was a repetition of Sir William's speech. Then they took another saying, Sir William asks the reason why we struck against the English, we think he ought to know better than anybody; yes, said they, it is Sir William that ought to know, but since the Senecas have made peace with him and the English, tell him it was them that first embroiled the Earth, and were the first cause of what has been done. Gave the belt.

They then took another belt and said, "Sir William and the Six Nations want that we should own our folly and find words to excuse ourselves that we may be again set right. You'll tell him by this belt, which you are charged to deliver to him, that for what is past, it's past, that we have yet done no harm since last summer, we have kept our young men quiet, for which reason we think the breach may be easily mended; and tell him also we shall keep them quiet this summer, when we think we shall be reconciled."

The two Mohawks who are come with Teata, say that they were told by the Hurons of Sandusky, that they would not tell Teata the result of a council they had had with the Shawanese, which was that they were to try to take Fort Pitt by treachery, and if they failed there were to go against the inhabitants on the Frontiers. That the Onondagoes that Sir William sent against the Shawanese came to one of their villages, where they were asked what they came for, they said "we come to scalp you"; then one Kayoughshoutong said "here, take these," giving them two old scalps that he had newly painted, "go home and tell Sir

William you have scalped some Shawanese." Upon which they returned; that the above mentioned Indian was the cause of their not striking against the Shawanese. But it was not so with the Tuscroras, for they lost three men.

One of them further says that before he left the Delaware towns he saw thirty small parties go out who were all intended to go to our Frontiers. They both say, also, that the Hurons at Sandusky laughed at Teata behind his back, and called him a fool for believing what Sir William said and bringing such a message.

That though he said they would be friends, it can never be until all the English, except traders go from this place, meaning Detroit, and then we believe we shall agree. That their God tells them they must make war and peace for seven years, at the end of which by force of treachery during that time, all the English will be drove away and then they will have peace and not till then.

That the Delawares and Shawanese and Hurons of Sandusky all say the English are fools, that they can make friends with us when they please, and next day tomahawk us. That the English always told them they had as many men as there was leaves on the trees, but we look upon one Indian as good as a thousand of them, and notwithstanding we are but mice in comparison to them, we will bite as much as they can. The two Mohawks' father says that the Hurons at Sandusky told them they were very sorry that Sir William was coming here, as they imagined by that he wanted to leave his bones here.

They also say that while they were at the Shawanee village the French from the Mississippi sent them a present of powder, of which he saw three barrels.

Mr. St. Martin, interpreter, told Maj. Gladwyn that Hurons of this place told him many times that if a peace was made with the Delawares, Shawanese and Hurons of Sandusky, that it would not be good, nor lasting.

*12th.* The schooner sailed at about four in the afternoon, and run out of sight from the fort before dark.

*13th.* This day Teata and several Hurons came to the fort and asked the commandant if they might not go once more to the Hurons of Sandusky, as perhaps though their ears had always been stopped till now yet they might be open at present.

The commandant told them they might do as they pleased, that he had sent their answer to Sir William Johnson with their belts, that it was not intended to force a peace down the throats of the Indians, nor was it intended for any but those who had sincerely repented of what they had done, and was really resolved to remain our friends for the future. That in his opinion they ought not to go, as they only laughed at the message taken by Teata, and him for carrying it.

*14th.* This day a Huron promised to set off with his little band of about twelve to bring in some Delaware or Shawanee scalps.

*15th.* This day Wabagommigot came in with some Chippewas and two prisoners and after repeating a good deal of what passed in council last fall, said that as the commandant had desired him several times go to his old village and to see him yet here, would perhaps make him think that he had no Intention to do what he had ordered him, but the reason was, that he had been trying to get all the prisoners that was among his nation and to gather his band together, which he had now almost affected; he did not speak for the whole nation, but for those who were with him who had heartily repented of what they had done and hoped to be received as he himself was. That there were some whom he advertised of what he (the commandant) had told him with regard to their quick repentance and of the council that was to be held at Niagara, but since they did not come in it was their affair.

He then asked for the two prisoners, saying it was nothing, but this war, that separated him from the rest of the nation, who were nevertheless part of his body, for which reason hoped they would be given up, as he then wiped away all the blood that had been spilt with the two prisoners he brought in. That he hoped in going home to his old village he might not hear it said that things went ill at the Detroit because Wabagommigot was refused that favour. That since the malefactors he then spoke for (meaning people he had with him) were come to their senses, and heartily repented of what they had done, and as they were set on by the Six Nations, hoped they would be forgiven and no more thought of it.

The commandant then asked him if he came in the name of the whole nation, he said no, but in part. "Then," said he "if you'll take my advice you'll go to Niagara before the council is over and make peace for yourself and band; you have no time to lose as it will be over in twelve days. And as to the prisoners I shall keep them till I get all mine in, as they belong to a band that has not as yet asked for peace nor brought in all my flesh. As to what he (Wabagommigot) might hear of things going ill here, nothing could go ill with us, but if anybody did anything that they ought not to do, it would be them that would suffer; that we were out of their power." He then repeated to him that it was necessary he should be at Niagara at the council, for which purpose he would give me a receipt, that he had delivered two prisoners, &c.; that the time was short and the sooner he went off the better.

The Frenchman that danced the war dance at Sandusky this spring with the Indians is named Thefault.

*25th.* This day Mindoghquay came in with about seventy of his people and about thirty Chippewas who brought in two prisoners, being the last they had amongst them, for whom the commandant gave them the two Indians he detained some time ago.

The Pottawatamies after all the promises did not go to Niagara, nor Wabagommigot neither.

*28th.* This day the schooner *Victory* returned from Niagara with another new schooner, the *Boston.*

*July 1st.* This evening at about ten o'clock one Reaume, a Frenchman, arrived from Michilimackinac with eighteen canoes of savages who came from the bay the 3rd June to go to Montreal, but when they arrived at Michilimackinac they were informed that ten canoes that were going there and an express with a belt informing them that they should go to Niagara where they would meet a great English chief, upon which they took their route this way, and several canoes from the nations thereabouts went across Lake Huron by way of Lake Ontario. They brought four Englishmen with them with all their packs, who had been amongst since last spring was a year.

*3rd.* This day some of greatest of the Huron chiefs of Sandusky came in with five prisoners to throw themselves at the commandant's feet, as they said, and after telling him that what they had done was in consequence of what messages and lies the Ottawas sent them, said that if he would have pity on them, he would see they were sincere, as his will was theirs.

The commandant told them the only way they had to get a peace, and if they did not benefit of what he said, it was their affair. He gave them a certificate that they had delivered five prisoners and that they had asked for peace, which they said they would take to Niagara with all the rest of the prisoners they had amongst them.

This afternoon the Michilimackinac chiefs and Foles a Voines came in told the commandant they came to take him by the hand and let him know they were glad to see him, and would come tomorrow to speak to him.

*4th.* This morning the above indians came in to the amount of fifty and told the commandant that they, the Renards, the Sieus, the Saquis, Puantes and Pians, were one body and one heart, and that, that heart was as well intentioned as it had always been; that he knew himself from their behaviour last year, that their and ours could be but one; that they were invited by the general last year to come to Montreal this spring, but that when they were assembled at Michilimackinac they received a belt from him, telling them that he stopped up the passage that way as the smallpox was amongst his people which they might catch and carry home to the destruction of their wives and children, but if they would go to Niagara they would find all they were in need of, for which reason they begged the rivers and lakes might be open to them as usual, showing the belt they received.

*5th.* This day some of the Hurons of this village came in with the chiefs of Hurons of Sandusky who were in the day before yesterday and brought with them some Hurons that arrived the day before to join their old village and brought in five prisoners, whom they said they would not have brought in till their chiefs returned from Niagara[69] had it not been to encourage those of Sandusky to do the same, as the commandant knew he was always sure of them, but nevertheless, though they had had some of them since they sucked, yet that the chiefs from Sandusky might be witness of their good intentions they brought them in sooner than they promised.

The Huron that went to strike against the Delawares and Shawanese returned this day without doing anything.

*7th.* This day Mr. Jadeau in repeating to the commandant some things that had passed between him and one Clermont (who had been sent with a letter to the Illinois, but went no further than where the Ottawas are in the Miami River) said that Clermont told him, "you do very well in serving the English, but I have my reasons for

---

69. These chiefs had gone to Niagara to hold a treaty with Sir William Johnson. The treaty was signed July 18, 1764, and bound the Hurons to deliver up all prisoners, deserters and Negroes or other slaves among them; to maintain a friendly alliance and to do their utmost to preserve His Britannic Majesty's interests and promote peace among the western tribes. They were promised pardon for all past misdeeds, and a free, fair and open privilege of trade.—*N.Y. Col. Hist.*, 7, 650.

what I do, and you will soon be obliged to save yourself in the fort. Another thing," said he "I'll tell you that you don't know, the English are all defeated in the Mississippi and there will be fourteen hundred men soon here, and all the Indians that are going to Niagara have agreed with the Ottawas to return with the army, and the Ottawas are to meet them on the lake and try to destroy them. That merchandise and powder was in the greatest plenty at the Miami River.

That one Borgard who came from St. Josephs brought them a barrel of powder and some corn, flour, &c. That there was one Clincincourt a French officer, who was sent by Mr. Deneyon with letters for the commandant here, was stopped by the Ottawas, where they keep him, neither giving him liberty to return nor come forward.

This afternoon a Saggina Indian who had been sent by his brother, as he said, to the Miami River to see what passed came in and informed that while he was there a French officer arrived there from the Illinois who was coming here with letters, but the Ottawas stopped him and took his letters from him, and sent for Cusieres' son to read them. After which one of the Ottawa chiefs told him that Cuesiere had told them that it was a letter from their father the French King, who desired his brothers the English to make haste and go away from this place, for he was coming in a great body and had a great many of his children with him, whose inclination he was not master of, and would not answer for what harm they might do. The officer they keep there and will neither let him go back or forward.

*10th.* This day part of the four following nations arrived here, the Saquis, the Renards, the Puantes, and the Saulteux of Lake Superior, some of whom came from the forks of the Mississippi (and from all appearance, and what they said) they came in expectation of getting rum. They were upwards of two months a coming; they brought upwards of sixty packs of beaver.

*12th.* This day at 2 o'clock the two schooners left this for the east end of Lake Erie.

*13th.* This day Mr. Clincincourt arrived from the Miami, who had been detained by the Ottawas.

*14th.* This day at about 4 o'clock in the afternoon the Schooner *Gladwyn* arrived from Niagara.

*21st.* This day Wassong, a chief of the Chippewas came in with a prisoner that he had promised to bring in, in the winter, but who had got frost bit and was not able to come. After telling that he was not concerned in the beginning; of the insurrection and asking pardon in a most submissive manner said: he did not pretend to excuse himself, that as he had told Mr. Labute in the spring he would behave as a dog that had offended his master, that if he was punished and was miserable he had nobody to blame but himself, and would still fawn till he was taken into favour again, for that he was as a dog that had been beaten and was running round his master with fear and respect, and would continue till he was pardoned, having since last fall resolved to die rather than disobey his brother's will. And asked what were the most salutary means to be well received by the general, since he had not been informed that he should have gone to Niagara. At the same time begging mercy in the most submissive manner and said if his brother could see the distress their families were in, he would have pity upon them and think they were punished enough.

The commandant told him the reason of the insurrection was because they had something then in their power which they would never have again, for if they had they would act the same part over again.

*22nd.* In the evening we were informed that the Sloop *Royal Charlotte* was aground on this side [of] the Whitewood; at 2 in the morning a detachment was sent with four *bateaus* to lighten her and get her off, which they did next day by four in the afternoon, and the 24th she arrived here.

*27th.* The Schooner *Boston* arrived from Niagara. 29 This morning at 11 o'clock the Sloop *Charlotte* set sail for Niagara with wind at N. W.

In the afternoon Manitoo, an Ottawa chief, with five other Ottawas, four of whom were from the Miami River, came in with three prisoners. The speaker said that God had been speaking with him a great deal this last winter, and that what he had said was the sentiments of all the chiefs, and begged to be pitied and heard. He then begged pardon for what they had done in a most submissive manner; the reason of their beginning he did not know, but he that set them on (Pontiac) was returned from the Illinois, but was no more heard by anybody in the nation; that God had told him he had done wrong, that he had made this earth for them and us to live quietly together in, and that Pontiac the causer of its being disturbed would not die but would burn in Hell eternally, as all those would do who did not follow the advice and obey the will of their brother.

God also told him he must not lie, steal, nor covet another man's wife, all which commands they would strictly adhere to for the future, and that their brother should see that what they said was true and sincere in the end, and hoped he would have pity upon them. That they would return to Sandusky to where their corn was planted, and after it was gathered would come and asked liberty to stay there another year, and that after that if their brother was convinced of their sincerity they hoped he would give them liberty to come and settle their ancient village.

The commandant told them if they did not know the reason of their beginning he would tell them. The reason was, said he, that you had at that time something in your power that you will never have again, for if you had I am sure you would make the same use of it you have already done, but if you bring in all those who set you on, black or white, I shall tell the general what you say, and it may be a step toward your getting peace, but it does not look as if you were very sincere, since this is the first of your appearance. But I suppose the reason of your coming is because your vain hopes of an army from the Illinois is vanished and you see yourselves without succour.

To which the speaker said the reproaches their brother made them were very just, but it was not the chief's fault that they did not come sooner, but his, for God had told him to remain quiet and not mind any more bad belts for that he would be forgiven when they prostrated themselves before their brother. And as a proof of their sincerity they would go and endeavour to bring in the people he mentioned.

*30th.* This day the Schooner *Victory* arrived from Niagara loaded with baggage for the 17th; she left Niagara the 20th, but had very bad weather. She sprung her bowsprit and broke her mast.

*31st.* Yesterday some of the Hurons came to dance before the commandant's door, and after they had done were going away, when one of them who stayed a little behind was stopped by a Royal American near Mr. St. Martin's house, where he coaxed him in and murdered him as it appears from all the circumstances of the affair; the soldier was immediately put in irons, and the commandant was going to send for the chiefs, when two of them came into the fort, having been informed of it by two other indians who stayed behind a little time with him that was murdered, who though they did not see the stroke, was near enough to hear it, as was also a corporal of the artillery.

*Aug. 5th.* This day *the little chief* came in and informed Mr. Labute that Seckaho had deceived the commandant, that he was gone back to the Miami River to where his corn was, and that after it was ripe, he heard that Seckaho and what people of his band would go with him, with those of Pontiac's band were going off to the Illinois.

*8th.* This day Mintiwaby from Saggina came in with six or seven of Mindochquay's band, and brought a prisoner that he had had all the winter, who Mindochquay told the commandant in the spring, would have then been brought in, but Mintiwaby was gone to Michilimackinac. He said that the Chippewas at Shaguomigan had sent a pipe to Mindochquay's band, and desired him to send it to Mochoquish who would send it to the Shawnies and Delawares with the following answer, to the invitation they gave them to join with them to strike against the English last fall as Mochoquish had sent the belt from the Shawnies and Delawares, namely, That they had no complaints against their brothers the English, and they had a greater regard for their wives, children and young men, than to enter into so bad a thing.

*10th.* This afternoon at about four o'clock, the Sloop *Charlotte* and Schooner *Gladwyn* arrived here, Commodore Loring and Capt. Grant came in the former.

*11th.* This day Marchioquisse, a Pottawatamie chief, sent in a turkey and some venison and desired the commandant would except of it, as he was unworthy of coming into the fort, but nevertheless he and the chiefs of the Pottawatamies of St. Josephs were getting the prisoners they had together to bring them in, in two or three days in case they would be received. And that if the commandant had not a mind to starve him, he begged he would send him two or three charges of powder and ball.

*12th.* This day *the little Chief* told Mr. Labute that Pontiac continued his usual discourse and was as ill intentioned as ever; that he had tried to animate all the nations about here, by telling them that there was absolutely a French army on the way here, from the Illinois, but that the commandant there could not come with them until he had received a letter from their father, which he expected every day. That Seckaho had sent three young men on to the Post Vincent [70] to meet them and bring him news.

*14th.* This morning a Pottawatamie came to the settlement and sent for Mr. Labute, to whom he told that he was sent by one of their chiefs to put his brother upon his guard, as the Shawanese and

---

70. Now Vincennes, on the Wabash in Indiana.

Delawares were come to join Pontiac at the Miami River, to come and attack this place, that they were not yet arrived, but one of their chiefs had seen some runners that came before to inform they were coming.

Mr. Labute was further informed by the little Chief of the Chippewas that Pontiac had much threatened the Ottawa chiefs who brought in some prisoners a little time ago and told them that his father was on his way March and as soon as he came he would have them all hanged that tried to make up a thing that he (Pontiac) had begun.

*15th.* The sloop sailed for Niagara.

*17th.* The Schooner *Boston* arrived in the mouth of the river from Niagara.

*19th.* This day at about one o'clock the Schooner *Gladwin* sailed for Niagara. At three o'clock Mr. Marsack came in and informed that he had been told by some Indians that some of the Hurons of Sandusky were gone to meet the army with the belts that were sent them by the Six Nations to take up the hatchet against the English, for that they might at least let the English fight their own battles, which they would tell them when they met them and desire them to return by the same belts that they desired them to take up the hatchet. That they were all ready to receive the English at Lake Sandusky.

*20th.* This morning Mr. Campeau came in and informed that he had overheard an Ottawa and two Foles a Voines speaking about the army, and the Ottawa asked where they were and which way they were coming; the others told him they were coming on the south side of the lake. What to do? said the Ottawa. To cut off the Hurons at Sandusky, said the others. O, said the Ottawa, they are all ready to meet them, the Miamis and all the Pottawatamies are assembled there, and they have sent their wives and children back in the woods, and have prepared their young corn and squashes on purpose that they may keep. That a Chibbaway was soon after sent off as he imagined to go to the Miami.

Mr. M'Dougal was told this morning by an Indian that most of the Chippewas and all the Pottawatamies were on the Miami River with the Ottawas and Miamis, and a good many other Indians.

This day and last night all the Ottawas and Foles a Voines, &c., that came from Michilimackinac this spring to go to Niagara returned.

*21st.* This afternoon the Schooner *Boston* arrived. Last night Mr. Jadeau came with a letter informing us that the Schooner *Gladwin* was aground near Isle Bois Blanc [71] upon which Mr. Grant was sent off with some men to get her off.

This night Mr. Colville, one of the masters of the vessels, came up to get a grappling and some other things for the Schooner *Gladwin*, as me had lost her anchors in getting off.

*24th.* Commodore Loring left this in the barge to go on board the Schooner *Boston* at the mouth of the river, for Niagara.

*27th.* This afternoon the army arrived under the command of Col. Bradstreet. [72]

*29th.* A party of men were sent to cut timber upon Isle Cochon for barracks, &c.

All the inhabitants were ordered to appear at nine next morning from fifteen years old upwards to renew their oaths of allegiance, which ran in the terms following. [73]

*31st.* This morning the Schooner *Victory* sailed for Niagara, with Maj. Gladwyn on board.

This evening the Hurons came to see the new commandant, and after their usual compliments gave him the name of the Little Deer.

*Sept. 2nd.* This afternoon fifty-five Ottawas, including women and children, arrived here according to their promise made to Col. Bradstreet, when he left the Miami River.

*3rd.* This morning the Ottawas came to Col. Bradstreet to give him their hands and told him they only came to tell him that the Chippewas and Pottawatamies were to come in next day and then they would speak for the whole. But without their saying anything about making peace, he told them that *if they were as well inclined for it as him* there would be one just at the mouth of the Mississippi.

*5th.* This day a council was held with the Ottawas and Chippewas, the Pottawatamies not having come in.

---

71. Isle Bois Blanc, or White-wood Island, lies in front of Amherstburgh, on the Canadian side of the Channel and 18 miles below Detroit. It is a little over a mile in length, and to one descending it is the last island on the left-hand side before entering Lake Erie.

72 Col. John Bradstreet had served with great reputation in the wars with France in America. He received a commission as colonel in Feb. 1762, and held at this time the office of quarter-master general. In 1772 he was promoted to the rank of major-general. He died at New York, Sept. 25, 1774, aged 63 years.—*Mass. Hist. Col.; Army Lists; Dunlop's Hist. N.Y.; Parkman's Pontiac.*

73. A blank here occurs in the MSS.

*6th.* This day the Pottawatamies arrived.

*7th.* This day the Ottawas, Chippewas, Pottawatamies, Miamis and Hurons signed the *Articles of Peace* given them by Col. Bradstreet, the contents of which is in the *Book of Councils.* Yesterday the Sloop *Charlotte*, the Schooner *Boston* and Schooner *Gladwyn* entered the river.

*10th.* This day the Schooner *Victory* arrived from Niagara.

*11th.* This morning the Schooner *Gladwyn* sailed for Michilimackinac.

*13th.* This morning Mr. Crofton arrived from Niagara in a *bateau* with despatches for Col. Bradstreet.

This afternoon news came by Indians, that the Shawanese and Delawares would not make peace, and that they had detained Mr Paully and the people with him, and were resolved to defend themselves.

*14th.* This morning at 8 o'clock the army embarked to go to Sandusky.

*16th.* This morning the Schooner *Victory* set sail for Sandusky, where she was to wait Col. Bradstreet's orders.

*17th.* This morning the sloop sailed for Niagara.

This evening Capt. Morris arrived here, having been sent by Col. Bradstreet to try to go to the Illinois, but was stopped by the Miamis who were going to burn him.

*18th.* This morning an express was sent to overtake Col. Bradstreet with letters from Col. Campbell and Captain Morris.

*27th.* The Schooner *Victory* returned from Sandusky for provision; in which came Mr. Cheppaton with orders from Col. Bradstreet.

*Oct. 6th.* This morning the Schooner *Boston* arrived after laying four days in the river with contrary winds.

*8th.* This morning Minechesne arrived from Col. Bradstreet with some Indians, who brought orders for Mr. Cheppaton to spare no expense in getting some Indians of each nation to take up the hatchet against the Shawanese and Delawares and for Minechesne to bring the *little* chief of the Chippewas in particular. As also orders to Col. Campbell to speak to the Hurons to send as many of their people as possible; his speech and answer to it is in the *Book of Councils* of this date.

This morning the Schooner *Boston* sailed for Fort Erie.

*11th.* This morning Mr. Cheppaton left this for Sandusky with thirteen Indians, who had taken up the hatchet against the Shawanese and Delawares.

*12th.* This morning Minichesne left this with eight Indians who had taken up the hatchet against the Delawares and Shawanese.

*16th.* This day we were informed by a man who came from Lake St. Clair that Mr. St. Clair[74] entered Lake Huron the thirteenth with the Schooner *Gladwyn*, and was soon out of sight, the wind being very good.

This morning the Sloop *Charlotte* arrived from Fort Erie.

*20th.* This day the Sloop *Charlotte* sailed for Fort Erie, with 121 packs of peltry, being the last of 1464 packs that were sent from this since last April.

*21st.* This day some Indians with Maisonville and J. Reaume arrived from Sandusky, who brought letters informing us that the army had left that place the 18th inst.

*22nd.* This day André the Huron arrived from Sandusky, who informed that he had been sent out on a party from Sandusky with twenty Englishmen and nine Indians to cut off a Shawanee village consisting of four *cabans*. That the morning after his first days march, four of his Indians who were of the Six Nations chose to stay awhile behind, and at midday when he halted he enquired for them, and was told by one of the Englishmen who stayed a little while with them that they were returned to the camp, upon which he pushed on without them.

The fourth day, knowing he was near the village, he sent two of his young people on before, who in a short time returned and told him they saw two Indians coming on horseback, who soon after arrived and told him they knew his design, but that the village was increased to ten *cabans*, and if he went on would be cut to pieces, and moreover that the Shawanese had asked peace from Col. Boquet and were gone with all their prisoners to meet him to the amount of two hundred, upon which seeing they were apprised of his design and were going to make peace he sent back his party and took two Indians and proceeded to the village, where he was informed that the four Indians that returned from the party informed a Huron chief who had made peace with Col. Bradstreet, who immediately sent off an express on horseback to the village, and that one of the two Indians that met

---

74. This was probably James St. Clair who was commissioned as a Captain in the 45th Regiment, March 10, 1761. Arthur St. Clair had previously been in the Regular Service but was then residing in Pennsylvania,

him was the brother of a Mohawk chief. That he was sure in case that his design had not been discovered, the Indians that were with him would not have fought. That in patting by the head of the Sandusky River he saw a Huron of Sandusky who told him he was arrived from the Frontiers of Virginia where he had been at war with a party of Shawanese and Delawares, who had taken thirty scalps, and that if he would not believe him he would give him two, that were pretty fresh to show to his father the commandant at this place, which scalps he saw.

*27th.* This day the Militia returned from Michilimackinac.

*Nov. 3rd.* This day the Schooner *Boston* arrived at the mouth of the river after been eighteen days from Niagara, and the Schooner Victory, who came out with her, they suppose was drove back.

*5th.* This morning Capt. St. Clair arrived here from Michilimackinac after laying up the Schooner *Gladwyn* in a small river near the head of the River Huron.

This evening the Sloop *Charlotte*, the Schooner *Boston* and Schooner *Victory* arrived opposite the fort.

*23rd.* This morning André and five other Hurons left this on a scout against the Shawanese and Delawares and were to encamp at the River Rouge for tonight.

This afternoon a soldier was killed and scalped on the road between the River Rouge and the fort.

*24th.* This morning a soldier was killed and scalped behind the fort near the edge of the woods.

Andrew returned this morning and promised (as he imagined it was Indians from Sandusky that took the two scalps) that he would fall upon the first Indian he saw from the other side of Lake Erie.

*25th.* This day we were informed that it was some St. Joseph Indians that took the scalps as they had seen them.

*26th.* This day two Pottawatamies of this place came in and informed that it was the St. Joseph Indians that took the scalps at the instigation of a Saqui who had been with them near twenty years, and whose son was killed this time twelve months at this place.

This was confirmed by many informations from many Indians.

*Dec. 14th.* This day Marchioquisse a chief of the Pottawatamies of this place arrived from St. Josephs with a letter from one Chevallier to the commanding officer, who informed the commandant that

Chevallier told him the King of France had sent over some merchants, whom he had ordered to sell things to the Indians at the following rate, *viz.*: if the English sold a blanket for four beaver they were to sell it for three; if they sold it for three, they were to sell it for two, and if the English sold it for two they were to sell it for one, and everything else in proportion. That there was five canoes of that merchandise already at St. Josephs, as much at Outattanon and a good deal gone to the Shawanese and Delawares.

After a good deal of discourse with the commandant about the scalps that was taken the 23rd and 24th of November he asked him in case the murderers could be brought before him to make a proper submission, whether he would not forgive them; to which he said if they were brought before him and made proper submissions he would not use them as they merited. Upon which Machioquisse promised to go and get some Sauteux and use all the means in his power to bring the murderers in and with the English prisoners that was at St. Josephs.

*January 21st,* 1764 [1765]. This day Andrew the Huron arrived from Fort Pitt with letters, for being informed that peace was made with the Shawanese and Delawares, he proceeded to that place instead of striking against them as he was directed when he left this. He said the Shawanese and Delawares told him there was three *bateaux* and two *perriaugres* arrived at the mouth of the Oenentois, from the Illinois, and they sent them a large belt of *wampum* desiring them to go immediately out of their river. That they had made peace with their father the English, and would not have any more to do with the French.

*Feb. 27th.* Andrew the Huron left this for Fort Pitt with Maisonville.

*Mar. 11th.* A small party from the Miamis took a prisoner that had straggled from the vessel at the River Rouge.

*17th.* Mr. Jadot was sent from this to the Miami to bring one Clermont and his family and some others to this place, as we had been informed they spirited up the Indians to strike here, but the Indians met him before he arrived there and disarmed his party, and sent him back.

*April 15th.* Col. Campbell sent them a message by some Chippewas (who offered themselves as volunteers) to let them know if they did not give up every prisoner they had and the arms they took from

Mr. Jadot's party, he would declare them his enemies; and the Chippewas who carried this message had orders from their Chief Seccaho, that in case they did not comply with this demand they might look upon them as their enemies as they would immediately strike against them.

The Schooner *Victory* sailed for Niagara, in which went Lt. Stewart and Sir Edward Pickering.

*May 8th.* This day the Chippewas returned from the Miami and brought word they would soon be in with their prisoners and desired their father not to be impatient; but by private intelligence we were informed quite otherwise.

*16th.* This day the Sloop *Charlotte* arrived from Niagara, in which came Lt. M'Dougal.

*17th.* This day some of the Ottawa chiefs from the Miami River came in and delivered a message to the commandant which they said they received from Col. Croghan, inviting them to Fort Pitt, begging he would write to Col. Croghan and tell him in case they did not come at the time appointed that it was because they were employed in trying to bring in the Miamis to make a proper submission to their father and with their prisoners.

And desiring if he their father chose they should go to the Miami he would get one or two of the Hurons chiefs to go with them.

In the afternoon one ——— a Mohawk who had been sent last fall by Sir William Johnson as a spy among the Indians came in with two Bennickees and informed the commandant, that as there was frequent reports at Sandusky that a body of French and Indians were coming by way of the Miami, they sent some young men as far as the Miami to see whether it was true, and as the above mentioned Indians were on their way here they met the Hurons returning from Miami, who told them that the 9th inst. Pontiac's nephew arrived from the Illinois who informed them that while Pontiac and the great Saalteur from Michilimackinac was there, six Englishmen, with one Maisonville a Frenchman, a Delaware, a Mohawk and a Huron from this place arrived there from Fort Pitt, whom Pontiac caused to be seized and brought them as far as Outattanon, where they were all burnt but two whom he was bringing to give to the Miamis. That Pontiac had seven large belts for to raise the St. Josephs, the Miamis, the Outattanons, the Pians, Mascoutons, and the Illinois, who were to assemble with some nations to the northward and make what efforts they could against

102

this place the beginning of next month, for which purpose Pontiac had besides the above belts a very large one which was for the hatchet from the French. That this undertaking was to be entirely by the Indians without any assistance.

St. Vincent, one of the above Indians further says, that being at the Shawanee town about twenty days ago, a French trader from the Illinois told him that he had received a letter from Maisonville when he was going down the Ohio, who informed him that he had been sent by the commanding officer at Fort Pitt, to go to the Illinois with some Englishmen,

20th. Three chiefs of the Ottawas with some young men left this with a message from the commandant to the Miamis and one for Pontiac.

21st. This morning the Sloop *Charlotte* sailed for Niagara.

This afternoon one of the Chippewas who were sent to the Miami the 15th March, came here and brought back the belts which the Miamis would not receive and told quite a different story from what their Chief Seccaho told on the return of the rest.

24th. This day the Indians from St. Josephs came to the settlement with a prisoner, and a belt from their chiefs, but the commanding officer would not receive them as there was no chief with, and as they had not fulfilled their promise.

The prisoner they sent in by two Pottawatamie chiefs of this place with the belt, which the commandant received and sent them word, when their chiefs fulfilled their promise he would receive them as his children, but not till then. This prisoner was gave to them by the Shawanese and Delawares two years ago, whom we knew nothing of, being one more than they said they had.

25th. This day the Huron chiefs with two Onondagoes came in and told the commandant that they came to speak to him upon the same Subject they had done the 17th instant, saying they had since been informed by some people from towards the Illinois that they were in danger, that the Indians the last time had only taken up the hatchet against the English, but that now they would take it up against the French and them, as they lived near the English and liked them; and that they should perish with them. They then desired they might give the commandant a little advice, which if found good he would have pity upon them and do.

They then said that as the Indians depended entirely upon what they could get or take from the inhabitants for subsistence, they thought it advisable that they should join in small parties and gather together their corn and cattle and make at different places small stockades where eight or ten families might secure themselves in, with their effects; that in proposing this to them the commandant would see whether they were inclined to be faithful or not, for if they objected against it, they were certainly inclined to fight, as the Indians would render themselves masters of them and would obliged them to do what they pleased and strip them of everything, in case they remained in the undefensible condition they were then.

They begged the commandant would desire the inhabitants on the south side of the river to join with them to make a stockade at the Huron Point near the priests house, that they might put their wives and children in for security, for notwithstanding they were a small number they would then laugh at anything the other nations could do, but if they were to remain they would be in their power and perhaps be obliged to do thing they had not inclination to do, for said they, what will not a man do to save his life, and when we see a knife at our throats we shall perhaps commit faults, for these and many other reasons they begged the commandant would propose to the people to put themselves in some kind of defence.

They further said they knew the inhabitants would be very angry at them if they knew they proposed such a thing, but they knew on their side that if they did not comply with it they would soon repent it, and perhaps would be very glad to take refuge in their little fort, in case they got one built. They said there was no time to loose, the sooner it was done the better. In the afternoon the commandant sent for the officers of the Militia, and acquainted them of the news he had heard and proposed to them to put themselves in the best state of Defence they could, agreeable to which he gave them some proposals in writing, a copy of which is amongst the orders issued to the Militia.

*26th.* This day the Schooner *Victory* arrived, having been sent from Niagara with Capt. Simpson of the artillery to take up the cannon left by Col Bradstreet last fall near the River au Roche, but was obliged to put in here for want of provision, having had a great deal of bad weather and not being able to go to the place. The vessel in very bad condition.

*June 6th.* The Schooner *Victory*.

[*The Diary thus ends abruptly in the middle of a page in the manuscript.*]

# Journal of the Siege of Detroit
# Introduction

Major Rogers arrived at Detroit on the 29th of July, 1763, with the detachment under the command of Capt. Dalyel, and shared in the gallant but unfortunate sortie made under the command of that officer a few days after, in which the leader and many of his men perished. The information contained in the following *Narrative* is entirely from hearsay, and only brings down the chain of events to the 4th of July, although dated nearly a month later. It is probable that Maj. Rogers began to write an account of the siege soon after his arrival, and that this was only partly finished when the sailing of two vessels (mentioned in *Diary of the Siege of Detroit*) offered a convenient opportunity for sending it to Sir William Johnson. At the close of the *Volume of Journals* published by Major Rogers in 1765, is an advertisement of a second volume to contain, among other things, an account of the Indian Wars in America subsequent to 1760. Subscriptions were solicited and the book was promised within a limited time, but from some cause unknown, it was never printed. It is reasonable to infer that the following pages were intended to form a portion of the book, and that this fragment, now first printed, may be the only part that has been preserved. It was found among the manuscripts of Sir William Johnson in the New York State Library.

F. B. H.

# Journal

*Journal of the Siege of Detroit*, taken from the officers who were then in the fort, and wrote in their words in the following manner, *viz.*:

The 6th of May; when we were privately informed of a conspiracy formed against us by the Indians, particularly the Tawa [1] Nation, who were to come to council with us the next day, and massacre every soul of us. On the morning of that day, being Saturday the 7th of May, fifteen of their warriors came into the fort and seemed very inquisitive and anxious to know where all the English merchants' shops were.

At 9 o'clock the garrison were ordered under arms and the savages continued coming into the fort till 11 o'clock, diminishing their numbers as much as possible by dividing themselves at all the corners of the streets most adjacent to the shops. Before 12 o'clock they were three hundred men, at least three times the number equal to that of the garrison; but seeing all the troops under arms, and the merchants shops shut, imagined prevented them from attempting to put their evil scheme into execution that day.

Observing us thus prepared, their chiefs came in a very condemned like manner, to council, where they spoke a great deal of nonsense to Major Gladwyn and Capt. Campbell, protesting at the same time the greatest friendship imaginable to them, but expressing their surprise at seeing all the officers and men under arms. The major then told them that he had certain intelligence that some Indians were projecting mischief, and on that account he was determined to have the troops always under arms upon such occasions: That they being the oldest nation, and the first that had come to council, needed not to be astonished at that precaution as he was resolved to do the same to all nations.

At 1 o'clock they had done speaking, went off seemingly very

1. Ottawa.

discontented and crossed the river half a league from the fort, where they all encamped about 6 o'clock that afternoon. Six of their warriors returned and brought an old squaw prisoner, alleging that she had given us false information against them. The major declared she had never given any kind of advice. They then insisted upon naming the author of what he had heard in regard to the Indians, which he declined to do, but told them it was one of themselves, whose name he promised never to reveal; whereupon they went off and carried the old woman prisoner with them. When they arrived at their camp, Pontiac their greatest chief seized on the prisoner and gave her three strokes with a stick on the head, which laid her flat on the ground, and the whole nation assembled around her and called repeated times "kill her, kill her."

Sunday the 8th, Pontiac and several other of the principal chiefs came into the fort, at 5 o'clock in the afternoon and brought a pipe of peace with them of which they wanted to convince us fully of their friendship and sincerity, but the major judging that they only wanted to cajole us would not go nigh them nor give them any countenance, which obliged Capt. Campbell to go and speak with them, and after smoking with the pipe of peace and assuring him of their fidelity, they said that the next morning all the nation would come to council where everything would be settled to our satisfaction, after which they would immediately disperse, and that that would remove all kind of suspicion.

Accordingly on Monday morning the 9th, six of their warriors came into the fort at 7 o'clock, and upon seeing the garrison under arms went off without being observed. About 10 o'clock we counted fifty-six canoes, with seven and eight men in each, crossing the river from their camp, and when they arrived nigh the fort, the gates were shut, and the interpreter went to tell them that not above fifty or sixty chiefs would be admitted into the fort, upon which Pontiac immediately desired the interpreter in a peremptory manner to return directly and acquaint us that if all their people had not free access into the fort none of them would enter it: that we might stay in our fort, but he would keep the country, adding that he would order a party instantly to an island where we had twenty-four bullocks, which they immediately killed. Unluckily three soldiers were on the island and a poor man with his wife and four children which they all murthered except two children, as also a poor woman and her two sons, that lived about half a mile from the fort.

After having thus put all the English without the fort to death, the ordered a Frenchman who had seen the woman and her two children killed and scalped, to come and inform us of it, and likewise of their having murthered Sir Robert Davers, Captain Robertson and a boats' crew of six persons two days before, being Saturday the 7th of May, near the entrance of Lake Huron, for which place they set out from hence on Monday the 2nd inst. in order to know if the lakes and rivers were navigable for a schooner which lay here to proceed to Michilimackinac. We were then fully persuaded that the information given us was well founded, and a proper disposition was made for the defence of the fort, although our number was but small, not exceeding one hundred and twenty, including all the English traders, and the works were nigh mile in circumference.

On Tuesday the 10th, very early in the morning, the savages began to fire on the fort, and vessels which lay opposite to the east and west sides of the fort. [2] About 8 o'clock the Indians called a *parley* and ceased firing, and half an hour after, the Wyndote's chiefs came into the fort, on their way to a council where they were called by the Tawas and promised us to endeavour to solicitate and persuade the Tawas from committing further hostilities.

After drinking a glass of rum they went off at three o'clock that afternoon. Several of the inhabitants and four chiefs of the Tawas, Wyndotes and Chippewas and Pottawatamies came and acquainted us, that most of all the inhabitants were assembled at a Frenchman's house about a mile from the fort, where the savages proposed to hold a council, and desiring Captain Campbell and another officer to go with them to that council, where they hoped with their presence and assistance further hostilities would cease, assuring us at the same time that come what would, that Capt. Campbell and the other officers that went with him, should return whenever they pleased. This promise was ascertained by the French as well as the Indian chief, whereupon Captain Campbell and Lieutenant McDougal went off escorted by a number of the inhabitants and the four chiefs, they first promised to be answerable for their returning yet night.

When they arrived at the house already mentioned they found the French and Indians assembled, and after counselling a long while, the Wyndotes were prevailed on to sing the war song, and this being done, it was next resolved that Captain Campbell and Lieutenant McDou-

---

2. The channel of Detroit River opposite the fort, ran but a few degrees south of west, although its general course is nearly south.

gall should be detained prisoners, but would be indulged to lodge in a French house till a French commandant arrived from the Illinois, that next day five Indians and as many Canadians would be dispatched to acquaint the commanding officer of the Illinois that Detroit was in their possession and require of him to send an officer to command, to whom Captain Campbell and Lieutenant McDougall should be delivered.

As for Major Gladwyn he was summoned to give up the fort and two vessels, &c., the troops to ground their arms, and they would allow as many *bateaux* and as much provision as they judged requisite for us to go to Niagara: That if these proposals were not accepted of, they were a thousand men, and storm the fort at all events, and in that case every soul of us should be put to the torture. The major returned for answer, that as soon as the two officers they had detained were permitted to come into the fort, he would after consulting them give a positive answer to their demand, but could do nothing without obtaining their opinion.

On Wednesday the 11th, several inhabitants came early in the morning into the fort, and advised us by way of friendship to make our escape aboard the vessels, assuring us that we had no other method by which we could preserve our lives, as the Indians were then fifteen hundred fighting men, and would be as many more in a few days, and that they were fully determined to attack us in an hour's time. We told the *Monsieurs* that we were ready to receive them, and that every officer and soldier in the fort would willingly perish in the defence of it, rather than condescend or agree to any terms that savages would propose. Upon which the French went off as I suppose to communicate what we had said to their allies, and in a little afterwards the Indians gave their usual hoop, and five or six hundred began to attack the fort on all quarters.

Indeed some of them behaved extremely well and advanced very boldly in an open plain exposed to our fire, and came within sixty yards of the fort, but upon having three men killed and above a dozen wounded, they retired as briskly as they advanced, and fired at three hundred yards distance till seven o'clock at night, when they sent a Frenchman into the fort with a letter to the major, desiring a cessation of arms, that night, and proposing to let the troops with their arms aboard the vessels, but insisting upon our giving up the fort, leaving the French auxiliary all the merchandise and officers' effects, and had even the insolence to demand a Negro boy belonging to a merchant to be delivered to Pontiac.

The major's reply to these extraordinary propositions was much the same as to the first.

Tuesday the 12th, five Frenchmen and as many Indians were sent off for the Illinois with letters wrote by a Canadian agreeable to Pontiac's desire. On the 13th we were informed by the inhabitants that Mr. Chapman, a trader from Niagara, was taken prisoner by the Wyndotes, with five *bateaus* loaded with goods.

The 21st, one of the vessels was ordered to sail for the Niagara, but to remain till the sixth of June at the mouth of the river in order to advert the *bateaus* which we expected daily from Niagara.

Upon the 22nd we were told that Ensign Paully who commanded at Sandusky was brought prisoner by ten Tawas, who reported that they had prevailed after long consultation with the Wyndotes who lived at Sandusky to declare war against us; that some days ago they came early of a morning to the block house, and murthered every soul therein, consisting of twenty seven persons, traders included; that Messrs Callender and Prentice, formerly captains in the Pennsylvania Regiment were amongst that number, and that they had taken one hundred horses loaded with Indian goods, which with the plunder of the garrison was agreed to be given the Wyndotes before they condescended to join them; that all they wanted was the commanding officer.

On the 29th of May, we had the mortification to see eight of our *bateaus* in the possession of the enemy, passing on the opposite shore, with several soldiers prisoners in them. When the foremost *bateau* came opposite the sloop, she fired a gun, and the soldiers aboard called at those in the *bateau*, that if they passed the savages would kill them all, upon which they immediately seized on two Indians and threw them overboard with him and tomahawked him directly, they being near the shore and it quite shoal. Another soldier laid hold of an oar, and struck that Indian upon the head, of which wound he is since dead. Then there remained only three soldiers, of which two were wounded, and although fifty Indians were on the bank not sixty yards, firing upon them, the three soldiers escaped aboard the vessel, with the *bateau* loaded with eight barrels of provisions and gives the following account of their misfortune, *viz.*:

That two nights before, about 10 o'clock, they arrived about six leagues from the mouth of the river where they encamped. That two men went a little from the camp for firewood to boil their kettle, when one of the two was seized on by an Indian, killed and scalped in an instant. The other soldier ran directly and alarmed the camp, upon which Lieutenant Cuyler immediately ordered to give ammunition to the detachment, which consisted of one serjeant and seventeen soldiers of the Royal Americans, three serjeants and seventy-two rank and file of the Queen's Independent Company of Rangers. After having delivered their ammunition, and a disposition made of the men, the enemy came close to them without being observed, behind a bank and fired very smartly on one flank which could not sustain the enemy's fire and they retired precipitately and threw the whole in confusion. By that means the soldiers embarked aboard the *bateaus* with one, two and three oars in each *bateau*, which gave an opportunity to the savages of taking them all except the two *bateaus* that escaped with Mr. Cuyler to Niagara.

Sunday the 5th of June, we were acquainted that Fort Maimi was taken, that Ensign Holms who commanded there had been informed by two Frenchmen who arrived there the preceding day of Detroits being attacked by the Indians, which he would hardly believe, but threatened to imprison the French for that report, that an Indian woman had betrayed him out of the fort by pretending that another woman was very sick, and begged of him to come to her cabin to let blood of her, and when he had gone a little distance from the fort was fired on and killed.

The serjeant hearing the report of the firing ran to see what it was, and was immediately taken prisoner. The soldiers shut the gates and would have probably defended the fort if one Walsh, a trader who had been taken prisoner a few days before, had not advised them to open the gates, alleging that if they did not comply the Indians would set fire to the fort and put them to death; whereas, if they opened the gates, they should be well treated. Whereupon the gates were opened, and the soldiers grounded their arms.

On the 10th of June we heard that Ensign Schlosser the commanding officer at Saint Josephs was taken prisoner and that all the garrison (except three men) were massacred. That the Indians came on the 25th of May with a pretence to council, and as soon as the chiefs had shaken hands with Mr. Schlosser, they seized on him, gave a shriek and instantly killed ten men.

The 12th we were told that Lieut. Jenkins and all the garrison of Outattanon, consisting of a sergeant and eighteen men were taken prisoners and carried to the Ilonies.

The 18th a Jesuit arrived from Michilimackinac and brought a letter from Captain Etherington and Lieutenant Lessley, with an account of their being taken prisoners. That Lieutenant Jamet and twenty-one one soldiers. That on the 2nd the Indians were playing ball as usual nigh the fort, where Captain Etherington and Lieut. Lessley happened to be looking at them, but were suddenly seized on and carried into the woods. At the same time the savages had purposely thrown their ball into the fort, as if that had happened by accident, and followed it directly into the fort, where a number of their women had tomahawks and spears concealed under their blankets, which they delivered them and put the whole garrison to death, except thirteen men.

The 30th we were informed that the blockhouse at Presque Isle was burned, that Ensign Christie and all his garrison, which confided of twenty-nine men were taken prisoners except six men, who it was believed made their escape to La Beuf.

On the night of the 2nd instant and Lieut. McDougall were lodged at the house I have already mentioned, about two miles from the fort, and made a resolution to escape, when it was agreed on between them that McDougall should set off first, which he did and get safe into the fort, but you know it was much more dangerous for Captain Campbell than for any other person by reason that he could neither run nor fee, and being sensible of that failing I am sure prevented him from attempting to escape.

The 4th a detachment was ordered to destroy some breastworks and entrenchments the Indians had made a quarter of a mile from the fort, and about twenty Indians came to attack that party, which they engaged but were drove off in an instant with the loss of one man killed (and two wounded) which our people scalped and cut to pieces. Half an hour after the savages carried the man they had lost before Captain Campbell, stripped him naked, and directly murthered him in a cruel manner, which indeed gives one pain beyond expression, and I am sure cannot miss but to affect sensibly all his acquaintances, although he is now out of the question.

The Indians likewise reported that Venango and Le Beuf is taken by the savages.

Dated at Detroit 8th August 1763.

To Sir William Johnson.

# Gen. Bradstreet's Statement Upon Indian Affairs

### INTRODUCTION

The following statement upon Indian Affairs is preserved in the Hand-writing of General John Bradstreet, in a volume belonging to the New York State Library, entitled *Bradstreet and Amherst* MSS., beginning at Page 190. These papers were found many years since in the garret of a house in Albany which Gen. Bradstreet once inhabited, and are of unquestionable authenticity.

During the Indian Wars which followed the conquest of Canada in 1760, General B. held the rank of quarter-master general, and his opportunities for judging of the merits or defects of the system under which Indian affairs were managed entitle his opinions to respect. The difficulties attending this service are clearly and forcibly stated, and the remedies which he suggests were dictated by sound judgement and enforced by strong argument.                                           F. B. H.

### GENERAL BRADSTREET'S STATEMENT

December 17, 1764.

Brief State of our *interiour* situation with the savages, the disadvantages occasioned by the Indian traders following them to their hunting country, castles and villages; the benefit to all His Majesty's subjects by confining the trade to particular posts and the danger of fixing those posts nearer the Colonies of New York and Quebec then St. Marys, Michilimackinac, La Bay, and the Detroit, &c., &c.

The savages retain their affection for the French Nation as much as ever, and have nothing more at heart than their return and power in this country, and are ready to execute anything in their power to answer that purpose, and detest the English so much, that the traders cannot quit the established posts to go and trade with them (as Canadians do, who run no risk, but on the contrary are well received) without being murdered and plundered; and experience also shews when they employ Canadians to carry on the trade for them they are cheated and ruined; which must in a short time put all the Indian trade in the hands of the Canadians in conjunction with the French and Spaniards from the Mississippi and the settlements of the Illinois, who at this time carry of great part of the trade between the Mississippi and the Great Lakes and the Ohio.

To remedy these evils and recover the trade which is much impaired, the savages debauched, become idle and neglect their hunting by spirituous liquors being constantly carried to their hunting countries and to fix the trade with equal advantage to all His Majesty's subjects, it is imagined it should be limited to particular posts and upon no account allow any traders to follow the savages to their hunting country, castles or villages, as it moreover gives their boat men and some of themselves a taste for a wandering and independent life, infects them with a habit of libertinism and many of these sort of Canadians remain amongst the savages now; from whom they are not distinguishable but by their vices and inciting them on to acts of cruelty against the English; and was their nothing to fear from the intrigues of foreign enemies the nearer the posts were fixed to the Colonies of New York and Quebec to more advantage would the trade be carried on, as the savages would then become the principal carriers themselves, which is a very expensive article.

But the disadvantage of confining the trade to posts nearer the Colonies then St. Marys, Michilimackinac, La Bay and Detroit would be, the savages of the northwest side Lake Superior would find it less troublesome to trade with the Hudson's Bay Company then to go to those posts, and those of La Bay, the west side Lake Superior and Lake Michigan would find it also less difficult to go to the Mississippi should the French and Spanish traders not go to them as they actually do now and they would also soon find the way into Lake Superior with their merchandise and so long as those traders come to the savages on the banks of the Wabash and Scioto Rivers, by the Mississippi and Ohio, our traders at the Detroit and Fort Pitt will benefit but little from them, those of St. Josephs and Miamis, which makes a considerable number of hunters and to these evils we may add a greater, namely, was the trade confined to posts as low as Niagara, the certain consequence would be, that all the fur trade and savages would fall into the hands of the French and Spaniards and it effected soon by means of the French inhabitants of Detroit, Wabach, St. Joseph and Michilimackinac and those vagabonds or Coureurs de Bois of Canada dispersed amongst them, who when left to themselves and able to act openly and without fear will not fail their old masters; the dreadful consequence of which would soon be severely felt by the inhabitants of the frontiers of several colonies.

From repeated information it can admit of no doubt but that the French by the Mississippi are using their best endeavours to bring all the savages to consider the Spaniards in the same favourable light to them as the French themselves; we must therefore lose ground every day with the Indians if we remain idle spectators of it; it would be of great use in helping to prevent it as well as that of a general confederacy of them against us when attempted were we to divide them by fomenting the quarrels generally subsisting amongst them instead of making them up and turn them to our own use and advantage and prevent as much as possible the intercourse of the savages of different districts, that is, those of the north west side Lake Superior to come down no farther than St. Mary's and Michilimackinac; those of La Bay, west Side Lake Superior and Lake Michigan to the posts of La Bay; those of St. Josephs, Miamis, Wabach and Scioto Rivers to the Detroit and Fort Pitt, and the Six Nations (if possible) to be kept from them all at the posts of Niagara and Oswego, as the meetings of different nations of Indians have too often ended in making up their old quarrels and plotting against us and to succeed in this important business, men of address with a perfect knowledge of the policy and craft of the savages should be employed.

The number of boats employed in the Indian trade annually from this province amounts to about 180 whose cargoes one with the other is in value £300 , at the New York prices; which makes for the whole about £100,000; out of which a large deduction is to be made from the profits of the trader for transportation and other expenses as may be conceived by the expense of one boat to Detroit:

| | |
|---|---|
| 3 Boatmen to Detroit, | £60 |
| *bateau*, Oars, &c., | 9 |
| Carriage over the little Falls and | |
| Fort Stanwix, | 1.12 |
| Do. Niagara, | 11. 8 |
| | ———— |
| | £82 |

And to Michilimackinac it amounts to £112, about; and enormous as this expense is it bears no proportion to that of following the savages to their hunting country during the Winter; which the English merchants of Canada are no strangers to—and to this follows the expense of provisions, which is always very scarce and dear at the posts.

At Michilimackinac pork sold this summer for two shillings and sixpence, bread four shillings and butter six shillings the pound, and at Detroit £5 a hundred weight, and this scarcity of provisions and expensive transportation will continue so long as the Detroit remains not properly settled; the encroachments of the French and Spaniards not prevented; the frontiers of several colonies not secure from the attacks of the savages, nor we have the full advantage of the fur trade but by Detroit being made a strong barrier to the colonies and that settlement encouraged or the whole of the Mississippi in our hands; which last will bring all the savages dependent on us for what they want; for whoever imagines the savages of the interior country will remain in peace and friendship with us whilst the French and Spaniards possess the Mississippi will find himself mistaken—indeed the former has not been found permanent though very expensive—and the large sum lately given at the Congress at Fort Stanwix will operate on the Six Nations and their friends only. From what has been said of the expense in carrying on this trade, it appears the method now practised is better calculated to enrich the *bateau* and canoe men than the merchants and is one of the causes so many fail; the regulating this, with justice to both, seems to be absolutely necessary; but the more vessels are employed in this trade to more advantage will it be carried on as it may be done for half the now expense and always with safety against the evil designs of any savages.

Detroit is here mentioned as being the most proper place for an establishment and barrier for the reason that its situation being most proper and convenient to raise provisions, awe and attack such savages as are most likely to be troublesome first, to them divide and keep them so, to take up the French and Spanish traders that may come on our side the Mississippi, for it is to little purpose to send troops to attack savages and take up people protected by them from so great distance as the colonies are, to return in a few months or to depend on small garrisons, be they ever so well ported, it being out of their power to do more than give protection to such as are within their works; and it is as bad policy to suffer the encroachments above mentioned and the savages to insult and murder without further notice than giving them large sums of money in presents to make peace for a few years, for which they have always held us in contempt and thereby encouraged to commit frequent depredations upon us to exact presents from time to time to make it up.

As the soil of the Detroit is as good as can be and plenty of it ready for the plough, provisions would soon be plenty and cheap there and the navigation of the lakes carried on by the inhabitants of that place in vessels at as little expense as in this province, which would be of great advantage to the trade, security to the posts as well as lessening their expense and without vessels neither one nor the other can be said to be safe and secure from falling into the hands of the savages.

Should the trade be limited to particular posts it would be of advantage to establish the prices of the merchandise and furs with equal advantage to both sides and to prevent impositions too frequently practiced by the traders; and perhaps the way of doing it less exceptionable to the traders and savages would be by two provincial commissaries of abilities and experience from the Colony of New York and Quebec with the Indian chiefs in presence of the officer commanding posts and those commissaries to reside at the posts, inspect the trade and report from time [to time] everything necessary and should it appear reasonable the traders and savages pay a proportion towards the general security of the interior country, the following duties may be laid by every province connected in the trade, *viz.*:

| On spirituous liquors | | 2s 6d sterling a gallon. |
| powder, | 6d do | a pound. |
| strouds, | 8s do | a piece. |
| blankets, | 1s do | each. |
| shirts, | 1s do | each. |
| silver trinkets 5p C$^t$ on first cost, | | |

which may amount to six or seven thousand pounds sterling *per annum* on this province only.

Some Court of justice is absolutely necessary to bring offenders to justice, oblige people to pay their debts and keep good order, it being impossible those ends can be answered by Provincial laws so distant as the colonies are, did their power extend so far.

It is submitted, if the designs of our enemies to draw the savages in general on us would not be more easily prevented and with far less expense if undertaken before any of them commence hostilities against us, than it can be afterwards, and if anything can be more effectual to answer this purpose than the savages seeing soon at the Detroit a respectable force fixed, the posts above mentioned properly established, themselves disunited and proper measures taking there to raise sufficient provisions for the full supply of the interior country. They know if the posts are supplied with provisions from the colonies below in boats only they have it always in their power to cut off the supply and even the retreat of those garrisons, and on it they chiefly depend for success in taking them and driving the English out of the interior country.

How fatal a sudden and well timed savage eruption would prove to the English Indian traders and frontier inhabitants of several colonies melancholy experience has made it too well known to need being mentioned here, and if the interior country is to remain in its present defenceless state all laws and regulations for the benefit of the trade will be of no avail.

It would be prudent to oblige all the French and Canadian people to remove from the Wabach, St. Josephs, Michilimackinac and otherwise dispersed amongst the savages to the settlement of Detroit to put an end to the tricks they play to our disadvantage.

The nations or tribes of savages surrounding the Great Lakes that have any knowledge of the English are at this time in a disposition to live well with them, respect them and beg for trade and vessels in every lake, hoping thereby that goods will be cheaper than it can be without them. They still love the French to a great degree and the French by the Mississippi and from the Illinois keep it up by extending trade to all nations they can and sending emissaries to propagate such tales as turn most to their advantage and prejudice to the English. These savages are numerous, proud, delight in and practice war from a political view, knowing that such as neglect keeping up that spirit must degenerate into effeminacy and become the prey of such as do not.

To insure a lasting peace, gain their affections and wean them from the French, strict justice, moderation, fair trade, with keeping them from frequent intercourse with each other, and a respectable force at Detroit is the way to obtain it, unless their whole dependence for the necessaries of life depended upon the English, which will never be the case as long as the French can come up the Mississippi in safety, land and extend their trade on our side with impunity, the preventing of which will in the execution be found difficult as the interest of the savages is to screen and protect them, and it is said to be carried on by the French East India Company.

It is absolutely necessary to make choice for the establishing posts for the security of trade, of such places as may be most convenient for the inhabitants of each lake to carry on their trade with ease to themselves, by which and their natural laziness will seldom go to their neighbours and without it they will be discontented.

At these posts men of sense, moderation and spirit should command, and each detachment for the small ones should not be less than one hundred good men. Niagara and Detroit should be more respectable, the former cannot do with less than three posts upon the Communication of fifty men each and the latter must have as many to make good the navigation to Lake Huron, the straits being too difficult for vessels, so that boats must be employed for that service and the officer commanding at Detroit should always have it in his power to detach from his garrison three hundred good men besides Militia to chastise any nation or band of savages the instant they deserve it, as the taking immediate satisfaction will make them respect and fear us and prevent a general war, so that Niagara cannot dispense with less than one battalion on the present establishment and Detroit near two battalions.

The posts necessary for Lake Ontario are already fixed except Frontinac instead of Fort Wm. Augustus,[1] the latter being useless, the Navigation to it dangerous and attended with great delays, and the former an excellent harbour and from it soon into the lake.

For Lake Erie Detroit is sufficient.

For Lake Huron Detroit and Michilimackinac.

For Lake Michigan Michilimackinac, the Bay and St. Josephs.

For Lake Superior, Falls of St. Marys with two other posts at the most convenient places, the Inhabitants being in that quarter numerous, particularly in the westward of it.

These posts of Michilimackinac, the Bay, St. Josephs, the Falls of St. Marys with the two other posts upon the Banks of Lake Superior will take one battalion, which makes four from Niagara westward.

All posts upon the banks of the lakes from Niagara upwards to be under the control of the officer commanding at Detroit and should government judge it improper to establish a Civil Government there and not encourage the colony, still some court of justice is necessary to the end offenders, inhabitants, Indians, Indian traders and others

1 About three miles below the mouth of the Oswegatchie. (See footnote 57, *Diary of the Siege.*)

might be brought to justice and punished by a law that might prevent litigious suits and satisfy the savages the strictest justice is done them at all times.

The savages have a contemptible opinion of all Indian traders, it is therefore necessary the officer commanding at the posts should not trade but inspect into the trade, prevent abuse and bring offenders to that justice the law may require; by this they will be respected and beloved by the savages and have it in their power to be of great use when the assistance of the latter may be wanted against His Majesty's enemies.

The officers at all posts which the savages frequent should be enabled to treat particulars, such as chiefs and well affected with a little rum, some pipes and tobacco, with provisions in cases of necessity; they have been accustomed to much more by the French and expect it from us, the expense is a trifle but the want of that may be attended with bad consequences; for Niagara and all trading posts above it twenty pounds sterling except Detroit, which should be thirty pounds annually.

The goods to be furnished the savages should be, if possible, as good as those they had from the French before the reduction of Canada, sold to them at the same prices or in that proportion if not so good, and the same prices given for their skins and peltry—and to enable us to carry on this trade to more advantage and greater safety than the French did, no transportation to be suffered upon the lakes but in vessels and government to furnish and keep up their vessels, the trader paying freight for his goods at the rate of one half what it would cost him if transported in boats. This would overpay the expense of the vessels for trade and those necessary for the public service and prevent drunken or evil minded Indians killing and plundering the traders, which cannot be avoided at times, if the transportation was carried on in boats.

The number of vessels necessary for the trade cannot be fixed, but by time, but the sooner there are two or three in the Lakes Huron and Michigan with two in Lake Superior the more pleasing it will be to the savages, as they will see no time is lost to put the trade on an advantageous footing for them. The execution of this I take to be of great importance towards sixing the inclinations of the savages in our favour. the savages should not be debarred spirituous liquors; it is their darling passion, nay they love it so much they will sacrificed their all to obtain it and will never live in peace with us without it, but still the quantity each trader should be permitted to take with him should be limited in the proportion of the goods he takes and might extend to fifteen pounds in spirituous liquors to every hundred pounds of other goods, paying a duty of two shillings sterling, per gallon, which they can very well bear from the enormous prices they fell it at.

The savages are subtle and the French intriguing, it therefore becomes dangerous to suffer the former to hoard up a large stock of arms and ammunition; but this cannot be prevented should every trader have it in his power to carry with him what quantity he may judge proper; upon these considerations and that the profits arising from the sail and returns would go a great way towards defraying the public expense for the protection of trade, would it not be best in the hands of government under the care of a commissary subject to the control of the commanding officer of each post with instructions as to the quantity to be disposed of annually. The honour of government will require these articles to be good and the prices should be established.

Here I must notice that from the Government of Pennsylvania all the Shawanese and Delaware Indians are furnished with rifle barrel guns of an excellent kind and that the upper nations are getting into them fast by which they will be much less dependent upon us on account of the great saving of powder by those guns, as it certainly diminishes the demand of such as have them more than half, and in their way of carrying on war by far more prejudicial to us than any other sort of gun; would it not be a public benefit to stop the making and vending any more of them throughout the colonies and prevent the importation of any into the colonies.

Should government judge it necessary to take the supplying the savages with arms and ammunition into their own hands; for the upper lakes a public magazine will be necessary at Detroit under proper officers to receive and send forward to the other posts, as likewise to receive the remittances back; and the commissary of the outposts should account annually with those of Detroit, subject to the inspection of the governor or officer commanding there.

Should New York be thought a proper channel for the conveyance up the country, a commissary should be there and one at Albany; but if on the contrary Canada should be thought best, Quebec and Montreal are proper places for offices for this service.

Of all the savages upon the continent, the most knowing, the most intriguing, the less useful and the greatest villains are those most conversant with the Europeans and deserve the attention of government most by way of correction, and these are the Six Nations, Shawanese and Delawares; they are well acquainted with the defenceless state of the inhabitants who live on the frontiers and think they will ever have it in their power to distress and plunder them; and never cease raising the jealousy of the Upper Nations against us by propagating amongst them such stories as make them believe the English have nothing so much at heart as the extirpation of all savages. the apparent design of the six nations is to keep us at war with all savages but themselves that they may be employed as mediators between us and them at a continuation of an expense to the public too often and too heavily felt, the sweets of which they will never forget nor lose sight of if they can possibly avoid it. That of the Shawanese and Delawares is to live on killing, captivating and plundering the people inhabiting the Frontiers, long experience having shown them they grow richer and live better thereby than by hunting wild beasts.

This campaign has fully opened the eyes of the Upper Nations of Indians; they are now sensible they are made use of as the dupes and tools of these detestable and diabolical set, the Six Nations, Shawanese and Delawares, and it would require but little address and expense (the foils and trade properly fixed) to engage them to cut them from the face of the earth (and they deserve it) or to keep the Six Nations in such subjection as would put an end to our being any longer a kind of tributary to them; and their real interest call upon them to destroy or drive the Shawanese and Delawares out of the country they now possess on account of hunting; this they know and would soon put either in execution if assured His Majesty would not suffer any other savages to live there. Happy will it be when savages can be punished by savages, the good effects of which the French can tell. That we can punish them is beyond doubt whenever wisdom, secrecy, dispatch and good troops in numbers proportionate to the service are employed.

The Pass of Niagara is of great importance and will always be an expense to government. The principal part of the trade, if the transportation is carried on in vessels will pass that way and from its proximity to the Chenusseo Indians, a part of the Six Nations and the greatest savage enemies we have, it will be difficult if not impracticable for some time to come, for private persons to keep up boats and carriage so well but that the trade will meet with delays; it would therefore be more safe and permanent in the hands of government who only can make transportation certain and by the traders paying a reasonable price for the carriage for their goods, &c., there will be no stop and the public service carried on there without expense.

This campaign upon the lakes has also laid open the hearts of the Six Nations and a black one it will appear for us if General Gage has sent the papers respecting them to His Majesty's Ministers, to which I hope he has tacked the immense expense they have been at to government this year exclusive of provisions, which is immense also. It will also been seen by them papers that the Upper Nations of Indians know that we are fully acquainted with the tricks the Six Nations play us and I believe they do expect to hear that that part of them called Chenusseo Indians get their deserts soon.

The French accustomed the savages of the Upper Lakes and rivers to send traders with goods to winter amongst them for which permit the trader paid a certain price each time; I believe the Indians will expect it will be so again; should government think proper to grant it then the trader can very well pay thirty pounds sterling for each large canoe so permitted, which will make a considerable sum annually; the pass to be given at Detroit only to prevent fraud.

I am assured by persons lately from the Illinois that exclusive of the French garrisons there, the inhabitants are 600 fighting men, have 1000 Negroes well accustomed to the use of small arms, averse to our taking possession of the country and have painted us out in such colours to the numerous savages near them that they, the latter, will certainly endeavour to prevent the troops getting there by the Mississippi even should the Indians nearer the sea allow them to pass, which they think they will not, unless well paid for it, which will not answer what may perhaps be expected. They add, that it is their opinion also, that all attempts to get possession of the Illinoes with less than 3000 good men will fail, and that those Troops should go down the Ohio River and the expedition carried on with such secrecy that they may enter the Mississippi 90 miles below Fort Charters before the inhabitants can have intelligence of it and time to apprise all the savages.

I am convinced the only way to establish ourselves amongst the savages with respect and safety is to begin by coming upon them by ways unfrequented, undiscovered and with such force as shall make such an impression as shall be lasting, and if a body of troops should be sent to take possession of the Illinoes those troops should visit all the principal nations of Indians upon the banks of ye Mississippi as near the sea as they live and endeavour to enter into an alliance with all they can and purchase their aid to make war upon those that remain stubborn to bring them to reason and open a free passage up the river. The shortest way to carry this into execution is by Fort Pitt, provided the troops are not to come from Canada, but if any comes from thence the best way is by Niagara to Presque Isle upon Lake Erie.

The colony of Detroit grows fast and the inhabitants have great influence over the savages; the removing them would occasion a general war with the Indians, and to leave them as they now are will take a great length of time before they become proper British subjects; it is therefore humbly submitted if it would not be best to permit and encourage British subjects to settle there as the increase of the latter would be so great in a few years that they must soon become one people by marriages, &c.

The spirit for settling the King's subjects there shew itself fully by a memorial of sixty officers serving in Upper Lakes in this campaign, praying His Majesty would be graciously pleased to permit them to settle 639 farms at their own expense, with such marks of the King's Royal Favour as His Majesty may think proper.

On receiving General Gage's orders to continue the war against the Shawanese and Delawares I demanded the assistance of His Majesty's new subjects, the Ottawas, Chepewas, Hurons, Sakes and Pottawatamies; four parties immediately went against them. One returned with one scalp which is sufficient for the whole to carry on and continue the war unless prevented by bad management by us.

Albany, 7th December 1764.

*Jn Bradshat*

# Papers Relating to the Indian Wars of 1763 and 1764, and the Conspiracy of Pontiac

### INTRODUCTION

Correspondence of military officers and others charged with duties relating to Indian affairs, during the Wars of Pontiac, necessarily embodies a large amount of information concerning the causes which led to hostilities, the alarms which those occasioned, the measures that were taken to suppress them, and the opinions that were entertained as to the changes necessary to prevent their continuance or recurrence. These letters place before us in vivid colours, the condition of the country, its resources and its wants, and narrate, without ornament, the simple facts which their writers wished to communicate. A portion of these papers are copied from the Bradstreet and Amherst Manuscripts, and most of the remainder from the manuscripts of Sir William Johnson, in the State Library. In making the selection we have avoided as much as possible including those ever before printed.

F. B. H.

### LETTER FROM GEN. AMHERST TO COL. BRADSTREET.
*[Bradstreet and Amherst MSS, p. 132.]*

New York, 22nd June, 1763.

Sir: Your express arrived here last night and delivered me your letter of the 19th with those enclosed; the answers to which I now transmit you, that you may forward them by the first safe opportunity that offers.

You do very right to be prepared for pushing up provisions to Fort Stanwix, which I would have you do though I am in hope we shall have ample supplies for the upper posts from Fort Wm.

Augustus.

I send orders to Captain Winepress to march with his company to Fort Ontario, as I now order about forty men of the 42nd and 77th Regiments, who are fit for garrison duty to Albany, where they will remain under the command of a captain of the 77th Regiment who will succeed Captain Winepress in the command of the garrison. There is likewise a subaltern of the 77th, with a lieut. and three serjeants of the Independents.

Major Gladwyn writes me of the 14th May, that the Detroit was inverted by a large body of Indians; but that the garrison were in high spirits and he was in hopes of being able to defend the place until he received some succour from Niagara, and Major Wilkins acquaints me he had immediately on the arrival of the schooner from the Detroit, sent off a reinforcement of fifty men with a lieutenant and non-commissioned officers, which I trust will have arrived in time to save the place.

I well know that you are always ready, however I think it necessary to acquaint you to be ready for moving at a moment's warning, as if the savages are not quickly reduced I believe I shall employ you on a command, which, I am certain will be agreeable to you.

> I am, Sir,
>
> Your most obedient Servant,

Col. Bradstreet,  *Jeff. Amherst*
D. Q. M. G.

P. S. Since I wrote the foregoing Mr. Leake has delivered me a return of the provisions, which, by the last returns, were at Fort Wm. Augustus, Oswego and Niagara, &c., of which I enclose you a copy, whereby you will see, that the quantities at these posts are very considerable.                                    J. A.

With Major Duncan's letter I received one from Major Wilkins to Captain Dalyell, which missed him by the way, of the 3rd instant: Nothing new then at Niagara; but one of the men that were missing, found, as I feared, dead and *scalped*, near the fort above the falls.

Although none of the letters require answers at present, I think it best to order the post to return; and I have directed Mr. Colden to order the rider, to make more haste than they have lately done and to be more ready to set out from Albany, as the service may require them, without waiting for any fixed time. Before I received your letter I had applied to the Lt. Governor (finding that my endeavours to accommodate matters with the persons employed by the elders and deacons had no effect, although I had spoke particularly to the chief justice for that purpose) to give the necessary directions to the attorney-general, not only to defend your suit, but to profecute the corporation of Albany, for pulling down His Majesty's fence, &c.

I am, Sir,<br>Your most obedient Servant,<br>Jeff. Amherst.

Col, Bradstreet,

D. Q. M. G. Albany.

P. S. I this moment receive a petition from one Crisp, which I enclose that you may be so good to give an answer. I imagine that his claim is not just or it would have been paid.

J. A.

New York, 20th July, 1763.

Sir:

The post came in last night with your letter of the 15th instant, and brought me likewise letters from Major Duncan and Captain Loring, advising me of the latter's arrival at Fort Ontario, on the 5th, with the sailors, and that he had fitted out the Johnson Snow, ready to proceed to Fort Wm. Augustus for provisions. Himself and the rest of the seamen were to sail in the schooner to Niagara.

THE SAME TO THE SAME.

*[Bradstreet and Amherst MSS., p. 134.]*

New York, 7th August, 1763.

Sir:

Last night I received your letter of the 1st instant.

You did very right to furnish Sir William Johnson with what provisions he required, for the use of the Indians.

I have no objection to your sending two or three oxen, at a time, to Fort Stanwix, for the use of that garrison, as you say you can supply them cheaper than they can be got from New England. Lt. Colonel Campbell must take care that there is a particular account kept of what is issued, according to orders, as there is no commissary from the crown at that post, the contractors commissary will be only to be paid for the flour; unless you fell the cattle to the contractors.

The dastardly behaviour of the *bateau* men is particularly unlucky at this time; for I have been impatiently waiting to hear of the arrival of the engineers' stores at Oswego: I hope when you sent them back, they have proceeded with all imaginable expedition.

I am, Sir,

Your most obedient Servant,

Jeff. Amherst.

Col. Bradstreet,

### THE SAME TO THE SAME.
*[Bradstreet and Amherst MSS., p. 135.]*

New York, 18th September, 1763.

Sir:

I am to own your letter of the 12th instant and I approve of your having supplied Sir William Johnson the provisions you mention as he expected to have a conference at his house with the Six Nation Indians.

Any bedding that may be wanted hereafter for the garrisons I can supply from hence, as there is a great quantity now in store, which came from *Martinique* and the *Havana*, but what you have forwarded to Oswego, will be so much the nearer for being sent to the Detroit, &c.

I am, Sir,

Your most obedient Servant,

Jeff. Amherst.

Col. Bradstreet,

D. Q. M. G.

### THE SAME TO THE SAME.
*[Bradstreet and Amherst MSS., p. 136.]*

New York, 24th September, 1763.

Sir:

I am to own your letter of the 10th instant; I have not yet come to the determination with regard to the small posts on the communication to Fort George: I can keep one man only in each of them, which I will contrive to do, to continue the possession; but you may send a proportion of candles for the garrisons of Crown Point, Ticonderoga, Fort George and Fort

Edward; the three last will have one company in each; and there will be four companies at Crown Point.

I enclose you a copy of public orders, which have been given here, and which I send now to all the posts, for making stoppages to all the provisions that may be issued to the troops, in pursuance of directions I have received from the Lords of the Treasury: It has already taken place in Canada, and I have ordered the stoppages to commence at Albany, the dependent posts and the communication to Fort George inclusively on the 1st October, for Crown Point and Ticonderoga are to be garrisoned by troops from Canada. The orders are to be made public at all the other posts; but I have thought proper to continue an allowance to the troops at Fort Stanwix and the dependent posts and to the several garrisons above, as I think it would be hard to put them to stoppages until the *Indian War* is entirely quelled and that they are on the same footing with the other troops: This regulation does not affect the provincials who must be subsisted, as usual, until the service will permit them to be sent to their respective homes.

I enclose you a packet addressed to Lt. Colonel Elliott, containing dispatches for Canada, which you will forward by one of your people, on purpose, to Crown Point; sending at the same time the letters to the commanding officers at Fort Edward and Fort George, When the companies from Canada arrive at Crown Point and Ticonderoga, Lt. Colonel Elliott, with the men of the 55th (Leaving compleat companies at Fort George and Fort Edward), will move down to Albany, where he will remain till further orders.

                    I am, Sir,
              Your most obedient Servant,
                          Jeff. Amherst.

Colonel Bradstreet,
D. Q. M. G., Albany.

THE SAME TO THE SAME.

                    New York, 28 September, 1763.
Sir:
A vessel having arrived here with the clothing for the several regiments in this country, I am sending that for the corps above as fast as possible to Albany, that no time may be lost in forward-

ing it before the winter sets in. One sloop is already loaded and will sail tomorrow morning: Ensign Crosthwaite, who is going to Albany, has the care of the clothing in her and will deliver you the bill of lading; so that you will order the clothing to be landed and put into the store at Albany, lending the enclosed letter to Fort Stanwix and Crown Point, as I have directed the commanding officers at those posts to send quarter masters and proper parties to conduct the clothing to their respective posts; the 17th, 46th and 80th to Fort Stanwix; from whence the two former will be forwarded to Oswego, for which I write to Major Duncan; and from thence to Niagara, &c., and the clothing for the other corps must be sent with the party that comes from Crown Point. Two other sloops will take the whole from hence; and you will pay the hire at the usual rate and according to what you may think just and reasonable. Swits's sloop, which fails tomorrow, has got many other things, I am told, on board; so that he ought to be paid accordingly; and I shall transmit you bills of lading of the others when they are loaded.

I am, Sir,

Your most obedient Servant,

Jeff. Amherst.

Colonel Bradstreet,
D. Q. M. G. Albany.

LETTER FROM ALEXANDER DUNCAN TO SIR WM. JOHNSON.
[*MSS. of Sir William Johnson, 7.*]

Fort Ontario, 1st October, 1763.

Sir:

A few days ago I was favoured with your letter of the 17th *ultimo* and yesterday that of the 26th reached my hands.

I have forwarded your letter to Major Moncries, from whom I have received a letter dated 26th *ultimo* at Niagara in which he informs, that they were then preparing to set out for Detroit, but that they were obliged to carry the provisions over the portage on men's shoulders and that it would be the 5th or 6th October before they would be able to set out. I have sent sixteen oxen which are with them before now, there is likewise a reinforcement of 260 men that I reckon have got to Niagara this day, these I hope will enable Major Wilkins to set out sooner and stronger than he expected; the whole are under his command I imagine will exceed 600 men, they go in *bateaux* and carry so much provisions as they can.

You will no doubt have heard that the savages attacked the schooner going up the river to Detroit on the 3rd *ultimo*, the master of the vessel and one seaman were killed and three others wounded, but the savages were beat off; they had once got upon the bowsprit and have hacked and cut the vessel a great deal on the bows and under the stern; there was only twelve men on board the schooner at the beginning of the affair, three of whom were sick. The Indians acknowledge to have left eight men and many wounded and by some of their canoes oversetting have lost sixty stand of arms.

Several canoes have lately arrived here from Canada with passports (to go to Detroit with ammunition and Indian goods) from General Gage; I have taken the passes from the traders and secured the ammunition and goods in the fort. The people in these canoes inform me that several traders have got passports to go up Grand River and that one canoe is gone to Toronto. I have informed Lt. Col. Browning of the latter, that he may send a party and bring away the traders from Toronto. Here follows a copy of the preamble to one of these passports.

> By the Honourable General Gage, &c., &c. Whereas Messrs. Wells and Wade have represented to me, that it is probable that the savages are dispersed from about Detroit, and therefore demand permission to send a canoe there under such regulations as I shall think necessary to be given.

It is not easy to account for Mr. Gage's conduct on this occasion, but I have send copies of all the passports that have fallen into my hands to Sir Jeffrey Amherst, let those two gentlemen settle that affair. Six canoes came here five of which were loaded, the other had put their loading on board the sloop at Fort William Augustus and they have no less than 75 barrels of gunpowder besides, &c.

Everything continues quiet here.

        I am, Sir,

                Your most obedient humble Servant,

                        *Alex Duncan*

To Sir William Johnson.

LETTER FROM GENERAL AMHERST TO COLONEL BRADSTREET.

New York, 1st October, 1763.

Sir:

As the last sloop with the clothing is not yet failed I take the opportunity of sending this by her (as she may reach Albany before the post) to acknowledge your letters of the 25th and 26th September by Captain Sowers; and to approve entirely of your readiness in forwarding the oxen, carts, &c. for Niagara: Your getting the *Tyers*, &c. made at Albany has likewise my approbation; and as they must be in want of provender for the cattle during the winter, they not having had an opportunity to make any hay, I should be glad you could forward to Niagara a sufficiency of corn, which you tell me you can do.

In a late letter to Lt. Colonel Elliot I directed him to send down the remainder of the detachment of the 17th Regiment, immediately on the arrival of the companies from Montreal, which I conclude he will have done; and that Captain Morris will have proceeded to Fort Stanwix; but should Captain Morris with that detachment be at Albany on receipt hereof or arrive afterwards you will acquaint him that it is my orders he proceeds, without delay, to Fort Stanwix; as Lt. Colonel Campbell has at present rather too thin a garrison; especially as, from the accounts I have received of the late affair on the carrying place at Niagara, there is reason to suspect that the body of savages who cut off our convoy were mostly Senecas. I hope the other five nations are not privy to this affair; although it is hard to say who are our friends or foes. The whole race of savages seem to be, more or less, concerned in this treacherous insurrection.

I am, Sir,

Your most obedient Servant,

Jeff. Amherst.

Colonel Bradstreet,
D. Q. M. G.

LETTER FROM CAPT. DANIEL CLAUS TO SIR WM. JOHNSON.

Montreal, 1st October, 1763.

Hon. Sir:

I hope mine of the 23rd *ultimo*, by Capt. Brown, came safe to hand, since which I had a deputation from the Missisagues living about Toronto; their message consisted of a large string and a belt of about 2000 *wampum*, by the former they expressed their great concern on account of the present unhappy disturbances about Detroit, &c., and that they abhorred and detested it and therefore had since the beginning kept out of the way in the environs of Cataracqui, that at the same time they were thereby reduced to the greatest distress for want of their necessaries being brought among them, and therefore requested and implored the general to let ye trader La Farge *alias* Tawaniawe the Swegachie interpreter, who used to supply them heretofore with necessaries come to their village this season that they might not be prevented from this winter's hunt for want of ammunition, &c.—— the belt.

General Gage without hesitation replied them that as to their possessions he could or would not so far doubt them, though he was sure of some canoes having been pursued by Missisague Indians and when overtaken and found they were French were told that they took to be English whom they lay in wait for. However be that as it would he should not give them an answer upon their message, that if they wanted to exculpate themselves they must address themselves to you as the principal person of their affairs who only had the power from the King to hear and settle such matters and as to sending a person to trade among them he would never agree to it, neither was it in his power, and so sent them away. They were three in number and had with them a Pany who deserted from hence when this place was taken and being found out by his master was taken from them by him upon the general's order and put into the provosts. A Frenchman that came from Niagara this summer informed the general that he was pursued by said Pany and coming up to him with his knife in his hand told him that if he was an Englishman would lose his life.

I afterward examined the Frenchman, whether any of these Indians were in company with the Pany but he was sure they were not.

I then spoke to them in my room, and made them as much sensible as I could of the heinous behaviour of those nations that occasioned the present disturbances, and that they must attribute every inconveniency they now laboured under to them only, and endure it till such a time as proper satisfaction was given for their vile and inconsiderate actions, etc.

I had their arms mended for them and gave them a little ammunition, tobacco and rum and dismissed them, though they expected some clothing, being in a manner naked; I also gave them a passport to go your way in case their nation would send them.

I impatiently wait for the return of the Caghnawageys as well on account of knowing the determination of the Six Nations who I hear had a numerous congress at your house, as my destination for the ensuing winter.

This goes by Major Abercrombie who I hear is to be one General Amherst's Family.

I am, with the greatest respect and compliments to the family,
Hon. Sir,
Your most dutiful
and obedient servant.

To the Honourable Sir William Johnson, Bart.
I beg leave to trouble you with the enclosure.

LETTER FROM MAJOR ROBERT ROGERS TO SIR WM. JOHNSON.

Detroit, October 7th, 1763.

Sir:

Major Gladwin has told me that he will enclose you all the proceedings at this place since the date of my last letter, as also every particular account concerning the Indian War, the first beginning, &c.

For these reasons and as I think it would come more correct from him than from me, I defer mentioning any other particulars relative to our condition at this place.

McCormick will deliver you this letter, he has a bill on Col. Croghan, I should be obliged to you if you would get him the money, for it would, serve me greatly to make my payments speedily.

Aaron the Mohawk Indian came into the fort this day, Daniel and Jacob is also in this garrison but I have not any intelligence from them but what Major Gladwin will communicate, though I soon shall and some that they tell me and no man shall at this place know but myself, but you shall have it in full from me, and one of the Indians you sent up will convey the said account, the other four is now in Sandusky where there is a grand council, but will return in a day or two; the schooner sails directly, therefore I cannot send to you their private information, but surely will do it by themselves the first opportunity.

There is about one thousand Indians in this settlement at present waiting for some troops that is coming up; I wish they may not get a flogging.

I beg you'll be so kind as to inform Mrs. Rogers if there is any likelihood of my coming down this fall, for my part I know nothing of the disposition for this place at present, neither does Major Gladwin.

> I am Sir, Your most obedient
> Humble servant.

To Sir William Johnson,

## THE SAME TO THE SAME.

> Detroit, October 7th, 1763.

Sir:

Since I wrote my letter, Aaron the Mohawk has come in and tells me that he was in the council yesterday and that all the nations here he says the Indian War begun through the Five Nations and that since the belt came here that Aaron says he told you was brought by one indian last fall, that a second belt came last March and told the indians to begin, and with that a tomahawk was delivered and the Indians that brought this belt from the Five Nations told and assured the Indians that they would begin at the time the corn was planted. The Five Nations was to strike from Niagara to Schenectady and the Toways and other nations to take the upper posts on the lakes, that the Senecas and Cahugees were the people that sent this message and further told them that they would meet them at the Windote's town early this spring.

Aaron tells me that the Hurons were obliged to strike the English as they were threatened by the Toways and other nations and that the Toways now tells the Hurons if they attempt to make peace without their consent or advice they will directly destroy them, and that if they attempt to come to the fort they will be considered by them as Englishmen.

Aaron says that they have seen our troops that are coming from

Niagara at the Long Point on the north shore, and that all the savages here are determined to attack them at Point a Plee.

Aaron says he will let you know further soon and what he has told you now you may depend upon is true, that the Hurons desire that you may know that the Toways and other Nations on the lake are now their masters, their numbers being so small they can't help themselves, they are going to the Huron River about thirty miles from this fort, where they intend to winter, and the Toways are resolved to winter at Miami River, the other four Indians that came up with Aaron are gone to Sandusky.

I am, Sir,

Your most humble Servant,

Robert Rogers.

*Endorsed.* Wrote to Jn Glen, Esqr. for 15 barrels pork and flour in proportion, 5 to be sent to Cherry Valley, 5 to Conradt Franks, 5 to Caghnawagey.

*Memorandum.* 10 pr strouds, 6 do. aurora, 6 do. blankets, 540 shirts; 12 ps stocking stuff, 108 lb. vermillion, 719 lb. verdi-grease, 100 pipe watches, 8 groce of knives, 20 yds ribbon, 6 ps silk handkerchiefs, 11 groce rings, 10 lbs beeds.

## LETTER FROM SIR WILLIAM JOHNSON TO COLONEL EYRE.

Johnson Hall, October 13th, 1763.

Dear Sir

I am to thank you for your favour of the 3rd inst., although the want of the *packet*, as you observed, must prevent your having any material news. I most heartily wish whenever it arrives it may bring the news of their being perfectly acquainted in England with the commencement of our Indian War, as without that they will be unable to take any proper measures and the first news which was sent home in June possibly did not appear very interesting.

About 2 days ago I had an account that a considerable body of Indians are assembling at the Susquehana with design to destroy this country from Schenetady upwards, or else to fall upon Esopus or Shamokin, &c. Both the former I look upon to be in their power and therefore believe it is probable they will put one of them in execution; for my part I cannot see what will prevent their success, as you know the nature of the country people sufficiently to suppose they cannot be kept in a body for any time, but must follow their several occupations, so that I have only to rely on the hopes of some previous intelligence and on the present favourable disposition of all the nations (except Senecas) many of whom are ready and desirous to join our troops, but how long they may continue in this disposition is uncertain, as the great success of our enemy's and the small opposition they have hitherto met with renders our friends very apprehensive of their resentment from their daily threats and may occasion their defection, especially as we are not able to give any necessary succour which might enable them to withstand our enemies.

I have from several hands the particulars of our unlucky affair at Niagara by which it appears that our troops were attacked in such a disadvantageous situation that they were hurried down the steep cliffs near La Platon unable to make any resistance and most of them perished, many of them were found sticking in the forks of trees; the Senecas of Cheneseo (who were the principals in this affair) have not brought in any scalps, with only one man wounded on their side. This is particularly unlucky at this time and I fear will be followed by more such blows if the greatest care be not taken.

I shall expect when anything occurs that you will let me have the pleasure of hearing from you,

as I am,

with sincerity, &c.

Col. Eyre.

LETTER FROM SIR WM. JOHNSON TO LIEUT. GOV. COLDEN.

Johnson Hall, October 13th, 1763.

Dear Sir:

I have just received an account, that a considerable body of Indians from towards the Ohio and the Seneca Country are assembling on the Susquehanna and that they are destined to fall either on Shamokin, Esopus, or to destroy the Mohawk River settlements from Schenectady upwards, the first of these places is capable of making a defence, but I can see little to prevent their success against the two latter, particularly in these parts from the sad state of the Militia and the great want of ammunition, &c.

I have acquainted Col. Hardenbergh of the danger of the settle-

137

ment of Esopus and as I have no doubt that one of these designs will be put in immediate execution, must beg the favour of hearing from you thereon as also of your answer to mine of the 10th of Aug. last concerning the vacancies and additions necessary for this regiment.

In the meantime I shall take every effectual measure for the obtaining the necessary intelligence on which the safety of this important frontier must chiefly depend, and on warning of the enemy's approach shall make the best disposition the nature of the country will admit of.

The many successes of our enemies, together with their large number, may prove of dangerous consequence by influencing our friends to join them through fear of their power, vicinity and resentment, especially as we are not able to afford them the assistance which allies should require, but I shall continue to use all my endeavours to prevent a defection, which as matters now stand must prove the destruction of this country as well as to cut off so essential a communication to the lakes.

I hope to have the pleasure of your answer and
> I am with great sincerity
> and esteem, &c.

Lt. Governor Colden.

## LETTER FROM GEN. AMHERST TO LIEUT. GOV. COLDEN.

New York, 15th October, 1763.

Sir:

In a letter I have this moment received from Sir William Johnson of the 6th instant, among other intelligence concerning the bad intentions of the Indians, he says he has learnt, "that the Senecas and Delawares were now daily marching to *Kaghraandote* on the Susquehana, a place appointed for their rendezvous; that when all were assembled their leader, *Quaghquoandax*, would then agree to fall on one of the following places, namely, Shamokin, Esopus or Cherry Valley; and the Mohawk River from Schenectady upwards."

I therefore think it highly necessary to give you this notice, that you may take proper steps for putting the Militia on their guard as it is absolutely impossible for me to spare one man from the posts above; for I have pushed on every man I could spare to Niagara and the Detroit; and you know I have none below. Sir

William Johnson, I doubt not, will take every precaution in his power for protecting the settlements on the Mohawk River. But the inhabitants everywhere on the frontiers cannot be too much on their guard and indeed the only thing they have to do is to be unanimous in repelling by force any attempts that may be made by the savages.

                  I am with great regard,

                        Sir, Your most obedient,

                            Humble Servant,

                                Jeff. Amherst.

Honourable Lt. Governor Colden.

LETTER FROM DAVID VANDERHEYDEN TO SIR WM. JOHNSON.

Sir:

I am this moment informed by Robert Lansingh, who came last night from the *Groote Imbogt* [1] that one *Dirk Ehl* at that place had received a letter from a kinsman, living somewhere on Delaware River, informing him that about 60 families were destroyed thereabout.

I fear that the Indians that have now been to N. York with Samuel Pruyn are spies, though they behaved very complaisant and civil to me and my house: my Negro wench tells me this morning, that the youngest of them, who talks the best English, had told her husband, Capt. Stephen Schuyler's Negro, that the Indians were all joined, and that they did not fear the great guns but enjoined him to keep it secret as the Negros would be in no danger. And by some traders I am informed that he is the same that caused a disturbance at Oswego and Niagara last spring a year.

I communicate these out of zeal for the service and am with unfeigned regard,

                    Sir, your Honour's

                        most obedient humble servant.

                        *David van den Heyden*

Albany, the 19th October, 1763, a 8 a. m.

To the Honourable Sir William Johnson, Bt. at Johnson Hall.

---

1 The *Groote Imbogt* (or Great Bend) was on the Hudson River, just below the mouth of the Catskill Creek, on the west side.

LETTER FROM F. DECOUAGNE TO SIR WILLIAM JOHNSON.

Niagara, October 22nd, 1763.

Honourable Sir:

In your last you desired to know whether Daniel and the rest of the Indians was gone to Detroit, the former has been up with two parties and has the character of a good man from everyone, but most people give an indifferent account of Aaron. There has been no Indians here; the traders at this post are all suttlers. Major Wilkins is gone with the last party and has taken with him all the belts and bands *wampum* to the Wapagamat Indians. I don't learn by any accounts that the said Indians have done any mischief at present. I have no more to relate at this juncture than have sent enclosed Mr. Stedman's account of what happened the 19th and 20th inst., the said person being present at the whole affair.

I have an intention to go as I think would be proper amongst some of the Wapagamats to get intelligence but believe it will be very dangerous, therefore beg your instructions by the first opportunity.

I am, Sir,

Your most obedient humble servant.

*Defouagne*

Sir:

I have further to inform you that all the Canadians who have passes from General Gage to trade are stopped at the different posts.

To the Hon. Sir William Johnson, Bt.,
at Johnson Hall.

LETTER FROM GENERAL AMHERST TO COLONEL BRADSTREET.

[*Bradstreet and Amherst MSS., p. 141.*]

New York, 29th October, 1763.

Sir:

I arrived here on Thursday morning and gave immediate orders for getting ready the iron work for the schooners that are intended to be built for the service of Lake Erie, &c. A sufficiency for one of 60 tons, with the rigging will be sent on Saturday next, and preparation shall be made for two more and sent up as fast as possible. I need not desire you to forward the whole in the best manner you can.

This will be delivered to you by *Bogardus* in whose sloop Mr. Napier has shipt the bedding as per the enclosed invoice and receipt, and you will please to receive the whole and order them to be safely stored to be ready for supplying any of the posts above: Though some of them have been used, Mr. Napier assures me they are as clean, sweet and good as if they had not been used. As Mr. Napier is accomptable for this bedding, it will be necessary that you send him a proper receipt for them.

Lt. Colonel Campbell writes me, that the bridges on the communication between Fort Stanwix and the Flatts [2] were broke down by the Oxen that were lately sent up; and that if they are not repaired before the winter, the roads will be impassable for sledges: I have wrote to Sir William Johnson on this head and requested him to endeavour to get the inhabitants to effect this useful service; but if you can anyways lend a helping hand it will be so much the better, for I fear we cannot depend much on what the country people will do, without they are pressed to do it.

> I am, Sir,
>> Your most obedient Servant.
>>> Jeff. Amherst,

Colonel Bradstreet,
D. Q. M. G.

THE SAME TO THE SAME.

> New York, 30th October, 1763.

Sir:

In all probability the sloop with the bedding will be at Albany before the post reaches you. I however enclose you a duplicate of my letter that went by her and I likewise transmit you a list of the ironworks that are getting ready for the schooner, and which with the rigging, will, I hope be embarked from hence on Saturday next.

I enclose a packet addressed to Governor Burton at Montreal, which you will please to forward by the first safe opportunity; and likewise a letter for Major General Gage which you will keep until he arrives at Albany, where you will soon see him, as I imagine he is on the route by this time and it might miss him,

---

2. German Flats.

were you to send it on.

On my arrival here, I applied to the Lt. Governor regarding the ruinous condition of the fort at Albany and represented to him how necessary it was to have it repaired in time, as 'tis shameful to see it: he has promised to make application to his assembly for that purpose; but as the fort is going in the mean time to ruin and that we may always want to keep a few men there, I would have you order the masonry or the parapets to be repaired, if it can be done at a small expense, as it will be too late before the assembly will determine. The coping them with wood, as the north curtain is and the work in the inside of the fort, may be done later in the season, and I hope will be done at the expense of the province.

> I am, Sir,
>> Your most obedient servant,
>>> Jeff. Amherst.

Col. Bradstreet,
D. Q. M. G.

## THE SAME TO THE SAME.

New York, 1st November, 1763,

Sir:

This will be delivered to you by Lieut. Godwin, whom I send to Albany, with a non-commissioned officer and three men of the Royal Artillery, which are all that I can spare from hence, and I think they may be useful in forwarding any artillery stores that may be sent to the upper posts, or giving their assistance to other services at Albany, and I write to Lt. Colonel Elliot accordingly.

To avoid any disputes about quarters, I would have you provide Lieut. Goodwin with a room in the hospital.

I have this moment received your letter of the 26th October, and with it I have one from Major Gladwin of the 7th October. Everything as well as we could expect at the Detroit: Moncrieffe, with the reinforcements, just setting off on Lake Erie the 14th and I hope they will arrive in time to give the barbarians a check before the winter sets in, though it is too late to expect much.

I have applied to the provinces of New York and Jersey, for two thousand men, to be raised early in the spring, 1400 from New

York and 600 from the Jerseys. Five companies of the former, of 60 men each, to be raised immediately for the protection of the communication between Albany and Oswego. How far my request will be granted I know not; but I shall acquaint you, as soon as I receive the governor's answer. In the meantime I would have you make the necessary preparations for the new boats, should the one you are building answer, of which you will be the best judge, and you must be sure of your success.

I may now acquaint you that His Majesty having been graciously pleased to give me permission to return to England, Major General Gages, with whom I am to leave the command of the troops and who will soon be at Albany on his way hither, will have full directions concerning the future operations; and you may consult with him regarding the new boats, as well as the preparations for the other matters; for by the time he arrives here i shall be able to judge of what assistance may be expected from the provinces and we must prepare accordingly. I have ordered two light six pounders to Albany.

I am, Sir,

Your most obedient Servant,

Jeff. Amherst.

Colonel Bradstreet,
D. Q. M. G., Albany.

EXTRACT OF A LETTER FROM WILLIAM EDGAR AT DETROIT TO SIR WILLIAM

November 1st, 1763.

I have lately received a letter from Hombach which came by an Officer from Illenois, who brought a belt and letter to the savages, with the account of the peace, between England and France, which neither the savages nor the French *here* believed till now. In consequence of which, our most implacable enemies, the Ottawas (who were the only Nation here disposed for continuing the war, all the rest having begged forgiveness for what they have done, of our worthy commandant) are now, with the others, suing for peace, in the most abject manner. Mr. Prentice is very well at Sandusky, as is Mr. Winston, at St. Josephs, and from the present disposition of the savages, I apprehend they will soon bring them in.

## Letter from Sir William Johnson to the Authorities at German Flats.

November 3rd, 1763.

Gentlemen:

As I understand that some Chenupsco [3] Indians (who are now our enemies) make a practice of coming to the German Flatts to purchase powder and other things which you know is not allowed, besides, when there, they have an opportunity of making their remarks and seeing our strength, you should in order to prevent ye like for the future, take up all such as you find of that nation and send them prisoners to Albany under a good guard, first being certain that they are our enemies not doubting but that your own prudence will lead you both to do everything of that kind with propriety and discretion. I need add no more. Letter to justices Frank and Harkemer to apprehend any Chenupscos who may come to the Flatts.

## Letter from Volkert P. Douw to Sir Wm. Johnson.

Albany, November 3rd, 1763.

Sir:

I thought it not improper at this time to acquaint you as being commissioner of Indian affairs that last night arrived here three Tennesie Indians directly from there castle as they say; they also say they waited on you as they passed in there way to Albany of which I doubt much; they have a small quantity of beaver with them but no person chuses to trade with them without liberty. I am at a loss how to act with regard to those Indians and should be glad of your direction therein by the return of the bearer.

I am, Sir,

Your most Humble Servant,

*Volkert P. Douw,*

To Sir William Johnson, Barnit.

---

3. Genesee.

## Orders

As the safety and protection of Schenectady depends in a great measure on the keep of a good guard in the town, it is Sir Wm. Johnson's orders that the commanding officer of the Second Battalion of Militia for the county of Albany do immediately appoint a guard consisting of a subaltern, serjeant, corporal and twenty men to mount at the block house in the Albany Street and to be regularly relieved every 24 hours till further orders, which guard is to post centinels at such places as the commanding officer of the battalion shall judge best, the centinels to be regularly relieved by the corporal of the guard every two hours and the officer to let no more than two men be at any time absent from the guard. every evening at sunset the officer of the guard is to have his men under arms, the roll called and men's arms, &c. examined and see that they are furnished with 12 rounds of powder and ball, no person is to be absent on pain of punishment and the town major is at the time he thinks necessary to visit the guards and centinels and make a report thereof to the commanding officer. The serjeant of the guard to visit the centinels frequently during the night and the officer on being relieved to make a report of the guard in writing to the commanding-officer who is to see these orders strictly complied with.

In case of an alarm the Militia are to assemble at the Dutch church and there to follow such orders as they shall receive from the commanding officer for the protection of the town, the guard turning out and continuing under arms until they shall receive the commanding officer's orders.

And the commanding officer is to transmit in writing to Sir Wm, Johnson a return of the state of the blockhouse and other fortifications about the town, as also of the number, state and quality of the cannon and ammunition, &c., immediately.

Johnson Hall, November 3rd, 1763.

Col. Vandyke, &c.

145

Dear Sir:

I came here yesterday and had the pleasure to find all your friends here well the *bateau* is in a hurry to go down which prevents my having the pleasure of waiting on you. Capt. Daniel, at parting, pressed me much to give an account of his behaviour whilst with me when I was guarding the wreck; I was there above a fortnight and in all that time he was but once drunk, always at my elbow, and very industrious to do everything to ingratiate himself with me, and so was Jacob, who was with him.

We were fired at for near two hours by 25 or 30 Indians, as they guessed from the tracks afterwards and Daniel kept close by me and showed great zeal we lost three men; the enemy came very near but we could not get one shot at them the behaviour of Aaron, &c. occasioned me to be solicited not to send Daniel up with the schooner, but I sent him; nor will I believe the Mohawks in general dishonest.

Fatigue and cold gave me an illness which though I have not yet quite recovered I am pretty well, only in a very bad weather I am pretty sure still of an ague fit. I am so far on my way to New York.

The troops for Detroit, about 600 men under Major Wilkins got out from the head of the rapids at the entrance into Lake Erie the 20th of October. Two boats were fired upon at embarking there and all in them except a serjeant killed or wounded; five were killed and one died of his wounds, as did also Lt. Johnson; there were a good body of men still ashore who pursued and engaged in the woods for some time and then returned in good order to the boats. This is the serjeant's account who remained unhurt, who said he saw this at a distance but knows no other particulars.

I don't know whether it is worth mentioning to you that whilst I was at Fort Stanwix I was told a squaw of the Oneidas that had just come said there was a report amongst them that 20 of their young men had been killed by our people in the Cherokee Country and that the Oneidas were holding a council about it. I am, with great sincerity, Dear Sir,

Your most obedient and very humble servant *Gavin Cochrane*
Fort Johnson, November 5th, 1763,

146

The number in the two boats that were fired upon were 14 exclusive of the officers,

## LETTER FROM GENERAL AMHERST TO COLONEL BRADSTREET.

New York, 6th November, 1763.

Sir:

I had last night your letter of the 31st October: The account given by *Silverheels*, I believe, is too true and I am not surprised the inhabitants on the Mohawk River are alarmed: They cannot be too much on their guard, until they can get an additional assistance, which I hope the province will furnish, when the assembly meets.

I have mentioned to the Lt. Governor how necessary it will be to get a law passed for impressing carriages, as well as billeting the troops on this occasion. But whether he can bring it to bear, or not, I know not. [4]

I am very glad to find you have such hopes of the boat answering; but am sorry to hear you have such bad reports of the stuff fit for building boats at Oswego; however I am apt to think the *bateaux* from Canada may answer; General Gage will know that.

General Gage, in all probability will be with you before this reaches Albany, and as he has no family with him, I hope he will have found all the assistance he could require on the route.

The sloop with the iron work, &c., as mentioned in my last, failed on the 4th. I enclose you a list of the whole, but the master went off without signing the invoice of the sails, cables and anchors: you have his receipt therewith for the iron work, and you will please to take care that he delivers the whole, agreeable

---

4. This Law was not passed. The only Acts passed by the General assembly of New York with reference to the Wars of Pontiac were the following:
"An Act providing for three, hundred effective men, exclusive of officers, to be employed against the enemy Indians, and for one hundred and seventy-three men, Officers included, to garrison the several forts such manner as the commander-in chief of all His Majesty's Forces in North America shall think proper, and also for three hundred effective men, exclusive of officers, to guard the western Frontiers of the Colony under the direction of the governor or commander-in-chief thereof. Passed Dec. 13, 1763."
"An Act providing for one hundred and eighty men, exclusive of officers, to be employed against the enemy Indians and other purposes on the Frontiers of this Colony, in therein mentioned."
Passed April 21, 1764.

to the enclosed list. I need not desire you to forward them in the best manner you can.

As Captain Loring, I imagine, will be down soon, I would chuse to wait for his opinion of the size of the other vessel, before I sent the materials; but should he not come soon, I shall order iron work, &c. to be forwarded for the same kind of schooner as the one for which the materials are now sent.

I am, Sir,

Your most obedient servant,

Jeff. Amherst.

Colonel Bradstreet,

D. Q. M. G. Albany.

MESSAGE OF LIEUTENANT GOVERNOR COLDEN TO THE

GENERAL ASSEMBLY OF NEW YORK.[5]

[*Gaine's Journal of General assembly, 2, 720.*]

Gentlemen of the Council and General Assembly.

The great and desirable work of peace, being by the wisdom and magnanimity of our gracious sovereign, happily accomplished since your recess; I cordially congratulate you on this joyful event, so highly glorious to His Majesty, and extensively beneficial to his people. His American subjects, who will derive from it a security, unknown since the first establishment of these colonies, must receive this mark of the royal attention to their interest and safety, with the warmest sentiments of loyalty, gratitude and affection.

The enjoyment of solid tranquillity is however unhappily suspended by the daring and unprovoked attacks of some of the Western Tribes of Indians, who under the specious appearance of friendship, have treacherously surprised some of our remote posts, and are in open war, renewing with relentless cruelty, that horror and desolation among the defenceless inhabitants, from which they were so recently delivered.

To suppress this dangerous defection, pregnant with the most fatal evils, before it becomes more extensive and formidable, is our indispensable duty.

The preservation of our own Frontier, should be our first and

---

5. The General assembly of New York met on the 8th of November, 1763, and on the Day following the Lieutenant Governor addressed to them the preceding message relating to the Indian War.

immediate care, every motive of policy, justice and humanity, unitedly demanding the protection of our fellow subjects, whose distant and dispersed situation must otherwise leave them an easy prey to merciless savages.

But barely to defend ourselves would be giving the enemy every advantage, and expose us to perpetual disquietude. It is necessary a force should be raised, sufficient to chastise these faithless people, that feeling the weight of our resentment, they may be awed for future by the fear of punishment; experience evincing, that destitute of every just and humane principle, nothing else can secure us against their continual ravages and depredations.

Since then, not only the prosperity of the colony, but the very existence of a great part of it, depend on the most active and spirited measures, no arguments can be wanting to animate you to a vigorous exertion of your strength in the accomplishment of this essential object.

I shall therefore content myself with laying before you a letter I received from His Excellency Sir Jeffrey Amherst, Commander in Chief of his Majesty's Forces, pressing this Government to furnish a proportion of men, to proceed early in the spring in conjunction with the regular troops, on this important service. Did the subject require it, his superior abilities, would render it unnecessary for me to enforce, what he so wisely urges for subduing that restless, fierce and cruel spirit of the savages, the source of the most dreadful calamities.

Gentlemen of the General Assembly

I flattered myself the ordinary support of his Majesty's Government, would have been the only aid required of you at this time. But the unexpected revolt of the Indians, renders a much greater expense unavoidable. Besides providing for the company now posted at Fort Ontario, Niagara and Detroit, which General Monckton, by the Advice of his Majesty's Council, a few days before his departure, directed to be continued on that service, I earnestly recommend you will grant the necessary supplies for raising, clothing and paying, a body of forces, sufficient with the other troops, to avert the dangers we fear; avenge the injuries we have received; and convince the savages of our ability to compel them to submission.

Gentlemen of the Council and General Assembly,

The enemy have already infested the border of Orange and Ulster, and though I am confident of the spirit and activity of the Militia, yet as this duty will soon be too severely felt, I assure myself, you will enable me to ease them; and by the most vigorous resolutions in this important conjuncture, secure to yourselves the great advantages of a peace, peculiarly calculated for the happiness of America.

Cadwallader Colden.

Fort George, New York, Nov. 9, 1763.

And then the letter mentioned in his honour's speech from Sir Jeffrey Amherst, was read, in the words following, that is to say,

New York, October 30, 1763.

Sir:

On a due confederation of the most probable measures for crushing the present insurrection of the Indians, and punishing the guilty as they deserve, I find it absolutely necessary to make application to the provinces most nearly concerned, that a respectable body of men may be raised, so as to proceed in the spring, in conjunction with such regular troops as can be collected, to put in execution such offensive operations as may be judged most effectual for reducing the savages, and securing peace and quiet to the settlements hereafter.

I am in great hopes that the provinces to the southward will cheerfully raise such quotas, as may be required of them, for reducing the Delawares, Shawanese, and other tribes on that side; and as I intend to assemble a respectable body of men early in the spring at Niagara, for the punishment of the Senecas and other savages on Lake Erie, &c. who have so treacherously commenced and are now carrying on hostilities against us, I think it but reasonable that the provinces of New York and Jersey, should contribute their shares towards a service of so much consequence to the future security of their respective inhabitants; and therefore I am now to lay before you, a requisition, which I am persuaded will not only meet with a proper reception from you, but that you will enforce the same to your council and assembly, backed with such arguments (if any arguments can be necessary on such an occasion) as will at once remove every obstacle that could be started to a compliance therewith.

The proportion I must demand from your province is fourteen hundred men, exclusive of commissioned officers, twelve hundred to be divided in four corps of five companies each, commanded by a field officer, who may have the rank of major; and each company to consist of a captain, and two subalterns and sixty men, including three serjeants and three corporals; the other two hundred to have a field officer, and to consist of four companies of fifty men each, with the commissioned and non-commissioned officers as above; for the service on which they will be employed requires that there should be a good many officers; the men to be clothed, but in a light manner; a cloth jacket, flannel waistcoat, leggins, &c. will be full sufficient; and it will be necessary that the whole are raised and ready to proceed to Albany by the first of March next.

But as the settlements on the Mohawk River, are. open to the enemy, and that it is not in my power at present to spare regulars for their protection, so much as I wish to do, I must recommend it to you, to use your influence with the assembly to raise five companies of the above mentioned quota with the utmost expedition, that they may be posted during the winter, on the communication between Albany and Oswego, and be ready for any service they may be called for, which may be a great means of preventing any incursions that might be attempted by the savages, and give that confidence to the inhabitants, which is so necessary to enable them to repel, by force in case of an attack.

Particular care should be taken that in recruiting the men, none should be raised but such as are able bodied; neither too young nor too old, but fit for the most active and alert service.

Although by an order from home, the regular troops are subject to a stoppage for the provisions issued to them, belonging to the crown, yet upon this occasion I will take upon me to order provisions to the provincial troops, that shall be raised and take the field; and they shall likewise be provided with arms, unless any of them chuse to bring their own arms, for which they shall have the same allowance as was made in former campaigns, should any of them be lost, or damaged in actual service. Tents will also be furnished to them as formerly.

The time of service may be limited to the first of November, although it is much to be hoped, everything will be finished

151

long before that period, in which case the men will be sent back to the province.

I am, with great regard Sir,
Your most obedient humble servant,
Jeffrey Amherst.

A true copy, examined by G. Banyer, D. Sec.

## LETTER FROM CAPTAIN GERRET A. LANSINGH TO SIR WILLIAM JOHNSON.

[*MSS. of Sir William Johnson, 7*]

Sir:

Agreeable to your orders I have been round the town to review the condition and state of the fort, blockhouses, cannon, amanition, &c., likewise the stockagadess; as for the fort is but in a verry consetreable condition, whants a good teal of preparing and the blockhouse at the widow Van Eps at the north side of the town is unfit for service, no shimble in nor flowr, at the blockhouse at Daniel de Graff at the southwest end of the town is entirely unfit for service is ready to fall down. The blockhouse at Mr. Ryner Mynders whants lettle repairing.

As to the blockhouse on the south end of Albany Street is fit to keep a wacht in, and the blockhouse which formley use to stand at Mr. Thomas Nixson door is intirely takeing away and no more of, and as for stoagadeges about the town there is about seventy of them mostly rotton; as for cannon in the Fort that belongs to it there is none fit for service, there is no cannon in the block houses not a single one, and there is a few cannon lying up the Albany Hill unfit for service which has been takeing out of the fort and blockhouse and have been tryed by soldier and conductors of the Royall Artellery and is found to be condemned; as for powder there is two cask of about 50 wieght each which belongs to the township of Schenectady likewise 30 wieght grave schot and about seventy or eighty small hand granades.

I am Sir
Your most obedient humble servant

*Gerret A Lansing Capt*

To Sir Wm. Johnson, Bart.

Capt. Lansingh's return of ye state of ye blockhouses, &c. at Schenectady.

A return of condition and state of the fortification of the township of Schenectady. November 11th, 1763.

## LETTER FROM T. DE COUAGNE TO SIR WILLIAM JOHNSON.
### [*MSS. of Sir William Johnson, 8*]

Niagara, 27th of November, 1763.

Sir:

I have received your letter dated November ye 3rd, 1763, wherein you write me word to be more particular or circumstantial than hitherto. You may depend I do everything to ye utmost of my power for my employer, likewise for His Majesty's Service, ye troops is come back thath was going to Ditroit with ye loss of one hundred men, ye got within less than one hundred miles was cafs away and lost there ammunition was forst to return for want; ye had to I am informed, but eight rounds a man thath ye could not proceed and have spoke to ye officer commanding, Major Browning, about ye Indians coming in, he has give out an order thath ye must not fire upon any small party of Indians upon no account and thath on their march in fight of ye garrison he says if ye should fall in with Fort Slhosser he can't be accountable what happens as they are daily killing our people. In your letter you say you do not understand what I mean by ye Voiseagamigate, Sir he is ye chief man North and West upon Lake Ontario and so far upon Lake Erie as ye big river, which is sixty miles from Little Niagara, ye Troops goes fishing every day and nobody hurt. I can't promise they do no mischief in there own country but what they do otherwise I cannot tell.

Sir, I have wrote you word before of Major Wilkins taken some belts of *wampum* from heare, he is come back, I have spoke to Colonel Browning for to gett them. In ye next letter I shall send word if Collonel has received.

D Couagne.

Sir ye Indians is arrived this day from Detroit which you will ye news more particular from them are ye vessel sails emediately.

LETTER FROM AARON THE MOHAWK TO SIR WM. JOHNSON.
[*MSS. of Sir William Johnson, 8*]

Fort Pitt, 1st December, 1763.

Sir:

Having been sent express by Major Gladwin from De Troite to this place, on arriving at Sandusky meeting with about 300 Shany and Delaware Indians, who ware at the same time holding a great Counsill and by which I understood and was told by them the breaking out of this warr was occasioned by the Seneca Indians who went about with a bloody belt and tomahawk to all the nations engaged in this troubles. The Taways also expressly told me that the Senecas were the beginners of this warr, they also desired me (the old men of the Delawar's and Shanees) to acquaint you that if you desire, that they would come down to you, and swear before you that this warr was begun by the Senecas. The old men of the Wiandots Nation want very much to see you, and if you desire they will come immediately, you being pleased to let them know. I had the misfortune to be robed of 4000 of *wampum*, a tomahawk and all the powder and ball I had by the Delawar's, Shanees and the Five Nations.

> Sir, remain with great respect,
> Your obedient humble servant.
> Aaron.

LETTER FROM JOHN STUART[6] TO SIR WILLIAM JOHNSON.
[*MSS. of Sir William Johnson, 8.*]

Charles Town, 10th December, 1763.[7]

Sir:

I am now to acknowledge the receipt of both your favours of 24th July and 2nd September, which my being at the congress with the Indians in this district prevented my receiving and answering sooner. I have a grateful sense of your polite and friendly expressions, and shall cheerfully embrace every opportunity of cultivating a correspondence with, and rendering you any agreeable service. I am sincerely sorry for the rupture with the Indians in your department, which is attended with so much bloodshed and desolation and necessarily with so much

---

6. Mr. Stuart was Superintendent, of Indian Affairs in the Southern Department.
7. Received Feb. 15, 1764.

trouble to you.

Immediately after the receipt of your last letter, I wrote to the Cherokee Nation, to know if they would send some parties against the Northern Indians according to their proposal to me at the Congress. As soon as I receive an answer I shall communicate it to you. Some officers of the independent companies in this province, who are on the point of being reduced, have offered to accompany such Cherokees as can be prevailed upon to go and act jointly with His Majesty's Forces against the Northern tribes. It would be a delicate point to propose any thing of this nature to the creeks at this juncture, when they are apt to construe every proposal as containing some hidden design; the impressions left on their minds by the French, and their jealousy on account of the late cession of Florida and Louisiana, not being as yet totally effaced.

The *Chactaws* have but newly entered into the covenant of friendship with us. Their country is a vast distance, I shall endeavour as soon as possible to inform myself of their disposition and the practicability of engaging them to send parties as you propose.

The *Chickasaws* are perpetually at war with the Northern Indians, but then they only act defensively, being reduced to 450 men at most, and surrounded by great nations with whom they never are upon terms of sincere friendship, for which reason they dare not weaken themselves by sending out strong parties, so far as they are able their friendship and attachment to us may be depended upon.

The *Catawbas* are willing and brave, but reduced by war and sickens to 60 or 70 gunmen. The Northern Indians infested them all last summer, killed and carried off several of them.

This may be depended on that I shall take every measure to induce parties from the Northern nations within my department to go and act jointly with His Majesty's troops employed against the nations at war with us, and shall be extremely glad to hear from you and receive the general's instructions relative to my conduct in this matter.

Our conferences at the late Congress ended with the most friendly appearance. The indians of every nation went away well satisfied, and made the strongest professions of attachment to the British interest. They are all appraised of the war between the Northern Indians and us, but know nothing of the particular events.

A minute journal of the proceedings at the Congress is now in the press. As soon I can be furnished with a copy for you I shall send it.

The *Tascaroras* inhabit a tract of 10,000 acres of land laid out for them in North Carolina. I have wrote to Governor Dobbs for a particular account of them and of their situation with respect to debts or whatever else may hinder or retard their going to join their people. Governor Dobbs told me when at the Congress, that they consisted of about one hundred men able to bear arms, women and children in proportion.

I am now to inform you, that on my return from Augusta, I received a letter from the Right Honourable the Lords of Trade declaratory of His Majesty's orders, that the agents for Indian affairs should correspond with their lordships in all matters regarding their departments, and should transmit them all such information as they should require. in consequence they have required from me a regular and constant correspondence upon those points. Their lordships have likewise directed me to transmit to them as soon as possible, a full and particular report of the state of Indian affairs within this department, and an accurate description of the several nations of Indians, their different interests, claims and dispositions and what will in my judgement be a proper plan for the future management and direction of these important interests.

The task imposed upon us I consider as arduous and what requires very mature consideration, on which I have not as yet been able to turn my thoughts, having a multiplicity of affairs to settle in consequence of the late Congress, it will give me the greatest pleasure to coincide with you in opinion, but to form *a general plan* by which a trade to the Indian countries may be at the same time *well regulated* and *free* to all His Majesty's Subjects, is not very easy. It will give me great pleasure to hear from you soon, being with most sincere regard, Sir,

Your most obedient humble servant,

*John Stuart*

## LETTER FROM T. DE COUAGNE TO SIR WILLIAM JOHNSON.
### [*MSS. of Sir William Johnson, 8*]
Translation.

Niagara, 15th November, 1763.

Sir:

Since my last which I had the honour of writing to you, by which I have mentioned the accident which happened to Major Wilkin's party which has retreated, Major Rogers arrived with his corps and two Mohawks, Daniel and Jacob, two days after.

The commandant has sent the man named Jacob with a Ranger to Detroit, and Daniel has decided to join the party returning with Major Rogers, to rejoin you, and who can relate to you all that has happened in these parts, as well as what has become of the other Mohawk. He has told me that the man named Ouapacamigatte a Missisague had a passport from the commandant at Detroit to come hither with a message, and I believe it would be *apropos* if the commandant would consent that I should send him with one or two others to speak with you upon this business. I believe that there is not here this winter any Indian whom I could send for some time. And I remember nothing further of which to appraise you. There are parties eroding every day to the other side of the river upon the lands of the Missisagues but they have not returned with, any scalps. The man named Roffin . . . . a Seneca of whom you speak in your letter has not arrived. I have spoken to his two sisters about him in a way that has flattered them much.

I have the honour to be with profound respect
Sir, Your very humble and much
obliged Servant,
De Couagne.

It is impossible at this moment to write to you in English, as everybody is engaged, and I cannot find a secretary.

## LETTER FROM COLONEL BRADSTREET TO GENERAL GAGE.
### [*Bradstreet and Amherst MSS., p. 169.*]
Albany, 20th December, 1767.

Sir:

I return your Excellency, enclosed, the papers you sent me relating to small arms taken by my order at Oswego for the Indians in 1764—with my certificate of the number. Those gentlemen's accounts and affidavits you will please to observe fix the time of my ordering those small arms to be taken in 1763—near twelve months before my arrival at Oswego.

I am,

Jno. Bradstreet.

His Ex. Genl. Gage, &c. &c. &c.

## LETTER FROM SIR WM. JOHNSON TO MAJOR GEN. GAGE,

[*MSS. of Sir William Johnson, 8*]

Johnson Hall, December 23, 1763,

Dear Sir:

Your Excellency's favours of the 30th *ult.* and 1st of this inst. were accompanied with two letters from the Lords of Trade, the one of September and the other of October last, enclosing me one of the King's proclamations, and expressing approbation of His Majesty and his minister and that of their lordships on my late representations, as also His Majesty's reliance on my endeavours to bring matters to a happy issue, and his orders that I should cause the proclamation therewith transmitted to be made public and strictly complied with throughout my jurisdiction.

I am hopeful that on receipt of my last letter, their lordships will be able still further to contribute towards the salutary points in view relative to Indians as I apprehend some additions may be added to the Royal Proclamation, which at present does not contain more with regard to them than has been already communicated to them by virtue of former orders, &c. transmitted to America. This proclamation does not relieve their present grievances which are many, being calculated only to prevent the like hereafter, although there are numberless instances of tracts which have indeed been purchased but in the most illegal and fraudulent manner, all of which demand redress.

I have made at this meeting the best use in my power of His Majesty's Proclamation for the convincing the Indians here of his gracious and favourable disposition to do them justice, and shall communicate the same to all the rest.

The Indians have been here for several days to the amount of 230, are now mostly departed for their respective nations, for which purpose I have dismissed them with a present. They are accompanied by several of the yet friendly Senecas from *Kanad-afego* [8] as also by three deputies sent from *Chenassio*, to desire to be informed of our present resolution, and to know whether the offer of peace which they have now made will be accepted of, in which they are seconded by all the rest who earnestly desire the same might be taken into consideration and after representing the manner in which the Senecas of Chenassio had been led into the war, intimated that should we now receive them into our friendship the generosity of the Indians would cheerfully join us in any operations against the rest, particularly against the *Shawanese* and *Delawares*, whom they represented as the principal authors of all the late troubles, to which after giving them ye most severe reprimand in ye presence of all ye rest, I answered them, that I could do nothing therein, but would lay the same before you. I must therefore request your direction and sentiments thereon.

This was the chief purport of the late conference, the rest of their speeches consisting of a repetition of their promises and assurances of their unvariable attachment to His Majesty.

On this subject I must beg leave to offer my opinion that the five friendly nations must naturally be very uneasy at any attempt against the Senecas, as they are a part of their confederacy, however justly they may deserve our resentment, but I am confident that the whole would readily join against their perfidious dependents, the *Shawanese* and *Delawares*, as well as any others who have acted as principals in the war. The Hurons of Detroit from the concurring accounts of all persons were with the utmost difficulty and by severe threats, persuaded to engage in the war by the Ottawas under Pontiac, who with the before mentioned Shawanese and Delawares have sufficiently shown themselves as principals in the war.

I imagine that any hostilities committed in or about Pennsylvania and Jersey must be done by the Delawares. [9] All those of that nation who have lately become our enemies, have lately removed from the Susquehanna to the Ohio amongst the Shawanese, and those who remain on or about the Susquehanna,

---

8. Near Geneva, Ontario County, N.Y.
9. The following sentence is here interlined in the original draft without apparent connexion with the text: "Wyaloosin is an Indian town a considerable distance from any settlement."

particularly from its source down to *Owegy* are our friends, and here I cannot help remarking that the absurdity of most of the accounts received from the provinces is apt to give a very unjust idea of Indian affairs. For instance, in one of the late New York papers you must have observed it is insinuated that a party who defeated Capt. *Westbrook* on the borders of *Pensilvania* consisted of Mohocks, which they pretended to know from their caps, and manner of cutting their hair.

The fidelity of the Mohocks deserves a better return, and the folly of such representations should certainly be removed, least it come to the knowledge of our friendly tribes who might entertain much rancour from such a falsity. The Mohocks do not wear caps, nor any nation of the confederacy except the Senecas and some Cayugas, the former learned that practice from their vicinity to *Niagara*, where such were usually worn during the winter, neither are the authors of that paragraph or any other persons capable of distinguishing one of these caps from another or knowing to what nation it belonged any more than they are of discerning one blanket from another.

The house of assembly have been very moderate in their resolves. I have received from the Lieutenant Governor in consequence thereof some blank commissions for raising two Companies of 50 men each to be stationed at *Schohare* and *Cherry Valley* which I shall give to such persons as I shall judge best qualified to answer their intention.

I am informed by letter from Niagara that Wabagommigot, chief of the numerous nation of the Chippewas who accompanied me to the Detroit in 1761, and has since behaved very well on his part and prevented numbers of his people from joining against us, proposes to visit me shortly on public business, which if he does, or that I am attended by any other district or enemy Indians, indeed I shall be glad to have your sentiments concerning my behaviour on that occasion and in what manner you think it most necessary to treat them.

I am &c.

LETTER FROM SIR WM. JOHNSON TO LIEUT. GOV. COLDEN.
[*MSS. of Sir William Johnson, 8*]

Johnson Hall, December 24th, 1763.

Dear Sir:

I am just favoured with your letter of the 7th inst. enclosing me two captain's warrants and two commissions as also three lieutenants' warrants and four commissions, from which I conclude that 'twas a lieut.'s warrant which was given to Mr. *Ten Eyke*. The rest of the warrants shall be given to such persons as I judge will answer the public expectations in the most expeditious and most effectual manner. The companies when raised shall be mustered agreeable to your directions, but the small pay of the officers in a country where people are accustomed to high wages and where men are now raising by Col. Bradstreet at much higher rates, will I fear greatly retard their completing, and I am a good deal surprised how your letter and enclosures could have been so long by the way.

The Indians who had been with me from all the Six Nations for several days are just departing for their respective habitations. They numbered 230, and were accompanied by several of the yet friendly Senecas from *Kanadasego* as also by three deputies sent from the *Chenussio* requesting to be informed of our present resolutions and to know whether offers of peace will be accepted of or not. In this they were seconded by the rest of the nations who after representing the manner in which the *enemy Senecas* had been drawn into the war, intimated that should they now be received into our friendship the whole of the Six Nations would heartily join us against the rest of our enemies particularly against the Shawanese and Delawares whom they represented as the principal authors of all the late troubles, and I know the disposition of these people so well as to foresee that any attempt against the Senecas must naturally create uneasiness amongst the rest of the confederacy, particularly the Cayugas and Onondagas who are more connected with them than any of ye rest.

I have just received two letters from the Lords of Trade (one dated in September the other in October last) enclosing me the King's Proclamation and expressing the approbation of His Majesty and his ministers and that of their lordships on my late representations as also His Majesty's reliance on my endeavours to bring matters to a happy issue, and his royal orders that I should cause the Proclamation therewith transmitted to published and strictly complied with throughout my jurisdiction, and I am hopeful that within a small period of time things may be settled on a still more satisfactory plan.

I am a stranger to what cause the assembly attribute the unhappy rupture, which is not a general defection of the Six Nations as is insisted, nor indeed of any others except ye Shawanese, some of the Ottawas and Chippewas, also Delawares. I shall not take upon me to point out the original parsimony, &c. to which the first defection of the Indians can with justice and certainty be attributed but only observe as I did in a former letter that the Indians (whose friendship was never cultivated by the English with that attention, expense and assiduity with which the French obtained their favours) were for many years jealous of our growing power, were repeatedly assured by the French (who were at the pains of having many proper emissaries among them) that so soon as we became masters of this country we should immediately treat them with neglect, hem them in with posts and forts, encroach upon their lands and finally destroy them, all which after the reduction of Canada seemed to appear too clearly to the Indians who thereby lost the great advantages resulting from the possession which the French formerly had of posts and trade in their country, neither of which they could have ever enjoyed but for the notice they took of the Indians and the presents they bestowed so bountifully upon them, which however expensive they wisely foresaw was infinitely cheaper and much more effectual than the keeping of a large body of regular troops in their several countries which however considerable could not protect trade or cover settlements, but must remain cooped up in their garrisons or else be exposed to the ambuscades and surprises of an enemy over whom from the nature and situation of their country no important advantage can be gained.

From a sense of these truths the French chose the most reasonable and most promising plan, a plan which has endeared their memory to most of the Indian Nations who would I fear generally go over to them in case they ever got footing again in this country, and who were repeatedly exhorted and encouraged by the French (from motives of interest and dislike which they will always possess) to fall upon us by representing that their liberties and country were in ye utmost danger and that a fleet and army, was arrived at Quebec, and an army coming by way of the Mississippi to their assistance, all which the Indians were persuaded to credit until their messengers sent to the Illinois returned and contradicted the report so industriously propagated by the French, which immediately struck at our trade, gave them some distant hopes of a re-establishment by embroiling our affairs and drew down the valuable fur trade by the way of the Ilyones and Mississippi and the indians once embarked in the quarrel were easily induced by their success and advantages of plunder to continue their ravages. In the midst of which however I have the satisfaction to find that my unwearied labours hath hitherto preserved the whole confederacy (Chenusseos excepted) with many other nations and thereby secured this very important communication to the lakes, also that by the River St. Lawrence, together with these Western Frontiers from the fate which hath attended the neighbouring colonies, to effect these important ends, as I have sacrificed all my tranquillity and domestic concerns so I have the pleasure to find myself rewarded in the favourable sentiments with which His Majesty and the ministry have been lately pleased to express themselves concerning my labours for the public welfare. The present unhappy rupture was long foreseen and frequently represented by me, but I had the mortification to find that it did not meet with sufficient credit, which neglect at length brought on the calamities in which we are involved and from which I apprehend we can never be free unless we remove the jealousies which the Indians entertain of us, and purchase their friendship with favours and notice, which friendship once obtained and established will enable us to withdraw our expenses by imperceptible degrees.

These are my sentiments on the present state of Indian affairs and the causes to which the hostilities are certainly to be attributed and I hope they may tend to the further information of any who may be desirous to enquire into the subject.

The petition which you sent me I was, informed of some time ago and that Geo: Klock a person of an infamous character at Conajoharie had made it his business to procure it signed by several persons (the greater part of whom I know to be his relations and retainers, and his own name is erased at the head of them) whom he persuaded thereto on promise of rewards and of procuring them commissions, which the ignorant people readily believed, I have however sent for the officers complained of and shall transmit you my further inquiries therein.

I am Sir, &c.

## LETTER FROM THE REV. SAMUEL DUNLOP[10] TO SIR WILLIAM JOHNSON.

[*MSS. of Sir William Johnson, 8*]

Cherry Valley, December 25th, 1763.

Honoured Sir:

Not reflecting upon you, because perhaps the matter does not lye alltogether within the compass of your power, we the inhabitants of Cherry Valley, think we are deserted, we hope not of God, but we think in a great measure of man, and exposed to the mercyless insults of our enemies without covert or relief.

You know General Amherst was condemned for not making some provision for the safety of the inhabitants by covering the Frontiers, and it was expected when he resigned that General Gage and your honour, or the persons to whom the care and management of these things were committed (you know best who they were) would have made an alteration before now. But things seem to remain in *statu quo*, with the poor and unhappy frontiers and the council of the heathen held sometime agoe seems to have had its accomplishment against all the places they intended, us only in this quarter escaped. Matters appear darker

10. In 1738, John Lindesay and others procured a patent of 8000 acres in what is now Cherry Valley, and soon after Mr. L. met in New York the Rev. Samuel Dunlop and prevailed on him to visit the tract, offering him several hundred acres upon condition of his using his influence with his friends to settle upon the land. The proposition was accepted and Mr. Dunlop visited Londonderry in New Hampshire, where several of his acquaintances resided, and induced numbers to emigrate to the new tract. Mr. D. was a native of the North of Ireland, and had travelled quite extensively in the colonies, particularly in the South. He left Ireland under an engagement of marriage which he returned and fulfilled. He opened a school for the instruction of boys, at Cherry Valley, and has the honour of beginning the first grammar school west of Albany within this state.

In the memorable massacre of November 11, 1778, Mr. Dunlop's wife was killed, but himself and daughter were spared by Little Aaron, a Mohawk of the Aquago branch. He was released soon after, but the combined effects of age, fear, and cold, led to a decline, which terminated in death about a year after.—*Campbell's History of Tryon Co.*

and darker with us, and the time now seems to be at hand to fetch us the intended blow, and Schoharry's being warned off we take to be a bad omen of our approaching ruin.

And if man neither can nor will help us, may Allmighty God, either ward off the blow or endow us with that firmness of spirit that may make us bear the thoughts of death without amazement, and bring our minds to an equal poise between the strong inclinations of nature to live, and the dictates of reason and religion that should make us willing to die when he pleases.

Death and a destroying enemy may curtail a few years of this mortal life, from those of us that are old, but thanks be to God can never destroy our immortal life. But it's a pity the young and rising generation should be cutt off, and the hand of the heathen embrewed in their blood, who if spared, might make some figure in the world and be usefull to generations to come, and therefore, if you can mediate any timous relief I beg you may.

For it is but a poor redress to come to our assistance when dead, and to bury our ma[n]gled corps when we are gone, which is but too often the senseless custom of the country where we live, though 'tis the best redress the case will then admit of. But the matter is to secure against the blow beforehand and therefore once more I would beg of you Honourable Sir that you would mediate some relief for us, or some way to secure us if in your power before it be too late. And if we fall, as Christ prayed for his enemies, *Father forgive them for they know not what they do,* so I pray God our blood may never be laid to their charge who had it in their power to help us and did it not. Please to give my kind compliments to Capt. Guy Johnson and all your good family. I add no more, but remain Sir your

  Humble Supplicant,

165

LETTER FROM SIR WILLIAM JOHNSON TO
LIEUTENANT GOVERNOR COLDEN.
[*MSS. of Sir William Johnson, 8*]
Johnson Hall, December 30, 1763.

Dear Sir:

Yesterday I was favoured with your letter of the 19th inst. in answer to mine of the 5th.

I have received particular information of all the late transactions at the *Detroit*, as well from the officers as from one of the Mohocks (whom with others I sent there to be of any service in their power), who is just returned from thence charged with several belts, &c. to me.

As the chief cause of the hostilities committed by the Indians was intended to procure themselves redress of some wrongs, and to obtain a better treatment, together with occasional gifts and rewards, for the admitting posts in their country, I am of opinion their offers of peace arise principally from an expectation that they will for the future obtain these desired ends which they could not get by any other means than by having recourse to arms, having found all amicable proceedings ineffectual.

For this reason I conclude they have made their late offers, and I likewise believe they would abide by their promises if we for the future gratify their expectations, but I am fully convinced they will never preserve peace on any other terms.

They know their own strength and situation too well to be as yet apprehensive of our resentment, and they will never want ammunition whilst the French can supply them by the variety of communications open to the western Indians and beyond our power to shut.

The Five Nations have had no occasion to alter their behaviour, which as it has saved this communication and the frontiers of this part of ye province, justly entitled them to all necessary supplies for themselves; more they did not require, nor are they so well affected to these nations who have made war upon us as to give them any ammunition even though they had plenty. Indeed the Indians are very chary of powder, and although they often waste it when they have plenty (yet that has not been since the surrender of Canada) yet they are not so weak as to part with it to others, betides they have never had more than

166

a bare sufficiency, often expended before their hunting season was near over.

If therefore they should be denied ammunition it would immediately confirm them in the sentiments which greatly contributed to produce the defection of the rest, and would counteract all my endeavours to remove that too general opinion for the suspecting their sincerity would make them dangerous enemies, and of this I have had repeated experience.

I wrote you pretty fully in mine of 24th by which you will see the difficulties which may arise in punishing the *Chenassios* and the advantages which will attend our turning our arms against the rest of our enemies, which will equally answer the important purpose of giving them a just idea of our abilities and resentment.

As I am well acquainted with the inclinations of the friendly Indians I know the lengths they are to be trusted on the article of ammunition, of which I am certain they will make no bad use. It is an article so hard to be procured here, that I have not had it in my power to give them what they flood in ye greatest need of, and the trade being now over they can have little if any from that quarter, although I must confess the danger they have run from the attachment to which we have hitherto own the safety of these parts sufficiently merits such a return from us as will shew them that they are not losers by their fidelity.

From what I have heard from the Senecas, as well as from the good disposition of the rest, I should be induced to hope that that these frontiers might enjoy a state of tranquillity, at least for a time, but as this must be very uncertain (especially if the peace offered by the Senecas is not accepted of), I apprehend the two companies for these frontiers may not be amiss but I fear they cannot be easily raised at this time, as I have offered the warrants to several who declined accepting of them, by reason of the lowness of the officer's pay, and the bounty now offered in Albany, &c. for raising men for other service. Be assured I shall give you immediate notice in case there appears a prospect for compleating them, as well as give you any further intelligence which may come to my knowledge worthy your information, and I have a particular pleasure in assuring you how much I am,

Dr Sir, &c.,

[*MSS. of Sir William Johnson, 8*]
[Copy.]

To his Excellency Thomas Gage, Commander-in-Chief of His Majesty's Forces in America, &c. &c. May it please your Excellency as we conceive some hopes from the accounts we have from Detroit of having a peace with the Indians in the spring, and as your Excellency has the ordering of everything on the continent, knowing your inclination of serving every person to the utmost of your power, and your Excellency's desire strictly to adhere to the good of His Majesty's Subjects, we humbly beg leave to petition your Excellency and represent to you the misfortunes we have laboured under from the plunder that was made by the Indians at the time that the forts were surprised, and to hint to you what we think may be to our private advantage without any detriment to the nation and wherein our losses may be in some measure repaid without any retardment to the public peace. According to the custom of trading several Indian Nations having taken up goods upon credit to a very considerable amount, and are all of them capable of making payment for the same, some of them having heard nothing of the Indian War had brought their peltries to discharge their debts, but on seeing the distress we were in their good intentions were laid aside and they took a part with our enemies. These are the Indians who have been most distressed during the time the war has continued, and we hear are most desirous of bringing things to an end. The Ottawas, the Chippewas, the Miamis, the Pouteoutamis, Saguinaw, Iroquis, &c. with all the Indians who trade on Lake Superior. If your Excellency thinks proper, when they propose terms of peace, to mention to them to pay their debts, if your Excellency thinks it will be no detriment to the public good it will make us some retaliation for the excessive losses we have sustained, will put us again on a good footing for trade and will relieve from great distress your Excellency's petitioners, and most dutiful and obedient servants

Signed,    Ja's Howard,              Hen'y Bostwick,
           Jno. Chinn,               Forrest Outres,
           Edwd Chinn,               Gorsen Levy,
           James Stanly Goddard,     Holmes and Memsen.
Dated 30th December 1763.

## LETTER FROM T. DE COUAGNE TO SIR WILLIAM JOHNSON.
### [*MSS. of Sir William Johnson, 8*]

Sir:

I have the honour to acquaint you on the 20th of November I got hear from the Seneke Castles the chiefs promised me that they would send the horses here. The Seneke Indians comes in evry day, brings in bevers and vennison and behaves very well, as also the Missisagues. I have no more to add, but if anything happen shall inform you, so conclude.

Your most humble servant to command.

De Couagne.

Niagara, January 4th, 1764.

## LETTER FROM SIR WM. JOHNSON TO LIEUT. GOV. COLDEN.
### [*MSS. of Sir William Johnson, 8*]

Johnson Hall, January 12th, 1764.

Dear Sir:

A great indisposition under which I have laboured for several days, and from which I am not yet recovered, prevented my answering your favour of the 28th *ult.* sooner.

In my letter of the 30th *ult.* I gave you my sentiments on the reasons which induced the Indians to propose an accommodation, as also concerning the article of ammunition, representing that none received any but those on whose confidence I might perfectly rely and to whom a refusal might prove of dangerous consequence, and that even the trifle of ammunition which they received was too little and too much valued by them to part with. In my letter of the 24th *ult.* I acquainted you with the occasion of my having been visited by the Five Nations accompanied by some Seneca deputies.

Last week arrived here several of the Senecas on the same errand as before, whom I acquainted that I was not as yet authorized to treat with them on terms of peace, they were followed by the Five Nations amounting to near 300, who came to repeat their offers of taking such steps against our enemies as I should direct, to which I have assured them in the best manner I could. But these Senecas having come contrary to my desire and not being desirous to give any satisfaction farther than a promise of assisting us against the rest, I have accordingly dismissed them until I hear from General Gage. I however apprehended a white man now amongst them, and who was formerly delivered up but went back to the Indians and has had as I am informed the treachery to act against us in the late operations of our enemies particularly at Niagara Carrying Place, I shall therefore commit him to jail.

The generality of the people have certainly great reason to be irritated against the Indians, and I am glad to find such a spirit of alertness as you express amongst them, though I fear they will not find it an easy matter to punish those who really deserve it, and the falling upon those yet our friends and who are consequently not aware of any such design, would I apprehend be very imprudent as well as disagreeable to you since it must inevitably involve us in a general quarrel.

The general thirst for revenge so justly raised amongst our people may without proper instructions direct itself to a wrong quarter as was lately the case in *Pensilvania*, to prevent which, as well as to promote the success of all the hearty volunteers I must observe that the greatest part of our enemies are removed a great way up the Cayuga or Tohicon [?] Branch of *Susquehanna*. Those of *Wawiloosin* (our friends) are gone chiefly to Philadelphia and the rest are removed to *Chughnot* on the *Susquehanna*, so that our enemies chiefly reside from Diaoga[11] up that branch, *viz. Singsink, Pepiquaghquey*, &c.

The meeting of these our enemies is very uncertain, as they have not made any long residence at any place since the commencement of hostilities, but the Indians of Canestio, a village between Chenussio and Fort Augusta, who are chiefly *renegadoes* of profligate fellows from several nations, and who murdered the two traders in November 1762, [12] are very proper subjects of our resentment and have been principals in carrying on hostilities.

I heartily wish that whatever party goes out, may be able to strike such a blow as will give the Indians in general a good

---

11. Tioga.
12. Upon learning of these murders Sir William Johnson sent up Lieut. Johnson to attend a meeting called at Onondaga to insist on the immediate apprehension of the guilty parties, but the Upper Nations did not attend and the rest of the Indians could do nothing but promise that if the Senecas did not apprehend the murderers they would themselves go in quest of them—*Letters of Sir William Johnson to Lieut. Colonel Wm. Eyre and Gov. Monckton.*

opinion of our abilities, but to give any hopes of success in my opinion it will be necessary that they should at least consist of 400 men, and those expert and well qualified for the service, acquainted with the woods and furnished with snow shoes and all other necessary articles. The distressing and annoying the enemy in winter if well conducted must prove very useful. I am now preparing some parties of trusty Indians for that purpose of which I hope the general will approve.

As the trade by reason of the war hath been at an end for some time I apprehend it will not be thought advisable to grant any passes till matters are better settled, whenever that may happen I am humbly of opinion that you will judge it necessary the traders should give security for their fair dealings, and also be permitted to trade at the principal posts only, as *Fort Stanwix, Ontario, Niagara, &c.* At these posts they will be in the most security and their conduct can be best enquired into, which if justly blameable and so represented by the commanding officer they may forfeit their recognizance, for the indulging them in a liberty of trading in the Indian's country or at their castles, will always produce complaints from the latter, of frauds and extortion, as well as render the traders liable to be murdered, and their effects seized on any future quarrel which may happen.

With some difficulty I have got persons to accept of the warrants for raising the two companies for the security of this frontier, and I am just now informed they are almost compleated with good men. I shall accordingly have them mustered and report to you thereon.

As Lt. Johnson, who by His Majesty's Proclamation is entitled to a grant of land, is desirous to know the limits within which you consider the same may be granted, I must request the favour of your informing me on that head, also your directions concerning the steps he is to take therein and whether he is entitled to his share as captain of the provincials in 1758, or is to abide by his title as Lieut, of the Independent Companies.

I am with very perfect esteem, &c.

P. S. I have great reason to apprehend that many mercenary persons inhabiting along the river sell ammunition and other articles to the Senecas, I could heartily wish you could interpose your authority to prevent the like for the future.

LETTER FROM SIR WILLIAM JOHNSON TO THE COMMANDING
OFFICERS OF THE NEW YORK PROVINCIALS AT GERMAN FLATS.
[*MSS. of Sir William Johnson, 8*]

Johnson Hall, January 19th, 1764.

Sir:

As some deputies from the Senecas, our enemies, who have
been here with a message from their nation to me, are now returning home and being probably not so well disposed as they
pretend, may be induced to do some mischief at or about the
German Flatts, these are therefore to desire you will be sufficiently on your guard to prevent them, and in case they should
attempt injury the persons or properties of the inhabitants or
the troops under your command, you will immediately seize
upon them (taking care that none escape) and send them down
prisoners to Albany, under a strong guard, sufficient to prevent
them from getting off.

In case you find it necessary to take this step it will require the
utmost precaution to be taken to prevent the greater part of
them from escaping, which will in a great measure defeat the
design proposed by making them prisoners.

I am Sir your most humble servant.

P. S. The inhabitants will enable you to distinguish the Senecas,
who are upwards of 20, but it will not be prudent to mention
my name as the occasion of their being apprehended at this
juncture. Should any of the inhabitants sell them any ammunition, clothing or other necessaries, you will immediately give
me notice thereof, and also prevent them for the future from
trading with any Indians who have been in arms against the
English.

LETTER FROM JOHN STUART TO SIR WILLIAM JOHNSON.
[*MSS. of Sir William Johnson, 8*]

Charles Town, 16th January, 1764.

Sir:

Since my last of 10th December I have not had the pleasure of
hearing from you. I have not as yet received any information
about the Tuscarora Indians, as soon as I do, you may depend on
its being communicated to you.

On the 24th *ultimo* 14 of our back settlers upon Long Cane
River were murdered, and we have since found out by seven

Creeks, who for some years past resided in the Cherokee Nation. The Creeks have sent me a talk upon the occasion and disclaim the murder and the murderers, who say they, the Cherokees ought to kill to show their innocence. I have sent off talks to all the nations within my district, but I must acquaint you that in this department every governor acts as if he were sole agent, they will hardly be directed by each other and do not consult me, so that it is odds but we counteract each other; this requires some regulation.

By next opportunity I will write you fully, it being my intention to keep you regularly informed of the occurrences within the department.

> I am with great respect,
> Sir, your most obedient
> Humble Servant,
> John Stuart.

## LETTER FROM SIR WM. JOHNSON TO LIEUT. GOV. PENN.
### [*MSS. of Sir William Johnson, 8*]

Johnson Hall, January 20th, 1764.

Sir:

I had the favour of your letter of the 31st *ult.* and fifth of this inst., together with the enclosures, and I heartily congratulate you on your arrival to your government, wishing that your Appointment may prove to your entire satisfaction.

The steps you have taken to discover those rash offenders were certainly very judicious as well as highly necessary and I am hopeful they may be attended with success for bringing them to justice.

I apprehend that after their first offence in murdering the six indians at Conestoga their mistaken resentment would have ended, and that first act was sufficient to create much uneasiness amongst all the Indians, but their last public insult to the laws and the government itself certainly demands the most strict enquiry as well as the severest punishment.

You may be assured I shall use every argument with the Six Nations, for removing the unfavourable ideas which they must certainly entertain of such a proceeding, as well as to satisfy them that your government highly disapproves of it and will severely punish the offenders, but I am aware of their sentiments on the subject and [am] greatly apprehensive it will stagger the affections of the five hitherto well affected nations, who consider the Indians of your government as connected with them and under their protection, and as the murdered have been all along peaceably inclined, the friendly Indians in these parts may be induced to doubt our faith and sincerity toward themselves from the unhappy fate of our late friends in Pennsilvania, which will cause them to expect the same treatment whenever it is in our power to destroy them. This I fear may greatly check the ardour they have lately expressed to me of assisting us against our enemies and even spirit up many to obtain revenge within your government.

The threats which the riotous parties have since thrown out, that they would destroy the Indians in the neighbourhood and under the protection of Philadelphia, favours so much of madness that I cannot account for them. Your gratifying the Indians request thereon of coming to me must therefore appear pleasing to them, but I have just received a letter from Lieut. Gov. Colden informing me that the council "have advised him not to admit them into this province." This will probably prevent me from seeing them, and I heartily wish their return back may not expose them to fresh insults, which would certainly occasion a general defection.

Several deputies from the enemy Senecas have been lately with me here, making some friendly offers of peace, but I am convinced that nothing but a good treatment accompanied with occasional favours will ever ensure a lasting peace from the jealous sentiments which our enemies entertain of the English and the presents the French have accustomed them to, for the toleration the Indians afforded them in their country insomuch that any future neglect on our parts will immediately produce a discontent and apprehension of our designs which will inevitably occasion a renewal of hostilities, so that a Peace made with these people without proper subsequent steps to remove these jealousies and establish a good opinion with the Indians is always liable to be violated to the great detriment of trade and the certain destruction of the Frontier inhabitants with their dwellings, and the expense in which the Crown must be involved to suppress such devastations will certainly amount to a much greater sum (independent of the loss the provinces must

174

sustain) than would conciliate the affections of the Indians and enable us to extend our settlements and trade with the utmost security.

I heartily wish that the law you have proposed may be agreed to by the *assembly*, as it appears to me highly necessary and essential as well to the credit as the safety of the province.

I am with great esteem

Sir, your most obedient humble servant.

## LETTER FROM SIR WM. JOHNSON TO LIEUT. COL. EYRE.
[*MSS. of Sir William Johnson, 8*]

Johnson Hall, January 29th, 1764.

Dear Sir:

I thank you for your interesting letter of the 7th inst. which I would have sooner answered but for the business in which I have been engaged for this fortnight past with a large number of the Five Nations and some Seneca deputies.

It would have given me much pleasure to have seen you on your return from *Niagara*. I dispatched a letter in answer to yours, with directions that it might be left at *Ontario* till you came back, which I hope you received although I understand you did not return by that post.

I cannot but coincide in opinion with you on the greatest part of what you have mentioned on Indian affairs, and I could wish for the good of the public that every person had been of the same way of thinking, which might have proved a means of preventing the many losses we have lately felt.

The causes to which the defection of the Indians may be attributed are:

First. Their jealousy of our growing power, and occupancy of the outposts where they neither met with the same treatment nor reaped any of the advantages which they enjoyed in the time of the French.

Secondly. The reports industriously propagated by many of the French, tending to set our designs in the most odious light and to represent the Indians as being on the brink of being enslaved.

It will not appear extraordinary that the French who had purchased the Indian's favour at a high price should obtain credit from such a representation, especially when there were but too many concurring circumstances to strengthen the belief of a people naturally credulous and jealous of their liberties. The indians began with remonstrances, represented many grievances and demanded redress. Their complaints I communicated from time to time with my sentiments and apprehensions thereon, but the inconsiderable opinion too universally entertained, of their small power and abilities occasioned it to be treated with neglect.

To particularize all their complaints would exceed the bounds of a letter; it will be sufficient to observe that I declared it as my opinion that the Indians would not be totally neglected, but that (after redress of their grievances) we should cultivate to the utmost of our power a good understanding with them, at least until we became more formidable and our frontiers better established, and this I thought we could effect at an expense infinitely less than any other method, and on principles the best adapted for securing peace, promoting trade and encreasing our frontiers.

The expense, difficulty and dangers attending other expedients, the stagnation of trade, destruction of our posts and frontiers, and the small advantages to be gained by a war with us, are now obvious to most people, and are so well represented in your letter that they need not to be enlarged upon.

The difficulty and even impossibility of securing our communications or maintaining our outposts contrary to the indians' inclinations is very clear to me, but I am pretty certain we can purchase all these advantages and secure their inclinations by a proper treatment which will gain us a sufficient credit with them, and awe of this country, as it will remove all their prejudices and which no other steps can effect. The inland small posts don't appear to me very necessary, they are too great a temptation to the Indians whenever they are induced to quarrel, and from their distance and difficulty of obtaining succours must always fall into their hands.

The same reasons induce me to think, that the persons and property of traders would be safe amongst them, for whilst there are any French there, they will certainly through jealousy promote a quarrel, and even were there none there the expense of transporting goods is so great, that they must sell at a price which would not be agreeable to the Indians as well as be guilty of many frauds not in the power of an officer to discover or prevent. Whereas the Indians (who think little of going a great way to purchase necessaries) would find them cheaper at our large posts, and the traders would be less exposed to risk.

Wherever we can have a good communication by water, we might tolerably well maintain posts, and if some small vessels are kept up on Lake Erie, Detroit or even Michilimackinac might be kept up, the latter being well situated for drawing down the northern furs.

After all that can be said, we shall be liable to many broils, till the French inhabitants and Jesuits are removed, the latter (being no longer a Society in France) we might very well appropriate their lands to His Majesty's use. I dare say they would be sufficient to endow a *Bishopric* in Canada, and for good missionaries, and I imagine an Episcopal Foundation in that country would greatly contribute to bring over the French, and make good subjects of them in time.

The late offers of peace made by some of the nations has been greatly promoted by the attachment the *Five Nations, Indians of Canada,* &c. have manifested during the course of the war, which makes our enemies dread they will accompany our troops against them in the spring, for they have much more reason to fear Indians than the best troops in the world.

Indeed the before-mentioned nations have made me so many offers of service that I have no doubt of their sincerity, and I am now sending out a considerable party of *Oneidas* and *Tuscaroras* who I hope will greatly distress our enemies, as well as convince them that we are not without *allies* of their own fort. This will likewise contribute to disunite them, a circumstance too important to be neglected.

Whenever the present unhappy trouble shall be ended by an accommodation, I trust such measures will be taken at home as may ensure a lasting peace to the northern colonies, on which subject I have lately received some letters from the *Lords of Trade* expressing His Majesty's favourable sentiments and those of their lordships concerning my late representations.

I am heartily sorry to hear that the animosities in England have not subsided, as such party differences must greatly prejudice public affairs and tend to divert the attention of the ministry from many important objects of public concern.

## LETTER FROM JOHN R. HANSEN TO SIR WM. JOHNSON.

[*MSS. of Sir William Johnson, 8*]

Schoharie, Capt. Thos. Eckkers,
February 1st, 1764.

Honoured Sir:

After Lt. Coll. Van Derhyden's mustering my men, I immediately marched for this place where I arrived with my men 28th of January, and have proceeded pursuant to your order in getting the men quartered in the most convenient manner with the advice of the justices and captains of Militia.

I have since sent one of my lieut's to the uppermost part of *Scohare* with a command of sixteen men, which was judged most necessary, whom I have ordered to be stationed in the best manner the situation of that part would permit off.

The remainder 34 men I have with advice quartered within a mile hereabout, if there should be any occasion to send out scouting parties there's no possibility of getting any snow shoes, at this place, if they should be wanted.

I am, Honoured Sir,
Yours at Command,
John R. Hansen.

To the Honourable Sir Wm. Johnson, Bart.

## EXTRACT FROM A LETTER FROM FERRALL WADE TO SIR WILLIAM JOHNSON.

[*MSS. of Sir William Johnson, 8*]

Philadelphia February 6th, 1764.

Sir:

Your favour of the 5th January was handed me a few days ago, which I should have answered before now but being in continual alarms on account of a number of people coming from the frontiers in arms with an intent to murder all the Indians in this city and under the protection of this government, but the opposition they met with by most part of the inhabitants being in a posture of defence obliged them to return as they came, excepting two, which was appointed to lay some grievances before the government,

# LETTER FROM SIR WILLIAM JOHNSON TO GEN. BURTON.

[*MSS. of Sir William Johnson, 8.*]

Johnson Hall, February 11th, 1764.

Sir:

Capt. Claus, my Deputy for Canada will deliver you this, as I would not send him to this duty without doing myself the pleasure of writing you, as well as giving you some account of the present state of affairs in this quarter.

The Indians of five out of the Six Nations who from the commencement of the present Indian war have shewn great zeal and attachment towards the English have thereby preserved these Frontiers and the importantant communication to Ontario, both of which must have inevitably fallen but for their fidelity.

As I am now impowered to comply with their request of going upon service, I have accordingly equipped a party of near 200 indians accompanied by several Indian officers, &c. who marched two days ago (notwithstanding the snow is here three feet deep) against the Delawares, Shawanese and others our enemies in that quarter, and I have great hopes that their operations will be attended with success, as it must appear evident that they are the best calculated to go in quest of one another, and that the engaging them as parties in the war, will effectually create a division among them which will prove a great check to their power hereafter.

As the Indians of Canada have likewise acted a very good part and made me offers of service when here last year, I shall likewise put their zeal to a trial, nothing doubting but it must strike a great damp on the spirits of our (hitherto elated) enemies, when they see the strength of our alliances and that they are liable to be attacked on all sides even by their own sort, which will greatly contribute to the success of the approaching campaign, and make our enemies very cautious how they violate a peace hereafter with a people who can employ one nation against another.

Capt. Claus will give you any further particulars necessary for your information on the present posture of affairs in the indian department.

I sincerely wish you an easy and agreeable Government and remain with much esteem,                           Sir, &c.

Hon. Sir:

My son returned home the 1st inst, when I was honoured with your warrant, instructions and favour of the 3rd January. I was extremely sorry to hear of your indisposition and sincerely hope you had a speedy recovery.

I make no doubt but my son at that time informed you of the conduct of the frontier inhabitants of this province (*See note following this letter*) who murdered six Connistogo Indians at their town near Lancaster, being all that were at home at that time except two boys who made their escape from them. The remaining part fourteen in number, women and children, being dispersed through the country were seized by the sheriff and magistrates of the county and confined in the workhouse of Lancaster, in order to guard them, but upon the back inhabitants receiving information of this, they again assembled themselves in a body and came down armed to Lancaster, broke open the workhouse and in a most inhuman manner butchered the whole, sparing neither women or children, an action I look upon not inferior to any of the cruelties committed by the savages since the commencement of the late or present war. As to my knowledge these Indians have lived all their lives within eight miles of Lancaster, in peace and quietness with their neighbours, and I do not believe were ever concerned against us.

The government made some faint efforts to find the heads of these people, which only encourage their impudence, as I am informed a few days ago, to the number of three hundred assembled themselves in arms and came down to Philadelphia in order to cut off some Indians the government have here, but upon some promises being made them by the government, they have dissuaded them from murdering those in Philadelphia and they are returned home again, and they now carry things to great length as to threaten the lives of sundry private people who have not agreed with them in opinions but condemned this as a most detestable murder, and not only contrary to the laws of government but Christianity, and everything that ought to distinguish us from savages, as this leaves us no room to find fault with their killing our innocent people in cold blood, as they may now say we are satiated in the same manner on them. I should be far from espousing their cause did I not think they were innocent, as no person has suffered more by the savages than I have done, and I should have thought the people who have thus behaved more excusable if they had cut off in Philadelphia maintained at the public expense, as there is some reason to believe that some of these have acted against us. But the others in a manner were become white people, and expected the same protection from us. I thought proper to acquaint your honour with this affair, as you might perhaps want to acquaint the Indians with the true circumstances relating to it.

My son presents his compliments to your Honour and begs if you have not sent a warrant for his account that you would be kind enough to forward one as soon as it may be convenient to you and if it likewise suits your conveniency I should be glad your Honour would accompany it with one to me for some money, as I am really at present in necessity.

I have nothing further to add, but that I am with greatest respect, your Honour's most obedient and very humble Servant,

*Thomas M:Kee*

*Note*: The disorders here alluded to have been known in history as the Paxton Riots, from having originated in the little town of Paxton on the East Bank of the Susquehanna, a place which had been burned, and many of its inhabitants butchered in 1755. A band of Rangers had been formed here under the auspices of the Rev. John Elder, under the command of Matthew Smith. The irritation of feeling towards the domesticated Indians on the Susquehanna, in consequence of some murders by unknown parties, led the government to gather the Moravian Indian converts of Nain, and Wecquetank near the Lehigh, and of Wyalufing near Wyoming, numbering about 140 persons, to Philadelphia for protection.

It required all its strength to protect the defenceless and peaceful Indians from the ferocious abuse of the excited frontiermen, and as they passed on their way to the asylum provided they were everywhere threatened, and at German town came nigh being murdered by the mob that followed them. They were

181

marched to the barracks but the soldiers refused to receive them and boldly set the governor's orders at defiance. After standing several hours before the barracks surrounded by the insulting mob, they were marched down the Street and conducted to Providence Island below the city, where buildings were hastily prepared for them by the Quakers.

About the middle of December, 1763, it was reported to Smith, leader of the Paxton Rangers, that an indian who had committed some depredations, had been traced to Canestoga, a small Iroquois settlement near the Susquehanna, and not far from Lancaster. Without waiting for a confirmation of the story or its circumstances, a resolution was at once formed, with the consequences detailed in the above letter. Mr. Elder used all his influence to divert his neighbours from their barbarous purpose, as they were about to set out for Lancaster, but with the fury of demons they rushed forward on their errand of blood. breaking into the jail on the 27th of December, they murdered fourteen men, women and children.

Before the magistrates and citizens could be rallied the white savages were gone, and nothing remained to be done but to give decent burial to the mangled and mutilated remains of these friendly natives. The news of this outrage quickly spread through the country and aroused the Quakers in particular to loud and bitter denunciations of the act. The memory of Indian murders, still fresh throughout the frontier counties, led many to sympathize with the rioters, to which they were rather instigated than deterred by the indiscriminate and sweeping abuse of the Quakers, which included not only the rioters themselves, but the whole Presbyterian Sect. Emboldened by this sentiment, the guilty parties openly proclaimed their achievement as in the highest degree meritorious, defended it by reason and scripture, and defied the civil authorities in any attempt at punishment.

They even went further, and reeking with the blood of the passive victims of their fury, they resolved to complete the work of death upon the Moravian Indians gathered at Philadelphia. An armed mob marched towards that city at about the last of December, with the avowed purpose of murder, if not of overturning the government and expelling the Quakers, whose sympathies with the Indians were bitterly denounced and whose motives were unscrupulously impugned. At midnight on the 4th of January, the authorities, hearing of the approach of this party, hastily marched the Indians through the streets, and having been supplied by their friends with a few necessaries, they were escorted to Trenton, and from thence to Amboy, with the view of sending them to the protection of Sir William Johnson; but before notifying either him or the Government of New York of this intention or asking permission.

At Amboy they were met by a positive order from the Governor of New York, forbidding their entrance into that province, and soon after from the Governor of New Jersey, requiring them to leave the territory of that province. They were marched back to Philadelphia under a guard of Regulars, and quartered in the barracks where the soldiers, conquered by the meek endurance and patient suffering of the Indians, received them. The Paxton Boys hearing of the return of their victims, rallied in great numbers, the city was thrown into uproar, and for several days it was the scene of intense excitement, and active preparation for defence.

The advance of the insurgents was checked by this show of refinance, and the affair finally ended in negotiation. The humane and sagacious Sir William Johnson, perceiving the perils that would attend the march of these Indians through the interior, upon application immediately devised a plan for their removal from Amboy to Albany, and their support among his friendly Indians until the tumult was over. The victims of these riots, shut up in their barracks, suffered dreadfully from the small-pox, which destroyed a third of their number. In about a year after their arrival, quiet having been restored in the back settlements, and peace with all the northern tribes, these converts were allowed to return with their missionaries to their wafted fields, and the sites of their burned cabins, on the banks of the Susquehanna.

The Government was too sensible of the exasperated feeling which prevailed in the interior to attempt any arrests until nearly eight years after, when Lazarus Stewart was apprehended on a charge of murdering the Indians at Conestoga.

Learning that his trial was to come off in Philadelphia, where conviction would have been certain, he broke jail, called a number of old associates around him, and setting the Provincial

Government of Pennsylvania at defiance, withdrew to Wyoming and joined the Connecticut settlers in that valley. It is not improbable that the desolation of that settlement by the Indians and their Tory companions in the revolution, a few years after, may have had some connection with their knowledge of the retreat of the former butchers of their kindred. (*Parkman's Pontiac; Loskiel; Hazard's Pa. Register; Rupp's York and Lancaster; Sparks's Franklin.*)

PART OF A LETTER FROM COLONEL BRADSTREET
TO GENERAL AMHERST.
[*Bradstreet and Amherst MSS., p. 146.*]

Albany, 20th Feb. 1764.

Dear Sir:

Your Excellency's favour of the 13th instant was delivered me yesterday. The boats for 2000 men only have long since been built and I directly stopt building any more untill your farther Directions.

To six the number of carriages [at] the Carrying Place at Niagara, it will be necessary to know whether you would have all the provisions, stores, &c. transported across before the troops proceed to any other service, and what number of days you would have taken up on that service only. General Amherst talked to me of leaving 600 men at the post to the westward of Niagara with 18 month provisions; if that is still to be the case, and our whole numbers amount to no more than 2000, it will require about 6000 barrells (for your Ex. knows we should not count by ounces but give a proper allowance for the kind of service) which will take 50 ox carts 15 days to carry it a cross at a full load of 8 barrells each trip, exclusive of everything for the vessels and posts to be established; but if accidents, which we certainly must expect from the distance the cattle have to go and the badness of great part of the road, of which Major Moncrief can inform you, the time required would be much longer.

As for the boats I shall begin to provide as many horses and carriages as shall be sufficient to carrying them over with the baggage of troops in proportion to the ox carts. By this your Excellency sees it is most probable the transportation at Niagara will last three weeks at least; a long time indeed, but it

184

would be impertinent in me to urge to one so well informed as you are of their treachery and good sense of the savages the absolute necessity of entering this inland country with a dispatch hitherto thought by them impracticable in us, and more particularly so should our strength fall so prodigiously short of the threats denounced against them and the pains taken to let them know it and therefore doubt not you will think it necessary to direct me to augment the number of carriages to do the work in the number of days you shall judge we ought to remain on that carrying place.

I take it for granted I must provide teamsters and waggons, but in this I shall not act untill I receive your Excellency's directions upon it.

I hope Gov. Murray [13] will not disappoint you, and I also hope the Eastern assemblys will think no credit ought to be given to an Indian peace but what comes to their . . . . directly from you, which I am persuaded they need not expect this spring.

## Letter from Henry Monture, Wm. Hare and John Johnston to Sir William Johnson.

[*MSS. of Sir William Johnson, 8*]

Kaunawau Kohare, Feb. 21, 1764.

Sir William:

Sir: The bearer hereof please to deliver eight dollars for which we war forced to do for the good of the service, for a hog for the warriours to make a feast as we could not do any otherwase as'tha said it was a customary thing and they hope Sir William would not make any differance now, and please to send paper and sealing wax up to their priest as I have used some of his paper and wax. A quire and stick of sealing wax. Please to send no more, but we remain

Your humble servants

Henry Monture,
William Hare,
John Johnston.

---

13. James Murray Had been appointed Governor of Canada on the 21st of November previous. He remained in office until June, 1766.

THE SAME TO THE SAME.
[*MSS. of Sir William Johnson, 7*]
Kuana Wahohare, Feb. 21, 1764.

Sir William:

After our respects to you we must inform you of the reason of our detainment here, at this place, we being in great confusion here ever since our arrival for reason why, because one Conokuiafi and one big Nichols of Oneida hast sent two belts through the Six Nations to the Sinackess to tell them of all our designs and force this castle to likewise comply with their evil purposes, and one young warrior called Wyyautaukeen from old Oneida has said he would very soon scalp some white people and then immediately fly to the Six Nations, and there is one of the head warriors called Cut the Pumpkin has sent word he will meet us at Teurogoa to try what we are, and he wishes to see Jacob the Mikouder [14] of Stockbridge as he is so long a coming when he could have the impudence to pretend to withstand him.

Last evening we received yours dated the 12th instant wherein we acquainted the Indians your giving your love to theire warriors and chiefs and then your desire of their exciting themselves in this affair, depending which should never be forgot, and would redound unto their credit hereafter, and your desire of our pushing on and not delaying our time in things of no consequence or moment, and likewise the hearty wishes of all the governors and chiefs of the country and prayer of all good people. The answer of the Indians to your letter: friend and loving brother Wawaukaugee, we return you thanks for your good will and complement to us and likewise the complement of the governors and chiefs. We should have been set out before had it not been for them belts sent by Conokgorasse and Nichols as we had reasons to think what would be the consequences that might likely attend us and this body of our enemy coming down against us, for which reasons brother, we must acquaint you that yesterday our Chief Warrior Cowaha set out for Onandaug in order to see if the Upper Nations would come down at the request of them belts and he to try his best to alter there minds and send them back, and at his return they imagen the

---

14. Mohegan.

whole party will joyn us.

However tomorrow morning early we set [out] from this on our march for Auqquage and what warriors have a mind to joyn us to proceed and the rest to follow us as soon as Gowaha returns. These Indians desire you would send for these fellows to know the meaning of their sending this belt and let some of these Indians come down also along with them that he may hear what they have to say for themselves. The aforesaid Cut the Pumpkin sent word by Capt. Monture to come along as he would be very glad to see him, and we hope Sir William will hurry all of them that is behind to push up to Auqquage to joyn us so as in case of a retreat that we will be able to push on them again and indeavour to rout them. The Indians of this castle request of Sir William that you would be so good as to supply their women with provisions if required at Fort Stanwix in a reasonable manner and that what few men there is left accordingly you will supply them with fire arms and ammunition, and such things as they will be short of in case of an attack.

No more at present, but our advice to you, to be on your guard in and on every part of the Mohawk River, Schohary, Stone Rauby and Cherry Vally. We remain your sincear and ever devoted humble servants till death.

Henry Monture,
William Hare,
John Johnston.

LETTER FROM ROBERT ME KEEN[15] TO SIR WM. JOHNSON.
[*MSS. of Sir William Johnson, 8*]

Cherry Valley, February 25th, 1764.

Sir:

I have thought proper to acquaint you with the present state of my company and have the pleasure to acquaint you that they are all in a good state and in high spirits.

I have kept a regular guard at Capt. Wells[16] ever since I arrived

---

15. Captain Mckean resided at Cherry Valley and early in 1776 raised a company of Rangers for the protection of that place. He was an enterprising and fearless partisan, and was mortally wounded in the summer of 1781 in an expedition against a Tory band in the border of Schoharie Co.—*Campbell's Tryon Co.*

16. Mr. Robert Wells and his family perished in the massacre of Cherry Valley, Nov. 11, 1778. The family consisted of himself, his mother and wife, and four children, his brother and sister and three domestics, not one of them (Continued next page.)

at this settlement, and reviews my men every week and has them stationed in the best manner I could for the protection of this settlement.

I should be glad if your Honour would let me know if it is necessary to send a monthly Return to the Lt. Governor.

I am Sir your most humble servant

*Robert McKeen*

P. S. In case of an alarm my men is always in readiness to assemble at the place appointed for an alarm post.

A monthly return of Captain Robert McKeans Company of Provincials now lying at Cherry Valley, February 25th, 1764.

Present for Duty.

| | |
|---|---|
| Captain, | 1 |
| Lieutenants, | 2 |
| Rank and File, | 50 |
| Total, | 53 |

Robert Mckeen, Capt.

LETTER FROM SIR WM. JOHNSON TO GOV. JOHN PENN.
[*MSS. of Sir William Johnson, 8*

Johnson Hall, February 27th, 1764.

Sir:

The express delivered me your favour of the 7th last night concerning the persecuted Indians now in Philadelphia. The rancours with which they have been pursued by the rioters is as extraordinary as it may be dangerous to the public, and least their designs might be put in execution I cannot but approve of your proposal of sending them hither, for should they fall a sacrifice to unjust resentment it must certainly occasion a breach with all the friend Indians.

The sending them through the back parts of the country at this time might subject them to the insults of the rioters, neither would it be practicable. I think the safest and best way would be, what you propose of sending them by water from Amboy to Albany, after which I shall dispose of them (although it will

escaped excepting John, one of the children, who happened to be absent at school at Schenectady. A Tory boasted that he killed Mr. Wells while at prayer.—*Campbell's Tryon Co.*

bring some expense on the Crown) amongst the friend Indians whilst the present ferment continues. I shall accordingly write immediately to Governor Colden, and represent the necessity of removing these indians for a time, as highly essential to our interests and the public safety, and I shall request the governor in case the government has no objection to their coming to give you notice that no time may be lost.

I am Sir your most obedient and most humble servant To the Honourable Governor Penn.

## LETTER FROM SIR WM. JOHNSON TO LIEUT. GOV. COLDEN.
### [MSS. of Sir William Johnson, 8]

Johnson Hall, February 28th, 1764.

Dear Sir:

I have just received your favour of the 17th inst. as also a letter pr express from Governor Penn representing the late audacious attempts of the rioters to murder the Indians under the protection of Philadelphia, as also his apprehensions concerning their future safety there, on which account he proposes sending them by land through his government or else by water from Amboy to Albany. The former may subject them to too many insults and hazards, and as I am well satisfied that should these Indians or any of them fall a sacrifice after what has already happened, it will prove highly prejudicial to our affairs as well as dangerous to the public security, I cannot avoid recommending the proposal of transporting them by water to Albany, after which I shall dispose of them amongst the Indians here till matters are accommodated. If it is judged advisable a line from you to Governor Penn will enable him to take the necessary steps without loss of time.

Whenever anything farther transpires relative to Mr. Lydius, [17]

---

17. Among the extravagant grants of land made by Governor Fletcher which have rendered his name a synonym for corruption, and occasioned among other things his recall and disgrace, was that of a tract covering eight hundred and forty square miles in the present County of Washington, N.Y. and the southern part of Vermont. This tract was granted Sept. 3, 1696, to the Rev. Godfredius Dellius, Minister at Albany, for the annual rent of one raccoon skin, payable annually, on the feast day of the Annunciation, at the City of New York. The grant was annulled by the General Assembly of the Colony, May 12, 1699, but Dellius denied the authority of that body, and continued to regard the claim as valid. He soon after sold his claim in Holland to the Rev. John Lydius, his successor (Continued next page.)

I shall let you know it. I am told that one of his sons has been lately through the country in company of a justice of the peace to obtain affidavits for what purpose I know not, but probably in support of his claims.

*Isle la Motte* [18] is supposed to be to the southward of the 45th degree of latitude, but perhaps on future observations it may appear in the *Quebec* Government. The lands above the Great Falls on Otter Creek may be good though a good deal out of the way for small a Tract.[19] There is a small piece of land within about three miles of Lake George, on the road leading from Fort Edward. Please to inform me whether it can be granted, but I find at the back of my patent here and at ten or twelve miles from the river, a small piece which is an intervale and I should be greatly obliged to you if you would grant it, on the Indians consenting thereto. Lieut. Johnson [20] will have a certificate shortly from Gen. Gage as you desire.

There are now several parties marched against the enemy, [21] one of these amounts to about 200 Indians, many more are collecting to follow them and my whole time is occupied in conferences, in fitting out parties, &c. The Indians will not be discouraged by the rigors of the season. The posts I have sent them to are the forks and branches of Ohio and Susquehanna, where many of our enemies reside, and the alacrity which our friend Indians manifest gives me great reason to hope I shall shortly have the pleasure of acquainting you that they have in a

in the pastoral relation at Albany. His son, Col. Lydius, to give additional claim to this title, made a settlement on the Hudson at Fort Edward and engaged in trade with the Indians. In 1744 this house was captured and burned by the Indians, and a son was carried prisoner to Canada. The writer refers in the text to efforts made by this family to substantiate their title to this tract (*Transactions of N.Y. State Ag. Soc.*, vol. 8.)

18. Now in Vermont, forming a part of Grand Isle County. It lies in lat. 44° 57m. and long. 3° 41m. E. from Washington. It is 28 miles N.W. from Burlington, 13 west from St. Albans, and contains 4,620 acres. It was first settled about 1785, and is celebrated for its extensive limestone quarries, which afford a black marble.

19. It will be remembered that at this period the Colony of New York claimed jurisdiction over the territory embraced in the present state of Vermont, and were granting lands in lavish profusion, in quantities of a whole township at a time. Sir William Johnson was peculiarly favoured in these allotments of the King's domain.

20. Referring to Sir John Johnson's son.

21. The success of one of these parties is related in a succeeding letter, dated March 2, 1764.

great measure destroyed and removed these dangerous enemies who have infested the neighbouring frontiers.

I am, &c.

P. S. One Mr. Tice of Schenectady has been mentioned to me as a very proper person for a Provincial Company I must beg leave to recommend him to your notice, should such be raised, as he has served as an officer for some years.

LETTER FROM HENRY MONTURE, WM. HARE AND
JOHN JOHNSTON TO SIR WILLIAM JOHNSON.
[*MSS. of Sir William Johnson, 8*]

Auqouge,[22] Feb. 28, 1764.

Sir William:

We have the pleasure to inform you of some part of our success, which if failed of some parts of the Mohawk River must unavoidably suffer, as we suspect Cherry Vally or Schoharey.

The prisoners we send to you as a token of our prosicuting your instructions as far as we are able; the Commander Sir William will singal out and several of them as principal murderers during the war and reward them according to their desert. The woman bringing down we adjudge as scheme that they might not be suspected they are murderers that has been and they have come some of them from Kanisteo. So we leave Sir William to act as he pleases.

We remain your ever devoted and humble servants

Henry Monture,
John Johnston,
William Hare.

Please to excuse the pen and haste, one of the prisoners a young man had the impudence to bring some English prisoners through this place.

THE SAME TO THE SAME.

---

22. Endorsed Oghquago, and variously written as Onohoghwage, Auqoage, Oucqoago, Oghquaga, &c. It was situated on the east branch of the Susquehanna in the present town of Windsor, Broome Co., N.Y. The hills here slope gently towards the river on both sides, forming a beautiful vale of three or four miles in length, and from a mile to a mile and a half in width, where the Indians resided in great numbers prior to and during the Revolutionary War.

[*MSS. of Sir William Johnson, 8.*]

Auqoauge, Feb. 28, 1764.

Sir William:

This day with pleasure we can acquaint you of our proceedings and success, after our arrival, which we shall deliver to you in the following maner from the Indians:

After our love and respect to you as governor and chief, and then to the commander of the several different places in America. First three days after our arrival at this our settlement we were informed that a body of our enemies were arrived here and going down under some pretence to the river, but on the contrary we suspect to do damage as they formerly have done to kill, burn and destroy, being noted for murdering, notorious villains. Last night we seized seven of there chief warriors here in our castle and the famous Captain Bull of their party, after some little resistance, bound them hand and feet. This morning we all set out for their encampment, and unbeknowing to them about day, seized eleven men of there warrors and eight women and three children, which make twenty-nine in number.

And now brother you see our fidelity in opening the door and we hope you will consider our care, and that we lay exposed to censure and ill will of all nations that are not found in the cause. We hope you will look into our case and listen to us as well as we listen to you, as we think we are equally bound to each other. Consider brother that this our settlement and Chininga and Chuknut are our bounderies of friendship so as we expect you will listen to our request, that is to send a party of men to Conawa Rohare[23] at Oneida and another party to this our settlement at Auqqoage of a safeguard for our women and children, and to hurry all partys of warriors to come to our assistance immediately as we are very weak at present and make no delay.

So after our arrival we found all our warriors as redy to execute and design as we were ready to propose, but we are sorry to think that the Oneidas differ so much in their way of thinking and that is one of the reasons we request a safe guard, and when we heard the sound of our brother warriors coming from you

---

23. Stated in a subsequent letter, dated March 2, 1764, from Sir W. Johnson to Colonel Bradstreet, to be within twelve miles of Oneida Lake.

and from Conawa Rohare it revived our spirits and was like a pleasing toy to a child or like a physick that refresh a sick or weak body, so as though we are delayed from proceding untill we get more assistance.

You used to say that your body was light and it was only the word for you to say march, and everyone must comply and you was never short of provision.

Tomorrow we send the prisoners by the way of Onida, for the reason that perhaps that some of the friends of the prisoners may meet each other and breed a quarrel. No more, but we remain

Your trusty brother Indians.

Attested by us,

> Henry Monture,
> William Hare,
> John Johnston.

LETTER FROM SIR WM. JOHNSON TO MAJ. GENERAL GAGE.
[*MSS. of Sir William Johnson, 8*

Johnson Hall, March 1st, 1764.

Dear Sir:

I have had the pleasure of your letters of the 13th and 20th *ult.* and embrace the first opportunity which time has permitted of answering them.

The exact number of Indians who may accompany the army must be uncertain, nor is it possible to know how many they will consist of. The present spirit amongst them gives me great hopes of a powerful assistance and I shall use every endeavour in my power to keep it up for this purpose. I apprehend however that I may rely with confidence on the attendance of 400 or 500, perhaps they may be twice that number, but it will greatly depend on circumstances and the time I shall have given me to collect them with the help of several proper Indian officers who must necessarily be appointed for that purpose. The friend Indians in general will readily join either against the western nations or the Shawanese and Delawares, and if affairs are not speedily settled between us and the Senecas, I have no doubt but they will march also against them.

I apprehend the Shawanese and Delawares will suffer greatly from the parties I have already sent out, and shall continue to send against them, which will make easy work for the troops on the campaign. These two nations appear the most determined but their party decreases, many of them have already fallen off on hearing the determination of our friends and I am hopeful they will (as affairs are now circumstanced) be unable to persuade the western nations to renew hostilities, especially as the latter will shortly discover that such a proceeding must involve them in a war with the friend Indians, which they would by no means relish. The like reasons will (I hope) have the same effect on the Senecas which will prove of great service to us, as the Indians in general would certainly proceed with greater alacrity against the rest.

Many steps have already been taken by the friend Indians to bring over the Senecas, to which their inactivity for some time past must be chiefly attributed, and I trust that the belts and messages lately sent to them will be productive of an accommodation of which I expect to have notice in a very short time, as the Upper Nations will shortly be down. I mean to treat with them outwardly as a misguided people whom we are desirous to compassionate and forgive on certain terms rather than to give them any confidence in their abilities by expressing a desire to promote a peace with them, and I trust this conduct will have a good effect.

I have sent out several parties since the first and shall continue to do so, as I have the pleasure to find that our enemies are already greatly alarmed at the resolutions of the rest.

### LETTER FROM HENRY MONTURE, WILLIAM HARE AND JOHN JOHNSTON TO SIR WILLIAM JOHNSON.
[*MSS. of Sir William Johnson, 8*]

Oucqoago. March 21, 1764.

Sir William:

This day the prisoners set out for your house by the way of Oneida, and all the Oneidas that came with us likewise return with them, as they said they had fulfilled your pleasure by taken of so many prisoners and chief warriors. Yesterday we received your two letters by an Onida, the one dated the 21 of February and the other the 23rd of February, wherein we acquainted them of your concern for their wellfare and your desire of our proceeding. They were very glad and made answer that they had done according to your will, which would be a welcome sight for you to see so many of your sworn enemies, as they had but one belt they thought they could return with honour. They pressured very hard for us to come along with them in company, but we confider of our errand refused, knowing at least sir that we was short as yet for the good work now in hand before us.

We then remain here untill such times as the arrival of other forces to joyn that we may strick the blow to purpose, which sir you will not neglect sending us a reinforcement as soon and as quick as possible, if you should think proper to send us a body of two hundred whites to joyn the body of Indians you are about to send us, we think with God's help we may destroy a great part of their settlements along the Dioago[24] River, the Ouqoagos are very harty and only wait for anything of a party to joyn

that they may strick the blow as they say their work is as yet before them. There is here in store six barrells of flour and about a hundred weight of sugar belonging to Mr. Wells of Cherry Vally, which sugar would be very usefull for any body of men to make Ouquickare and the flour likewise in case required. We send you one Capt. Bull, the famous head warrior belonging to the Sqoashcutter, a great villain, and the rest of his crew of warriors.

We hope Sir William will not take any excuses from them but punish them with severity as they deserve. Two brothers, Fidlers, excepted, being by all accounts not party concerned, as Capt. Monture knows them very well. As to our speedy return it is uncertain, as Sir William must judge by circumstances, but you may depend on our pressing it on as far and as fast as possible we can, and with God's help we hope is short of give you pleasant detail of our success. We remain your ever devoted and humble servants till death.

> Henry Monture,
> William Hare,
> John Johnston.

P. S. Be so good as to forward the party. The priest of the parifs here gives his compliments to you and all his family.

---

24. Tioga.

LETTER FROM SIR WILLIAM JOHNSON TO COL. BRADSTREET.
[*From the Original in the Possession of M. M. Jones, Esq. of Utica.*]

Johnson Hall, March 2, 1764,

At night,

Dear Sir:

It gives me great pleasure that I now inform you of the success of the first party I lately sent out against our enemy, an express being just arrived with letters acquainting me that on the 26th *ult.* in the evening, near the main branch of Susquehanna, as they were pursuing their rout, they received advice that a large party of our enemies the Delawares, were encamped at a small distance on their way against some of the settlements hereabouts, upon which intelligence they made an expeditious march to their encampment, which they surrounded at daybreak, then naming upon the Delawares (who were surprised and unable to make a defence) they made them all prisoners to the number of 41, including their chief, *Capt. Bull*, Son of Teedyuscung, and one who has discovered great inveteracy against the English, and led several parties against them during the present Indian War. They are all fast bound and may be expected here under an escort in a few days.

The indians of Onoghquagey and Canawaroghere, the latter within twelve miles of Oneida Lake, are very uneasy least our enemies should take advantage of the absence of their men, and destroy their families, on which account they are very felicitous for a guard till their men return, and I apprehend if their request is complied with, it will give new spirits to the parties and encourage more to go on service.

I have therefore mentioned it to the general, and am of opinion it may be easily done by parties from the Provincials at German Flatts.

I am of opinion it will be best to send the prisoners to New York as the best place of security, there to remain till something be done with them.

I am with great respect,

Sir, your most obedient

humble Servant,

Wm. Johnson.

[*MSS. of Sir William Johnson, 8*]

Capt. Eckerson's, Wisersdorp, [25] March 12, 1764.

Honoured Sir:

Received yours of the 3rd inst. and have since proceeded according to your directions, in dispatching a sergeant with ten men of my company and six of the Militia in company with six Indians for Ouaghquago last Saturday. Yesterday five of the Indians, all Mohawks, returned here to me, with two Indians which they say are their prisoners, and told me for what reason they had taken them, they at first refused to tell me, and insisted that I should take them and send them down to your Honour, and if I would not that they would immediately kill them. I then requested of the head of them, one Joseph a *Sachem*, that he would send one or two of his men along with the prisoners to your Honour. He told me he could not do that for he was afraid if he did not go off with his warriors and our men to Onoghquago that his brethren there would suffer.

He then cautioned me in particular about the prisoners and in particular against one of these named *George O'Moke* and said that the said *O'Moke* had threatened one of their old Indians and a squaw and sayed as soon as the young men their warriors was gone against their brethren the *Delawares*, that they then would kill their wifes and children here. This morning two of the Mohawks again returned to me, who having heard that I should have ordered the prisoners to be untyed and sayed if I ordered any such thing and the prisoners should escape, that they would be afraid to go to Onoghquago for fear of the severall threats made by the prisoners.

The sergeant who I have gave the command of those men assigned for Onoghquago I have gave particular instructions agreable to my own instructions received from your Honour; the sergeant is pretty well acquainted with the Indian tongue. His instructions are, that he shall act no farther than what is agreeable to heads of that tribe or as your Honour may further direct him.

---

25. Weiser's Dorp was on the site of the present village of Middleburgh, Schoharie Co. It was named from Conrad Weiser, a prominent early German settler.

The remaining part of my company are all fitt for duty. I have placed so the best advantage in case of an attack with our arms in the best manner. The company having never received any pay yet since they have been raised causes an infinite trouble, notwithstanding all I can do to the contrary to prevent it.

I am honoured sir,

your most obedient servant to command.

John R. Hansen.

To the Honourable Sir Wm, Johnson, Bart.

### Extract of a Letter from Sir William Johnson to Lieutenant Governor Colden.

[*MSS. of Sir William Johnson, 8*]

Johnson Hall, March 16th, 1764.

Dear Sir:

I have had the pleasure of your very kind favour of the 19th inst. and in addition to the success of my first party, I have the pleasure to acquaint you that another party of only ten headed by Thos. King, which I had lately sent out, met with a party of nine Delawares, who were singing their war song against the English, on which they immediately killed and scalped one and took three prisoners, who are now on their way here. This is a small affair, but as 'tis the first who has been killed by our Indians, it will prove of some consequence, and I have reason to expect good news daily from the other parties.

The first prisoners taken arrived here yesterday, and this morning I sent down fourteen men of them to the care of Coll. Elliot at Albany. One of the stoutest remains wounded at Aughquago, and I was obliged to give them people five prisoners for their good behaviour, others to the Oneidas, Tuscaroras, Onondagas and Mohawks, and to detain four myself which I distributed amongst the most deserving to replace persons deceased, for which purpose the rest were given according to the Indian custom.

The consternation our enemies are in on account of our employing Indians against them is very great, and will I hope soon be the means of bringing the disaffected to our terms. Near 400 Senecas, &c. are coming here to make some proposals, as the Onoghquago's are very apprehensive that their families may suffer by the enemy in the absence of their warriors, I thought it very necessary at this time to comply with their request of a guard, and accordingly sent them an officer and thirty men from the Cherry Valley and Schohare garrisons with six Militia, and the general having given me the direction of the future security. These deputies with numbers from the Five Friendly Nations now here, amount to about 500. From the latter I shall send out several parties amongst the Shawanese and Delawares, who are the only nations at present that have not made any offers of accommodation.

I received several letters in autumn and the beginning of winter from the Lords of Trade, one of which contained orders of a like nature with those you mention, which I answered some time ago as well as I could under so much hurry and business. As I understand the board have the regulation of trade, &c. under present confederation, I apprehend it may be too late to lay matters of that nature before them so as to answer the design. All that I thought necessary on that head was, that the Indian trade should be free to all His Majesty's Subjects and carried on at only the principal outposts, where the traders should be under the protection of the garrison and thereby avoid the risk they often run of being robbed and murdered, their goods being a great temptation to Indians if they are in the Indian villages, and such robbery or murder might prove the foundation of a future war, as the Indians seldom stop at the first crimes, neither is it easy to persuade them to make any restitution.

Another matter of consideration is, that the traders at the principal garrisons by being under the eye of the commanding officer would not be so ready to overreach them, fearing a discovery, whereas in their villages they are often imposed upon and apt to redress themselves. The commanding officer could also banish the trader on proof of extortion. The rest I observed to their lordships regarded the state of the department, the interests, dispositions and numbers of the indians.

I am much obliged to you for the particulars you communicated concerning the nations to the southward, as also about the Tuscaroras, and should be glad to hear further from you on that head.

It gave me concern to hear of the hostilities committed by the southern Indians and I heartily wish a speedy stop may be put to them as well as that the several governors may act such a part as may enable you to bring them to reason, for whilst people act upon different plans it is impossible for a superintendant to discharge his trust as he would wish. The French are probably at the bottom of the affair, as they have been to the northward, for it gives them sensible pleasure to foment differences between the indians and us, from which they are apt to flatter themselves with reaping an advantage.

I shall not omit acquainting you in a little time, with any material transactions in this quarter, and am,

&c.

LETTER FROM SIR WILLIAM JOHNSON TO JOHN STUART.
[*MSS. of Sir William Johnson, 8*]

Johnson Hall, March 18, 1764.

Sir:

I have had the favour of your letters of the 10th December and 16th January last, which I should sooner have answered but for the extraordinary hurry and business I have been engaged in, the great resort of indians and the variety of their affairs occupying my whole time, nor especially at this season can they be neglected with prudence.

Since the command of the army devolved upon General Gage I have been impowered to make use of the services of the friendly nations against our enemies, and have sent out in different parties above 300 of them. The first of these parties surprised at the North Branch of Susquehanna 41 Delawares with their chief. I delivered over several of them amongst those who attached to our interest to replace their deceased relations, and sent 14 of them with their chief to Albany under a guard, from whence they will be forwarded to New York. A small party of ten has since fallen in with a scalping party of nine enemies (who seemed destined against some of the Frontiers of Pensilvania), of these they killed one and made three prisoners, whom I daily expect. The killing of this Indian by a party of their own sort will greatly promote the cause and interest our friends more heartily in our behalf.

These parties have already mown their importance, the enemy are greatly alarmed, numbers have retired towards the Twightwees, and the rest knowing that indians are best calculated to destroy them, have forsaken their castles and will shortly be reduced to great extremity if not totally subdued.

The Chenussios and other enemy Senecas have sent me several deputies from each of their towns with proposals of peace, which will not be granted them but on terms most advantageous to our provincials at the German Flatts. I have ordered Aughquago to be reinforced by a detachment of a captain, two subs and sixty men, and sent the like number to Canowwaroghere, a village of Oneidas, whose men are all going out against the enemy. These garrisons for the Indians will not be required for above four or five weeks and will greatly forward the service by the encouragement it will give the Indians.

I cannot but agree in opinion with the council, that the Wyaloosins, &c. might give bad impressions to the rest, but I was determined and prepared to guard against that and hoped to be able to remove any unjust suspicion they might conceive having (without vanity I may say it) a greater influence now over the many nations in our alliance than ever. However as General Gage informs me that he has proposed an asylum for them in Burlington Barracks, I think it will answer very well for the present.

Capt. Duncan [26] of Schenectady has requested I would represent to you his request, whether he may have his proportion of land, he sold out of the 44th Regiment, but thinks he may claim some title on account of the service he performed last year, as will appear from Lt. Campbell's certificate.

EXTRACT OF A LETTER FROM HIS EXCELLENCY THE HONOURABLE MAJOR GENERAL GAGE TO MAJOR GLADWYN, COMMANDING AT THE DETROIT, DATED NEW YORK, 23RD MARCH, 1764.

[*MSS. of Sir William Johnson, 8.*]

You will there be informed, I accepted of the proposals of peace, which the Indians of Detroit had made you, and I am now to desire, if you find the savages amicably disposed, and sincerely inclined to conclude a peace with us in earnest, that you would give them notice in a proper manner to repair to Niagara by the end of June, at which time Sir William Johnson will be there to meet them. You will best know what is most proper

---

26. John Duncan, a merchant of the City of Schenedtady. He died at Albany, on the 5th May, 1791, aged 69 years.

to do, on such an occasion, shall therefore add, that it may be necessary to acquaint them that the representatives they send to this business need not be apprehensive of receiving any insults from the troops which they will probably meet in their way, as when we find they are sincere in their overtures the troops will have orders not to molest them, and they should likewise have notice to collect all the prisoners and deserters which they may have amongst them, who should all be delivered up to us on this occasion. If you think of any proposals proper for Sir William Johnson to make on this occasion of peace, you will write to Sir William on that head.

LETTER FROM JOHN CAMPBELL TO SIR WILLIAM JOHNSON.

[*MSS. of Sir William Johnson, 8*]

Fort Stanwix, March, 31, 1764.

Sir:

I am favoured with your letter of the 17th March, concerning the women of the Oneida village, called Canowoarohere, being in great distress for the want of provision on account of the absence of their men. I have therefore agreable to your letter this day supplyed the women of said village with a quantity of provisions supposed to serve them till the return of their men, which I dare say will meet with the general's approbation, it being so very necessary and prudent to treat them with civility at this present juncture, which is the most effectual method of gaining their affection and of cours to promote the good of the service.

I had the satisfaction of seeing Capt. Bull when the prisoners passed here, whom I think the best looking Indian I ever saw. He is quite the fine gentleman.

The success that attends the partys that you have sent out gives me infinite pleasure, as it must to every person that has the good of the service at heart, and heartily wish that the like good fortune may constantly accompany your unwearied attention to His Majesty's Service.

I hope Mr. Johnson has remembered to apologize my going away so abruptly from your house the morning I left it without my paying my respects to you, which I beg you will excuse as I was afraid of disturbing you so early in the morning.

I am with the greatest esteem Sir, your most obedient, humble servant.

John Campbell.

P. S. I have received orders from the general to be in readiness to take the field with the 17th Regiment next campaign.

## LETTER FROM WHITHAM MARSH TO SIR WILLIAM JOHNSON.
[*MSS. of Sir William Johnson, 8.*]

Bayard Hall, April 2nd, 1764.<br>¾. p. Merid.

Sir:

Although I had not the happiness of receiving some more agreeable news by Capt. post, yet I cannot help acquainting you that last Monday I visited Capt. Bull in jail. He confesses the Shawaneze are rascals, and that the Chenussaes sent for him and other Delawares. This was confirmed in the morning of this day in presence Mr. Nic's Bayard, Senior at the jail by *Joe Newtimas*, who may remember at Easton. When I asked whether any *white men* of Pennsylvania (you well know who I mean) had desired them (ye Delawares) to strike us, Joe answered, *he did not understand the question.* Bull owned there were 22 Indians who made inroads into the Jerseys, by whom poor Westbroke (at whose house we layed) was killed. I much want to get at the bottom of the Delaware scheme, I am sure some *quaking devils* originated the business. Excuse me Sir, for saying no more now, as the post rider waits in the entry. I am with all due deference and respects to your families your

Most obedient and humble Servant.<br>Witham Marsh.

P. S. Darlington sends by me when I embark a great curiosity of shellwork. It is a grotto.

## LETTER FROM COLONEL BRADSTREET TO GENERAL AMHERST.
Albany, 6th April, 1764.

Dear Sir:

I have received your Excellency's packett of the 1st instant and shall obay your commands in everything in my power. I have already informed your Excellency that Major Hogan could not enlist but sixty men to serve to the first of May, and that they were not fit for service; and I may now add, that they can't get any more this way, nor have they tryed for some time past.

That I may know the exact number of boats to take from Schenectady, I beg to know if there is any more troops to go besides the following, *viz*.:

| | |
|---|---|
| 17th Regiment, | 314 including the Draughts. |
| Yorkers, | 300 |
| Connecticut, | 250 |
| Jerseys, | 240 |
| Canada, | 300 |
| | 1404 |

I set the 17th Regiment at 314, as I am assured they cannot at this time make out but 140 men fit to go on service, but they have some which may do in garrison.

What exploits may be expected of 1400 men, one half of them new raised Provincials, and the half of the other half but lately the subjects of the French king, acting in the centre of the savages surrounding the great lakes, known to be our inveterate enemies, I know not, but sure I am, if the whole were of the best troops His Majesty has, the number is far from being equal to service; however it is my duty to obay and to doe the best I can for the service. After the 55th has given 174 men to the 17th, they will have about 230 good men left. If I could be allowed two detachments of 50 each out of them, to be replaced from the Provincials, it would be of great service, but your Excellency is the best judge and I hope will excuse this liberty.

I mentioned your Excellency there was but 50 barrells of powder here, including what was sent from New York, since which Sir Wm. Johnson has had ten barrells. I beg to be allowed sufficient for the service and practice.

There is no muskets arrived from New York yet and but 300 in store here.

Permit me to ask your Excellency if there is to be no kind of staff allowed us.

LETTER FROM COLONEL BRADSTREET TO MAJOR DUNCAN.

Albany, 30th April, 1764.

Dear Sir:

Seven days after the letters from Niagara got here I received a letter from Col. Browning, by which I find it absolutely necessary to send the Grenadiers and another company of the 55th Regiment from hence to Niagara, they are compleat to 45 rank and file with two subalterns to each, and I must beg of you to add to them as many officers and non-commissioned officers as you possibly can from your garrison, and to make them in every respect, as respectable as possible. I suppose Capt. Daly will join his company as soon as possible after knowing it has gone on service.

Some York Provincials are also on their way to you, but in order to get up the boats I am obliged to send them half manned; then you'l please also to send on to Niagara and you will be the best judge what provisions to put in each boat, of the whole, as they leave you.

If the Canadian *bateau* men should have made their second trip from Swegache [27] before I get up and any provisions remains there pray send them back for it, or at least as many of them as will be sufficient to bring it away, and let the others push on to Niagara, not only to land their provisions at the landing but to be employed in carrying the provisions at the fort to landing, &c. and if any make the third trip they must do the same if you think it necessary and safe.

Pray endeavour to get an exact state of all the provisions from Swegache to Niagara as soon as you can, that we may provide in time if more is wanted.

By mistake Lieut. Grant has taken a new mainsail belonging to the schooner on the Onida Lake; be so good to write for it by the first conveyance and send it her.

Pray caution all the detachments that leave you for Niagara to be watchful, for it may possibly happen if the savages find they can't do much to the people employed at the vessells or on the carrying place they will endeavour to surprise our people on some place on the banks of Lake Ontario.

Please to let me know if the Canadian *bateau* men have arms, if they have not and that you can supply
them that go to Niagara with the provisions, pray do it.

Sir Wm. Johnson tells me he has sent some friend Indians to as-sist at Niagara which will prevent your being troubled with so

---

27. Oswegatchie, now Ogdensbrrgh, St. Lawrence Co., N.Y. A flourishing Indian Mission at this Place, formed in 1749 by Francis Picquet, a Sulpitian Priest, was mostly broken up by the conquest of 1760. There was a strongly fortified island in the river three miles below, and as it lay at the foot of navigation from the lake this station possessed great importance.

many as was first intended. I make no doubt but the Draughts and Yorkers are near leaving Oswego for Niagara and that you gave the arms with the Draughts. I will settle it with the artillery officer and Col. Campbell will give the proper receipt for them when he gets to Oswego.

Major Duncan.

LETTER FROM COLONEL BRADSTREET TO GENERAL AMHERST.

Niagara, 4th August, 1764.

Dear Sir:

The Indians of the bay, those of Arbrecroche, some Cheppawas and Mississages now here have so settled matters with Sir William Johnson, that he acquainted me he thought it absolutely necessary to send those people home well satisfied, and that it could not be done without allowing them to trade for everything, except arms and ammunition, which has been allowed them as you will see by the enclosed order and regulations. The prices were fixed by three Indian traders and inspected by Sir William. For the greater security of the troops to be posted at Michilimackinac, I thought advisable to desire Sir William to tell the above savages they need not expect trade to extend so far as this country without posts and garrisons to protect the traders and see that justice is done them; on which they desired Michilimackinac should be re-established and that they would endeavour to protect it.

As to the Genesea Indians a message arrived at Oswego from them before we left it to Sir William Johnson, desiring four boats with provisions should be sent them to Irondequoit in which part of them would proceed with all the English prisoners they had to this place. The boats and provisions by Sir William's desire I ordered thither directly, but they were so far from keeping their words, that they were not there to receive them, but on being sent to, sent men and horses for the provisions.

For some time after this, the accounts we had from them were, that they seemed more inclinable not to keep the peace they made last winter but continue the war; but at length they finding the troops remaining here and suspecting it was on their account and having no time to hunt for provisions and thereby starving, they took the resolution to set out for this place in different parties, and the 18th instant we were informed of their being on the way, but that they were bringing but four of our people instead of thirty which they had prisoners amongst them with many other circumstances mowing plainly necessity only makes them submit more than inclination; whereupon Sir William and myself were of opinion, that suffering any longer such insults might or would be attended with bad consequences, at this time in particular, as the eyes of the Upper Nations was upon us and would judge of our strength and spirit from what passed upon this occasion, and that it was for His Majesty's Service we should send them word that unless they would punctually fulfil every article they promised at the making the peace last winter, they had no business and that we did not desire to see them; and determined also, if they returned, it was absolutely necessary to march against them and treat them as they deserve.

It appears to me, the true cause or reason for this conduct of the Senecas proceeds from their utter abhorrence to us, that they do not think the other part of the Six Nations in general will hurt them, that we live a great distance from them and that the Shawanes, Delawares and their friends can do them great damage, and consequently it is their interest to be well with the latter. But to return to their conduct; on the 21st July they sent in two men here to tell us, that upon receiving the message we sent them, they had sent off runners to bring in all the prisoners and that the principal part of their men, women and children would be here the 23rd, and on that day came in about 60 men with about 150 women and children, and said the remainder would immediately follow and do everything that could be desired of them; but they did not arrive untill the 1st instant with nine prisoners only; nor would they have been here then had they not feared we should march against them, which they were several times given to understand.

The second Sir William Johnson called them together, they acknowledged their faults and insist on it that they will be very good for the time to come, and that they will deliver up the King and War Chief of the Delawares and Shawanes and be amenable for the future conduct of the rest which they took under their protection this spring, provided we grant them peace also, which is agreed to. I expect to see this place clear of savages in a day or two so as to be able to proceed with troops to the westward; and I think it prudent to take with me as many Indian warriors as will go, it being certain the savages round Detroit, &c. will take it much amiss in them, which if properly managed will be of infinite service to the nation whenever either those to the westward or Five Nations break out again; their additional expense in going on will only be provisions, and although one half or more may be suspected of loving their own colour better than us, still I think it my duty to risk it for the advantages which may attend it hereafter. It will be impossible to know the numbers of them until they are in the boats.

LETTER FROM COLONEL BRADSTREET TO GENERAL AMHERST.

Niagara, 5th August, 1764.

Dear Sir:

I have received your Excellency's Letter of the 2nd instant and I will send to the savages of the Illinois as soon as I get to Detroit and shall not fail to do all I can for Pontiac. You will see by the inclosed letter from Major Gladwin, the Sanduiky savages have lately offered to make peace; had I not been stopt here, I should not have received that letter and perhaps might have had the good fortune to have cut up that band, which I think would have been more for the public good than making peace with them.

From very good information I find it impossible to get to the Siotio River by water, but from Prisq Isle Shataquau and so round by Fort Pitt, which would take up so much time; even was there water at this season, which there is not for many miles at first setting off, that I do not think we shall have time to undertake it, and I have great reason to think Major Gladwin has been misinformed, when told that the Shawanes and Delawares Indians were but two days' march from Sandusky, as the same savages who gave him the information now tell me that they are still at their old castle near the Ohio, except a few, and this is confirmed by others. But you may depend upon my marching to them by land if it is possible for us to undertake it, which perhaps may be about the time Col. Bouquett on the move this way.

I am not without hopes of falling on Mr. Pontiac's friends and shall push first for that. The Putewatamas have also offeerd peace, which I am sorry for, as I think I could not well fail of making them repent of what they have done as well as those of Sandusky, if not prevented by being so late.

Untill I came here no place of security for the vessels of this and of Lake Erie was found and they were under the necessity of coming to anchor in the open lake and exposed to every storm and to be lost; add to this they had more than twenty miles to send for their loading; but on examining the north shore a proper place has been found to secure the vessells by the help of a wharf just above the rapids; a post is now building there and all that can be done towards finishing under our circumstances this season will be done; and to avoid giving offence to the Senecas savages to whom the land belongs, I have desired S. Wm. Johnson to ask it of them and they have granted it.

I enclose your Excellency returns of the troops with a plan and report of what we have done for the security of the Carrying Place and vessells from hence to the rapids on Lake Erie.

P. S. I cannot discarge the teamster and waggoner although that business is done, being obliged to employ them at clearing the wood of each side the road over the carrying place, *bateauing* provisions to Fort Erie, making hay, &c. and have employ which is absolutely necessary for many more than I had then.

This instant I have received the enclosed from Major Gladwin, saying the Outawas ask peace and have brought in three prisoners. Fear has brought all these civilities about, but how long they will last when the danger is over time must tell. The enclosed staff of the baker here will appear strong to your Excellency and believe you will approve of my ordering the man to be paid no more than what he receives from the troops and direct Mr. Lake to pay it being a great saving to the Crown.

Col B. to the General, Niagara.

LETTER FROM COLONEL BRADSTREET TO GENERAL GAGE.

Presque Isle, 14 Aug. 1764.

Dear Sir:

Agreeable to your instructions to grant peace and His Majesty's protection to such savages who shall lay down their arms and beg for peace, I enclose you what has passed between me and the deputys of all the nations of Indians, who inhabit the lands of Sandusky, Scioto Plains, Muskinhem, the Ohio, Presque Isle, &c. and your Excellency may depend upon my marching to the Plains of Scioto if I find they intend to play me the least foul trick. Surrounded as I shall soon be by numbers of savages who ask peace from fear only, makes it impossible for me to fix any other plan than acting as circumstances occasion, so that I can now only say that I shall do everything in my power for the honour of His Majesty's arms and the benefit of the nation. I am, &c.

J. Bradstreet.

P. S. I send this by the way of Fort Pitt; out of 574 Indians which was said at Niagara I should have with me, we have 255,100 of whom belong to Canada.

His Excellency Gen. Gage,

LETTER FROM COLONEL BRADSTREET TO GOV. JOHN PENN.
[*Bradstreet and Amherst MSS., p. 155.*]

Presque Isle, 14 Aug. 1764.

To Governor Penn.

Sir:

As it may be agreeable to you and the people under your Government to know as soon as possible of the peace concluded with all the nations of Indians, who have done you so much damage, I enclose you a copy of what has passed on the occasion. I am, &c.

Jno. Bradstreet.

P. S. Perhaps under present circumstances of the troops acting from your quarter and the advanced season, it may be agreeable to the southern governments to have early information of this affair in which you will please so act as may be most agreeable to you.

LETTER FROM COLONEL BRADSTREET TO COLONEL BOUQUET.
[*Bradstreet and Amherst MSS., p. 159.*]

Presque Isle, 14th Aug. 1764.

Sir:

Agreeable to Gen. Gage's Orders to me to grant peace and His Majesty's protection to all savages that may lay down their arms and beg for peace, I enclose you what has passed between me and the deputys of all the nations of Indians who inhabit the lands of Sandusky, the Scioto Plains, Muskinham, the Ohio, near this place, &c. and doubt not if you are in readyness to march you will first receive Gen. Gage's directions how you are

to act after his receiving my letters and articles of peace.
> I am, &c.
> > Jno. Bradstreet.

Col. Bouquett.

> Presque Isle. 14th Aug. 1764.

Sir:

I send you enclosed copy of a peace I have made with all the nations of savages upon the banks of the Ohio, Scioto Plains, &c., &c., and letters for Gen. Gage, &c. which I must desire you to forward with the utmost dispatch.

> I am, &c.
> > Jno. Bradstreet.

LETTER FROM COLONEL BRADSTREET TO SIR WM. JOHNSON.
[Bradstreet and Amherst MSS.]

> Detroit, 28th Aug. 1764.

Dear Sir:

I have only time to say by Major Gladwin we have shown the savages in this quarter we could have cut them up in part at least had they not asked peace, that the Outawas, Petewatamas, &c. Chepewas are to be all in six or seven days to end the general peace and comply with everything I demand, amongst which Pontiac is to be given up to be sent down to the seacoast and maintained at His Majesty's expense the remainder of his days. Major Gladwin will tell your Ex. the sad state of this place respecting the quarters for the troops. I shall do all I can towards building barracks, it being absolutely necessary. The troops you ordered for to garrison Michilimackinack with two companys of fifty men each which I have raised out of the inhabitants here, go of tomorrow and one of the vessells shall be got into Lake Huron, though no more than six feet water is as yet found over the barr in Lake St. Clair, and no pains shall be wanting to know how to fix the navigation from Niagara Falls to Michigan Lake, &c.

Inclosed you have a copy of the peace made with the Shawanes, &c. and I shall be at Sandusky at the time appointed for the chiefs and prisoners to be there and to march against them to Scioto if they do not fulfill their engagements.

From very good information I found necessary to give the inhabitants and savages of the Elliones and the nations on this side of it to the Miamis to know that unless they carry themselves well to His Majesty's troops who were to take possession of that country, they might expect to hear from us and ye savages of the Six Nations, those of Canada, the Shawanes, &c. that we have made peace with, together with the nations surrounding this place soon, for which purpose I have sent Capt. Morris of 17th Regiment and savages with the usual belts. Should Capt Morris succeed he is to push on to all the nations of savages on the banks of the Mississippi to the sea, as your Ex. will see by his instructions a copy of which is herein enclosed, as also the oath the inhabitants are to take.

## LETTER FROM COLONEL BRADSTREET TO LIEUT. SINCLAIR.

Detroit, 12th Sept. 1764.

Sir:

You are hereby required and directed the beginning of May next to receive on board the Schooner *Gladwin* a load of provisions for the garrison of Michilimackinack and with it proceed to that place, and as soon as you have delivered it you are to sail for the bottom of the bay where we had a fort, and from thence round the Lake Michigan, steering up the River St. Josephs as far as you can, making throughout the whole voyage such remarks and observations as the importance of the service you are ordered on requires for the safety of the future navigation of those lakes, observing the same on Lake Huron, the whole of which you will report in writing to Lt. Col. Campbell or officer commanding here on your return and receive from him directions for your further conduct.

As you will doubtless see many savages before you return you will inform them, that the reason of your failing round those lakes is to find out if it is practicable for vessels agreeable to my promise to them at Niagara.

I am, &c.

J. B.

Lt. Sinclair.

LETTER FROM COL. BRADSTREET TO LT. COL. CAMPBELL.
[*Bradstreet and Amherst MSS., p. 155.*]

Sandusky, 10th October, 1764.

To Lt. Col. Campbell.

Sir:

Your letter by chain, without date, I have received and I have great pleasure to find you have in so short a time gained so much influence over the Indians as you mention. I doubt not but you will improve it as His Majesty's Service much requires it at this time to correct the Shawanes and Delawares; but I must observe for the good of the service, that it is absolutely necessary that every person that may have Influence with the Indians should be employed to gain their affection and to engage them not only to keep the peace with us but aft for us against the King's enemies. The savages love the inhabitants of Detroit in general and the latter may by gentle treatment be brought to exert themselves in our favour with the former with little or no expense to government; but after all, affability and attention in the officer commanding at Detroit is absolutely necessary, to the savages in general, particularly those going out to war, without which all will go wrong.

You will please to use your utmost endeavours to make up and send out against the Shawanes and Delawares all the parties of Indians in friendship with us you can possibly collect and continue it until further orders, unless you shall receive letters from Col. Bouquett telling you to desist, he having made peace with those two nations of savages, the Shawanes and Delawares, and you are to fit out all such parties as you send out against those two nations in the manner the French did those Indians they sent to war, and pay for every scalp or prisoner brought in by them, you send out four blankets, four shirts, four pair of stockings and one pound of paint. The goods wanted for this service you are to purchase as occasion requires and add it to your other public accounts. You will also employ such of the inhabitants of Detroit in each party as you think can be trusted. Mr. Royome, that was with Capt. Morris, offers his service.

I shall send you what I can from Niagara this fall, and set off for that place this day. Much depends upon the manner you receive those Indians now going against the Delawares on their return; if they do anything pay them for each scalp or prisoner as above mentioned, and if not successful be kind and give them what will send them home satisfied, with some rum to the chief of the party. At the request of the Ottawas, Chepewas, etc. I have appointed *Chain* an interpreter to those nations, he is much beloved by them and will be of great use in getting parties to go out and go with them when necessary. You will allow him one man's provision to be given to his mother when he is on service and pay him the same pay and in the same way as you do the other interpreters. You have enclosed copy of my letter to the officer commanding the places at Fort Chester with the instructions to Godfrey and Maisonville whom I order thither and when they return the latter may proceed to me with the answer if he thinks proper, otherwise you will forward the officer's letter and the answer from the Indian Nations they speake with.

You have the copy of the peace, &c. with the Hurons on of this place to be added to the one made at Detroit, and it being highly necessary to acquaint all the nations of Indians we possibly can that our continuing the war with the Shawanes, &c. is owing to their sending out parties, killing and taking our people prisoners after having sued for peace and neglecting to come to Sandusky with their prisoners and chiefs to ratify that peace agreeable to their. . . .

You will therefore use every means in your power for that purpose, and I send an order to Mr. Morsac having great influence, he being well acquainted with the Upper Nations, to proceed to the Falls of St. Marys for that purpose, also as you will see by the copy of his instructions herein enclosed, all passes that I thought proper to give when I left Detroit for carrying on the Indian trade you will allow to be carryed into execution, giving instructions to the people to acquaint all the Indians when they go of the perfidious behaviour of the Shawanes and Delawares, and to use their utmost endeavours to prevent any bad impressions being on them by the . . . .